DATE DUE

Who's

Afraid

of the

WTO

?

Kent Jones

Who's Afraid of the WTO

WTO

?

OXFORD
UNIVERSITY PRESS

2004

OXFORD
UNIVERSITY PRESS

Oxford   New York
Auckland   Bangkok   Buenos Aires   Cape Town   Chennai
Dar es Salaam   Delhi   Hong Kong   Istanbul   Karachi   Kolkata
Kuala Lumpur   Madrid   Melbourne   Mexico City   Mumbai   Nairobi
São Paulo   Shanghai   Taipei   Tokyo   Toronto

Copyright © 2004 by Oxford University Press, Inc.

Published by Oxford University Press, Inc.
198 Madison Avenue, New York, New York 10016

www.oup.com

Oxford is a registered trademark of Oxford University Press

Library of Congress Cataloging-in-Publication Data
Jones, Kent Albert.
Who's afraid of the WTO? / Kent Jones.
   p. cm.
Includes bibliographical references and index.
ISBN 0-19-516616-7
1. World Trade Organization.   2. Free trade.   3. International economic relations
4. Globalization.   I. Title.
HF1385.J67   2003
382'.92—dc21   2003048292

9 8 7 6 5 4 3 2 1

Printed in the United States of America
on acid-free paper

In memory of my father,
Albert Hyatt Jones

Preface

As a result of recent antiglobalization protests, the World Trade Organization (WTO) has come into the public spotlight and become the subject of intense and highly emotional debate. At the same time, the public discussion of international trade and the trading system has too often proceeded on the basis of sound bites, flickering images of street protesters, and superficial and uninformed commentary. This volume attempts to rectify the situation by providing an analysis of the most contentious issues surrounding the debate over globalization and the WTO in light of that institution's role in the world economy. Until recently, the analysis of WTO issues was largely an academic undertaking focused on technical issues, the province of legal and economic scholars in both the writing and the reading of the literature. The emergence of the WTO as the subject of public debate has given rise to the need for a discussion of the basic background and activities of the institution that is accessible to the informed layperson, as well as those with interests in business and political aspects of trade policy. Gaining a detailed understanding of the WTO is indeed a formidable task, requiring extensive knowledge of international law, political economy, and negotiating practices. Yet its basic motivating principle is simple: to establish a global framework for governments to negotiate for the gains from trade. This is the simple institutional fact that serves as the foundation for any informed discussion of the global trading system.

While the direct inspiration for this book came from the current debate over globalization, the idea for it has much deeper roots. My long-standing interest in the evolution of the world trading system began with my studies at the Graduate Institute at the University of Geneva. The weekly seminars on trade policy, run by Gerard Curzon, Jan Tumlir, and Richard Blackhurst, gave me my first real lessons in the political economy of trade, with lively discussions and debates among professors, students, and the many visiting scholars who attended. Understanding international economic institutions, I discovered, required a synthesis of economics, law, and political science. This multidimensional approach to analyzing the global trading system found a conceptual framework in the so-called new institutional economics, which revealed to me the powerful motivations that countries have in establishing international organizations devoted to rules and negotiations. This is also the single unifying idea of the book. The viability of the global trading system depends on the integrity of a dedicated and highly focused institutional agreement on rules and obligations. The way to deal with other issues of great importance in the global commons is to work toward similar agreements and commitments in those areas, based on a consensus of the participating countries.

I am grateful to Jeffrey Schott, Martin Drewe, Richard Blackhurst, Thomas Niles, and Melissa Wong for their comments on all or parts of the manuscript, and to numerous others for suggestions, arguments, and criticisms on the ideas that eventually went into this book: Sylvia Ostry, Keith Maskus, J. Michael Finger, Richard Eglin, Joel Trachtman, Ross Petty, Beth Yarbrough, Paul McGrath, and R. David Simpson. The usual caveat applies: none of the above is responsible for the views expressed in this volume, or any oversights and inaccuracies, which are my responsibility alone. I also thank Ingo Walter and Stephen McGroarty for their help in bringing this project to fruition, and Babson College for its support. The lion's share of administrative and technical support was provided by Linda Katz, with help from Angel Lee. Finally, I am thankful to my wife, Tonya Price, and my daughters, Ana-Lisa and Diantha, for their forbearance during the long process of researching and writing this book.

Art Credits

Chapter 1: Miel, reprinted with permission of Cartoonists & Writers Syndicate/
cartoonweb.com

Chapter 2: By permission of Chip Bok and Creators Syndicate, Inc.

Chapter 3: (a) Pritchard, reprinted with permission of Cartoonists & Writers Syndicate/
cartoonweb.com; (b) Henry Payne, reprinted by permission of United Feature
Syndicate, Inc.

Chapter 4: Kevin Siers, reprinted with special permission of North America Syndicate

Chapter 5: Reprinted with permission by Kirk Anderson

Chapter 6: Reprinted with permission of John Sherffius and courtesy *St. Louis Post-
Dispatch*

Chapter 7: Danziger, with special permission by Tribune Media Services International

Chapter 8: Reprinted with permission by Kirk Anderson

Chapter 9: © Chappatte, in *International Herald Tribune*—www.globecartoon.com

Chapter 10: Michael Shelton, reprinted with special permission of North American
Syndicate

Contents

Who's

Afraid

of the

WTO

?

Introduction
The Fear Factor

Who's afraid of the World Trade Organization, the WTO? The list appears to be long. Many workers—and the unions that represent them—claim that WTO agreements increase import competition and threaten their jobs. Other groups emphasize the role of the WTO in the allegedly ill effects of globalization in general, and they claim that, in particular, it weakens labor standards by encouraging a "race to the bottom" by countries seeking to attract foreign investment in export-oriented industries. Many environmentalists share this concern, claiming that the WTO encourages pollution and prevents governments from defending national environmental standards. Human rights advocates see the WTO as a protector of commercial interests over all others, ready to block any efforts to impose trade sanctions in defense of human rights. Still other groups fear that the WTO compromises national sovereignty, taking away a country's right to govern its trade and even its own domestic policies. The list goes on. Some WTO critics believe that the WTO damages the interests of developing countries by imposing free-market trade policies on them before they are ready. Anticapitalist protesters regard the WTO as a tool of big business, particularly multinational corporations. From various anti-WTO sources we hear that the organization is exploitative, undemocratic, unbalanced, corrupt, or illegitimate. These groups paint their protest in vivid colors; other groups interested in reforming the WTO use more subtle, pastel hues. The growing interest in the connections between trade and nontrade issues has spawned proposals to broaden the scope of WTO rules to include environmental, labor, and human rights standards in trade agreements. Numerous nongovernmental organizations (NGOs) have called for increased access to WTO negotiations and dispute settlement processes

3

in order to make the organization more "democratic" and responsive to social concerns. In sum, the WTO has become an increasingly prominent target of skepticism, criticism, and anger since its inception in 1995. In the words of an anti-WTO protest slogan in Seattle, many groups want to either "fix it or nix it!"

All of the recent turmoil surrounding the WTO contrasts sharply with the staid image of multilateral trade diplomacy in general and a history of trade negotiations played out in relative obscurity. The organization was established in 1995 as part of the set of agreements reached in the Uruguay Round of trade negotiations that had begun in 1986. The WTO's predecessor was the General Agreement on Tariffs and Trade (GATT), founded in 1947 as part of a new postwar economic order that also included the World Bank and the International Monetary Fund. Over the next forty-seven years, the GATT sponsored eight rounds of trade negotiations that reduced average industrial tariffs among its members from 40 percent to just 3 percent. The GATT began with just twenty-nine members (or contracting parties, as they were known), including the United States, the United Kingdom, other European countries, Canada, and a small number of developing countries. Its membership grew to 131 countries by the end of the Uruguay Round, and the WTO as of 2003 included 146 member countries.[1]

The WTO is an organization based on a consensus among its members that countries benefit from trading with each other, and the members are therefore willing to promote trade through multilateral negotiations and a system of trade policy rules and dispute settlement. Only governments can be members of the WTO, and all of the rules, negotiations, and procedures are driven by consensus: no rights or obligations can accrue to any member country without the implicit agreement of the entire membership. This principle keeps the organization focused on the one issue that forms the basis of that consensus: the mutual gains from trade. It also means that the WTO as an institution has no independent power. The WTO Secretariat's activities are strictly defined by the collective membership, and its staff is therefore small and has a limited budget by the standards of international organizations. There is no WTO army and no WTO jail. When a dispute arises, enforcement of the WTO agreements and rules among its members occurs through mutually agreed procedures that include consultations, further negotiations, and the possibility of limited retaliatory measures, which are rarely used in practice.

It is ironic that the WTO, with nearly universal membership and a strong consensus on the benefits of trade, should generate such controversy. Yet it is important to recognize that trade policy has never been free of political conflict, especially when trade has been part of a larger and often disruptive process of economic change. The rapid globalization of markets and competition, accompanied by a new public awareness of global social and environmental issues, has compounded these concerns. We live in an age of anxiety over the disruptive effects of changes in technologies, social and cultural influences, political forces, and market conditions. Globalization encapsulates popular notions of vague but potent fears of disruption and displacement: it stands for those forces beyond our control that we would like somehow to master, or at least keep at bay. The WTO, in its link with the market forces that drive international trade, has in many ways become a lightning rod for those anxieties and fears. And so the fear of globalization has contributed to a fear of the WTO.

This is a book about the WTO and the issues that have sparked heated debate over its role in the world economy. It is supportive of the WTO system, but not without a critical evaluation of it. The WTO faces challenges today that go well beyond the scope of its traditional role, established under the GATT, as keeper of the global trading system, and therein lie the seeds of conflict. For in addition to (or, in some cases, instead of) the gains from trade, many countries and interest groups have other goals to pursue: global environmental quality, the protection of human rights worldwide, and increased economic and social welfare among the world's citizens. Many advocates of these goals view the current system of WTO rules and procedures as a barrier to progress.

This book takes the view that global trade policy rules can coexist with and reinforce social and environmental goals—but not without the creation of new global institutions. Above all, it seeks to present an accurate picture of the WTO as a consensus-driven international organization designed to achieve gains from trade for its members, not as an instrument of world government. Reconciling trade and nontrade goals and creating a framework for progress will require effective domestic policies within countries, as well as an expanded set of international agreements.

Work on this study began as an answer to the protesters at the December 1999 WTO ministerial meeting in Seattle, who challenged the current institutional model of an interdependent, globalized economy. Protesters in Seattle and at other recent economic summits have included both well-meaning WTO skeptics and not-so-well-meaning WTO bashers. The bashers tend to be ideologically opposed to capitalism and therefore see irreconcilable conflicts between human rights, social justice, and the global environment, on the one hand, and a market-driven trading system, on the other. For them, it seems, the conflict over the WTO is akin to a struggle of good versus evil, with no compromise possible.

The WTO skeptics, however, are in principle concerned about the impact of globalized markets on their jobs and the state of the world, and they question the role of the WTO in a world of multidimensional issues and problems. They fall into a number of different groups, based on both economic and non-economic interests and priorities. Some, for example, are worried about losing their jobs as a result of international competition; others own factories and capital assets threatened by imports. Still others see the profit motive associated with international trade as a dangerous force that is being allowed to override environmental and social concerns. Implicit in this sentiment is the acknowledgment that the flow of goods and capital in global markets is indeed a powerful force. Economists tend to emphasize the ability of markets to create wealth and improve welfare for most, if not all, citizens. Yet the worry persists that the global economic imperative will sweep away everything in its path, crushing all non-economic elements of human aspiration and allowing the rich to dominate the poor.

Common to nearly all of the WTO protesters is a fear of market forces allegedly controlled by elites, faceless bureaucrats, or oligarchs. According to this view, markets—and in particular, multinational corporations—often run roughshod over the interests of society at large. Much of the fear is associated with the uncertainties of change, as markets expand, competition supplants existing companies and jobs, and the profit motive sparks a supposed race to the bottom in terms of environmental regulations and wage rates.

The following pages will discuss these fears in more detail, but in general, an understanding of the WTO and of a possible solution to the problems must begin with a recognition of the compelling nature of trade, investment, and competition. These activities cannot be easily suppressed, and if they were, the reduction in market activity would be harmful to the world economy as a whole. The importance of trade leads to an even more compelling point. The most daunting problems raised by the staunchest WTO critics—global environmental quality, human rights, living wages—all require that a sound economic foundation be in place in order to find solutions. Higher standards of living for the billions of impoverished people, many suffering under repressive regimes, would contribute mightily to their well-being and provide the basis for their governments to improve their social and environmental policies. Such improvements are unlikely without an open trading system, especially one that improves global economic integration for poor countries.

At the same time, it is important to recognize that there are other factors besides putting bread on the table. Improving the lot of the world's population will also require the development of democratic institutions, improved environmental quality, and enlightened government attitudes toward human rights, to name a few. Economists are often chided for asserting a simple-minded laissez-faire economic determinism as the requirement for all government policies. Let us recognize now that the solutions, like the problems, are multidimensional, combining economic, political, social, cultural, and health factors. The necessary global institutions to deal with these problems must be correspondingly multifarious.

An open trading system is a key element of global economic growth, which can in turn make solutions possible. Those who would be harmed most by a weakening of the WTO are not the rich countries, which can deal from a position of power and strike their own deals. The real losers would be the poor countries, which would be left without a rules-based system of global market access.

September 11, 2001

While globalization has generated fear and anxiety over the repercussions of integrated markets and structural changes in the world economy, terrorist groups such as al-Qaeda seek to undermine the world economy itself by using fear as a weapon. They have concentrated the fear of globalization and refocused it on anybody involved with the broader scope of business, government, or travel. Are you afraid that trade might harm the environment? Worry now about working in or near a commercial or government building that may be the target of an attack. Are you concerned that world competition will cause your wages to be set in Bangladesh? Consider now the risk of just stepping into an airplane and the greater risk of traveling overseas. The danger comes from distant lands such as Yemen and Afghanistan, drawn into our world by a nightmarish process of globalized communications, travel, weapons sales, and finance and stoked, ironically, by a hatred of the economic system that supports them. As sworn enemies of the United States and its allies, the terrorists' goals on September 11, 2001, were to undermine the U.S. government and the global economic system, one of the principal mechanisms for U.S. influence in the world. Their targets were of great symbolic significance in this regard: high-profile government buildings in Washington, D.C., and the World Trade Center in New York.

The attacks tell us something about what is at stake in globalization and the functioning of the world economy, because the terrorist plan was to stop globalization dead in its tracks. They also pointed out how nationalities, social groups, and people of various income levels are connected in the global economy. The attacks also indicated the potential importance of trade in reinforcing and expanding an antiterrorist coalition among governments.

The suicide attacks by al-Qaeda terrorists sought, in spectacular fashion, to sow fear and panic in the global economy and to undermine the U.S. government. A potent symbol of globalization, the World Trade Center, for example, housed some 400 businesses from many different industries, most of them involved in some way with the international economy: import-export trade, banks and financial institutions, legal, business, engineering, and other consulting services, telecommunications, insurance, manufacturing, retailing, and education.[2] Terrorism tries to generate widespread fear, and the symbolic targets of September 11 were instrumental in pursuing this goal. Fear and uncertainty are poison for any markets, and the real damage that terrorism can inflict on the world economy derives from a sense of panic that will cause investors to stop investing, consumers to stop consuming, commerce to cease, and markets to stop functioning. Market damage in this regard has already included airline travel and the international movement of people in general, now subject to increased and costly security measures. In addition, the targeting of commercial and government buildings has increased insurance and security costs for business and public properties in general.

Most of the Western economies were already either in recession or on the brink of it on that fateful day, and the attack on the largest city in a country until then considered impregnable to foreign aggression could only heighten anxieties in markets worldwide, increasing sensitivities to risk. It showed that the world economy has much to lose from the spread of terrorism, to the extent that it can have a chilling effect on economic activity.[3] In a broader sense, the terrorist attacks also threaten some basic freedoms we associate with a market-based economic order: the freedom to conduct business and to travel without intimidation.

As U.S. trade representative Robert Zoellick emphasized (Zoellick 2001), it is imperative that governments take the lead in turning away these threats to global economic security and freedom. To respond in fear, by closing off borders and insulating the national economy or by reducing the international engagement and investments of countries around the world, would be to fulfill the terrorists' purpose. In order to meet the terrorist threats, governments must increase both international cooperation and economic integration. Resolute policies to pursue trade liberalization and integration represent the most direct economic counteroffensive against international terrorism on this scale. In this regard, the tragedy of September 11 appeared to stiffen the resolve of the United States and other major trading countries to bring the WTO ministerial meeting in Doha, Qatar, to a successful conclusion in November 2001, thereby launching the next round of multilateral trade negotiations.

The victims of the attacks also showed in a profoundly symbolic way the connections among nations, races, and income levels within and between countries. To many of those ideologically opposed to Western capitalism, the buildings in New York were surely thought to house the demons of capitalism: executives from American multinational corporations, commercial banks, and Fortune 500 companies. Were the terrorists perhaps hoping to collapse the twin towers full of CEOs, financial manipulators, and otherwise millionaire executives that collectively represent America's plot to dominate the world economy, to the detriment of Islam and, in general, the world's poor?

The truth of the matter is that the victims—in the planes, in the World Trade Center, and in the Pentagon—came from a variety of backgrounds and countries. Along with military officers, company executives, and bond traders were office workers, maintenance and administrative staff, and food service employees, as well as the many police and firefighters who tried to rescue them. In the long series of obituaries of victims carried in the *New York Times*, one is struck by the number of middle-class and working-class people from various ethnic groups. For the most part, these were people going about their everyday business. Their varied backgrounds show that these victims of a murderous attack on "Western capitalism" were not limited to an elite; they came from all walks of life. In addition, they came not just from America, but also from sixty-two other countries around the world. Among the 3,000 dead, as many as half were from foreign countries, many of which had offices for their national trade delegations in the towers. Victims included large numbers of Europeans, Russians, Latin Americans, and Asians. A large number from Muslim countries, such as Bangladesh and Pakistan, also perished.

Thus the terrorist attack, in targeting the hub of U.S. capitalism, claimed victims from the whole spectrum of the American and the world economy: black, white, Hispanic; people of the West and of the East; Christian, Jewish, Muslim, atheist; rich, poor, and all of the groups in between. The register of the dead shows the depth and breadth of social representation in modern commercial life and the world economy. Their common fate signals a common destiny for the rest of us: we are all part of the world economy and have a common stake in its stability and growth.

Avoiding the economically destructive consequences of terrorism and of other sources of international conflict will require a firm and viable global trading system. This is because economic institutions serve to reduce the risk of doing business, while the prospect of international conflict, which includes both the outright violence of terrorism and the subtle intimidation that accompanies trade disputes between countries, tends to increase that risk. Recent challenges to the existing world trading order have served to increase the urgency of developing and expanding international economic institutions. Global trade cannot be allowed to become a victim of fear and conflict.

The immediate concern of governments in the wake of the terrorist attacks was to protect their countries from further attacks. Achieving this goal will require increased cooperation among governments in law enforcement, security measures, and, in some cases, military intervention. In addition, working toward a long-term resolution of the conflicts that spawn terrorist campaigns suggests the need for more effective means of defusing tensions among states, cultures, and ethnic groups. In both the short term and the long term, there will be a need for a deepening of international legal, political, and military institutions to deal with common threats to the global community, from both terrorism and conflicts between countries.

The long-term economic implications may yet transcend the military aspects of the "war on terrorism." It is difficult to generalize about the underlying motivations of the terrorists themselves.[4] Social, political, historical, religious, and economic factors may play a role, but such aggression is ultimately a psychological phenomenon and is committed by individuals. Yet, whatever impulses drive such violent acts, terrorist groups such as al-Qaeda tend to find popular support in poor countries in which economic deprivation has created fertile ground for hatred of the dominant and easily identifiable outside forces, such as the United States and Western capitalism. This factor complicates efforts to combat terrorism on a global scale. In this regard, there are two important links between the WTO and antiterrorist strategy.

While it would be naïve to assume that terrorism, or any form of deep-seated conflict, can be quelled with economic progress alone,[5] a rising standard of living may help to dry up support for terrorism. Trade, in combination with effective economic policies, would be instrumental. In this regard, the question arises as to how countries that breed or harbor terrorists might eventually be brought into the community of nations through economic integration. The countries most commonly associated with state-sponsored terrorism, for example, are not WTO members.[6] They continue to be excluded from the WTO partially because of their terrorist leanings. However, at some future point, it may be worthwhile for major trading countries to consider a strategy of negotiating to bring these countries into the WTO. The strategic purpose would be to use diplomatic recognition and the benefits of membership in the WTO and other international economic organizations as incentives to draw these countries into the world community, and even into an antiterrorist coalition. The costs of supporting terrorism consist of isolation and the forgone economic benefits of trade and growth. At the same time, strengthened international organizations can bring pressure to bear on their member states—once they are inside—that do not comply with established standards of civilized behavior.

A number of countries in which terrorism is suspected of breeding *without* state support are also outside the WTO, such as Algeria, Ethiopia, Lebanon, Somalia, Uzbekistan, and Yemen.[7] These countries and others still outside the WTO deserve increased support for WTO membership, as they can benefit greatly from increased integration into the world economy and the prosperity it can bring. In these and other developing countries, rising economic welfare through trade may also provide the framework for a more stable and democratic political environment.

The fear of global terrorism has been the unwelcome by-product of conflict in an integrated world society. There is widespread global consensus on the need to counteract, and if possible to eliminate, the scourge of terrorism in order to preserve and expand the hard-won gains from economic and cultural integration. This goal is attainable, however, only with the help of more extensive international cooperation and coordination at many levels. International institutions dedicated to the many different dimensions of global integration will therefore be needed. Their purpose will be to create systems of shared access to prosperity, security, and conflict resolution.

| Economic Change and Fear

Countering global terrorism through international cooperation and economic integration addresses one dimension of the anxiety over globalization. There is another sort of fear, no less palpable, that comes from the uncertainties of rapid economic change. Many of the changes that have occurred as a result of a more integrated world have been severely disruptive economically. International trade and investment have in this regard vastly increased the availability and variety of goods and services to people worldwide, expanding incomes and welfare significantly for large populations. Yet this process of economic transformation requires economic adjustment, and this often involves difficult and painful displacement, which engenders its own special type of fear. It is the fear of change, of obsolescence, of losing control over one's security and one's way of life. It is often the fear of physical deprivation. These are ageless anxieties that accompany nearly all economic change.

Yet the new, globalized economy brings even more challenges. Increasing prosperity has contributed to a growing awareness of the global environment and human rights. Closer communications have brought the plight of the poorest populations into the living rooms of workers in the West. They ask: are we supposed to compete with workers in these countries for jobs? If my country imposes costly environmental protection laws, do not the poor countries without such laws have an unfair advantage on the world marketplace? Do not multinational corporations take advantage of the situation, shifting jobs there and eliminating them in the industrialized countries? Can we force those governments to improve the environment, working conditions, and human rights, so that we can all compete on a level playing field? Since everybody trades, why not use trade as leverage? Why can't the WTO let our governments use trade sanctions to get these countries to clean up their acts? Why can we not use the WTO to make those countries adopt environmental, social, and human rights standards?

These questions reflect genuine anxieties over the consequences of greater industrialization and trade in the context of divergent pollution standards, persistent poverty, and human rights abuses worldwide. They also provide scenarios for serious international conflicts over policies and practices among countries that trade with each other. Yet the questions tend to conflate the multidimensional aspects of global problems and challenges into a unidimensional solution: using trade restrictions to force conformity with global standards that are often asserted unilaterally. This approach risks missing the target and, as noted earlier, tends to make everyone worse off in the process. What this book proposes is that countries sit down and conclude international agreements on environmental and social agendas, and then concentrate their efforts into developing and strengthening international institutions that deal specifically with the problems.

It is understandable that many will object to proposing a proliferation of more and more international agreements and institutions as the way to solve the world's problems. Yet there is a compelling logic behind this approach, based on the limited scope of consensus that countries can reach in any given treaty or organization. Much of the animosity toward the WTO stems from allegations that it does either too much or too little—the assertion of too much power over its members' trade policies, for example, but too little mention of environmental and social standards in its trade rules.

Ultimately, clarifying the extent of the WTO's power—what it can and cannot do—will help to put the larger issues and conflicts into perspective.

This issue points to an important problem of public perception and understanding. The activities of the WTO are obscure to most people, veiled behind the opaque language of trade specialists and esoteric procedures, and often held behind closed doors. Who elected the WTO to control world trade? Aren't the participants a bunch of faceless bureaucrats with no accountability? They seem to set things up for the benefit of multinational corporations and big businesses. Surely they do not care a whit about workers who lose their jobs because of imports from countries that do not treat their workers or the environment right.

These frustrated questions also deserve clarification and thoughtful answers. The increased public profile of the WTO demands a more accurate discussion of its function and purpose. In a world that is growing smaller, conflicts of all sorts become more sharply defined and widely felt. Their impact penetrates more deeply across borders. We need to better understand the limitations of the systems in place—and the necessity of developing new ones—for dealing with these conflicts.

Presenting the WTO as an international organization that functions on the basis of consensus, as this book will do, is not the same thing as endorsing all of its practices and agreements. As the reader will see, many WTO agreements can be improved upon, and developing countries, in particular, have valid complaints about governance within the organization. At the same time, it is fair to say that any improvement in the world trading system will have to emanate from the governments of WTO member countries, not from the WTO Secretariat.

Whatever improvements can be made in the WTO, the overarching themes of these pages rest on the fundamental importance of the world trading system itself. We are all part of the world economy, and trade is the basis for increased economic opportunities and growth. Trade liberalization should proceed, not in spite of, but because of rapid economic change, and not against, but in support of, the environment, human rights, and social progress. The WTO is uniquely designed to promote trade to the benefit of all its member countries and their citizens. Other goals of the world community in both economic and non-economic areas require similar types of organizations and agreements. The clear designation of responsibilities among global institutions provides the best framework for resolving conflict.

Organization and Scope of the Book

This volume begins with a review of the issues raised at the WTO ministerial meeting in Seattle, including those presented so loudly out on the streets and those that emerged more quietly within the meeting itself. Chapter 2 presents the underlying economic principle of the WTO—the gains from trade—and how the WTO agreement translated that principle into an international set of trade policy rules. The main opposition to trade liberalization and the goals of the WTO comes from the adjustment problem, which is the subject of chapter 3. Chapter 4 discusses the basic organization and operation of the WTO, emphasizing the consensual nature of the rules it enforces and the activities it undertakes as part of its mandate.

The next chapters turn to the major issues confronting the WTO system. Chapter 5 focuses on national sovereignty and the extent to which countries voluntarily sacrifice sovereignty in order to gain economic benefits from trade. Chapter 6 focuses on trade policy and the environment and the ways in which differing goals in the two camps can be reconciled. Chapter 7 offers a review of human rights and labor rights and the possible roles of trade and trade policy in promoting them. Chapter 8 focuses on the interests of developing countries in the WTO system, and chapter 9 discusses the roles of nongovernmental organizations and multinational corporations in global trade policy. The concluding chapter summarizes the case for a focused WTO dedicated to trade liberalization, with recommendations for improving the world trading system and rejuvenating the political coalition for trade in the face of globalization and nontrade issues.

The agenda for this study therefore focuses on issues of practical interest and importance to the public, business, and policymakers. It does not presume to offer any new or profound scholarly insights into the history, organization, or underlying legal or economic theory of the WTO. Nor does it give a comprehensive overview or analysis of the content of the WTO agreements. The presentation of trade theory and trade policy proceeds informally. Discussions of dispute settlement provisions and procedures, as well as cases, are tailored to selected key issues and are not intended to be comprehensive. The historical accounts of the GATT, the WTO, and trade policy are limited to the needs of the argument at hand.

Many other authors have pursued academic analyses of all these elements of the WTO. But this book has a different purpose. The citations and references are intended to introduce the interested reader to some of the specialized works in economics, law, politics, and history of international trade. This study therefore offers a more modest but broader—and, hopefully, more compelling—approach in order to present the most important features of the WTO to the interested layperson. The primary goal is to improve the public's awareness of the workings of a global trading system, the way it functions, and its impact on all of our lives.

One more note on the presentation. Much of the public debate over the WTO, especially since the first major anti-WTO protests in Seattle, has taken place on Internet Web sites and in editorial cartoons. The discussion therefore draws frequently on Web site materials and goes to some effort at times to analyze the messages contained in several editorial cartoons, since these caricatures have a remarkable ability to influence and shape public opinion, for better or for worse.

Ultimately, a book that emphasizes current policy issues aspires to have some impact on the public debate or at least to make a meaningful contribution to it. Especially in this case, because of the controversial nature of the subject matter, it is the intention of the author that this book will contribute not only to the debate, but perhaps also to a reconciliation of conflicting points of view on WTO issues. At the same time, one cannot ignore the fact that extreme WTO critics are calling for its dismantlement.

Yet strategies of simply tearing down or weakening the WTO (and other economic institutions) would be both dangerous and counterproductive in terms of pursuing progressive nontrade goals. Trade will continue to be one of the most important forces in the world economy into the foreseeable future, and thereby also the single most compelling source of a global consensus. In other words, trade rules are a "public good," no less than improvement in the global environment, peace, and human rights. It is up to the governments of the world to harness the proven readiness of countries to pursue trade liberalization to best effect: to secure a strong base of economic prosperity and growth from which to pursue other goals of the global commons. This will occur only if creative efforts are made to develop the needed global institutions for negotiating the issues with each other, not against each other.

1

Flashpoint Trade
The WTO under Fire

MIEL
THE STRAITS TIMES
Singapore
SINGAPORE

Senior trade officials from nearly all of the trading countries of the world gathered in December 1999 in Seattle, Washington, to discuss the future course of trade negotiations. They were met by thousands of antiglobalization protesters, who did their best over the next few days to disrupt the meeting. When everyone finally went home, the WTO meeting was widely regarded as a major disaster, and many doubts arose as to the ability of the organization to continue its program of promoting open markets and increased trade. This chapter examines the discontents of the protesters and the degree to which the Seattle meeting could be judged a "disaster."

There is an editorial cartoon drawn as a laconic commentary on the Seattle meeting of the WTO that appears to reflect the popular view of the impact of the street protests there. It shows the WTO—embodied as a shocked and befuddled white, bald, middle-aged trade diplomat—with a black eye, the O of WTO forming the periorbital bruise. The drawing is striking and clever but raises several questions. Did the WTO really suffer a setback in Seattle? If so, was it the result of merely a public relations problem or of more fundamental problems regarding the organization, its global impact, and its political support? Who inflicted the black eye? And finally, the underlying public policy issue comes down to this: did the WTO *deserve* to get a black eye?

| *Setting the Stage for Trouble*

The World Trade Organization is an international institution that sets rules for its member countries' trade policies. It also acts as a forum for multilateral trade negotiations and provides a mechanism for settling disputes between members. The ongoing day-to-day business of the WTO is conducted in Geneva by standing trade delegations from the member countries in conjunction with a small staff of independent WTO civil servants and administrators. The Seattle meeting, however, was one of the organization's bi-annual big events, a meeting of trade ministers and senior trade diplomats to discuss major trade policy issues. The original agenda for the Seattle meeting was to launch the next major multilateral trade negotiations. This outcome was not to be.

The WTO ministerial meeting appeared at first to be an unlikely place for protests to erupt. Such meetings are held periodically—the previous ones took place in Singapore in 1996 and Geneva in 1998—and rarely garner much attention outside of the international business press and the specialized circles of trade policy and trade law analysts. While important in terms of international trade negotiations, they typically focus on issues of limited interest to the public at large, such as agendas for upcoming negotiations, progress reports on previous agreements, finalizing interim negotiations, and forming working groups on specific issues.

The activities of the WTO are typically characterized by mind-numbing detail and obscure legal language: the final agreement of the Uruguay Round of trade negotiations, concluded in 1994, comprises 1,000 pages of treaty text and 26,000 pages of tariff tables. These matters are the province of trade lawyers, diplomats, and other specialists in commercial policy and negotiations. Important, yes, but not the sort of material that would be expected to garner much public attention. While the person-in-the-street may vaguely acknowledge the importance of global economic issues, this sort of bureaucratic pow-wow would strike most people as simply boring.

Much of the protest on the street in Seattle—and most of the consternation among the delegates inside the meeting rooms—could be traced to specific aspects of certain trade agreements concluded in the Uruguay Round of trade negotiations, which had lasted from 1986 to 1994 (see display, "The Legacy of the Uruguay Round"). The ambitious set of agreements that came out of these talks had far-reaching effects on the global trading system and national trade policies.

The Uruguay Round created a new full-fledged international organization, the WTO, which replaced the looser and narrower agreement that had preceded it, the GATT. The WTO was established as a consensus-based organization. In principle, the major provisions of WTO rules and agreements cannot be changed without very large majorities or even unanimity among the member countries. Here are some of the main results of the Uruguay Round:

1. The WTO expanded the scope of rules covering trade issues and established adherence to all aspects of the negotiated agreements as a "single undertaking." In other words, any negotiated agreement under WTO auspices is a package deal. Many members that finally signed the Uruguay Round agreement did so recognizing that some issues would require follow-up negotiations. This situation created a built-in agenda of implementation issues and other topics for future negotiations.

2. The traditional outcome of multilateral trade negotiations—tariff reductions—continued with the Uruguay Round agreements. WTO members reduced many tariff and nontariff restrictions on trade, continuing the trend in general trade liberalization begun in the first GATT trade round in 1948. However, some tariff trade restrictions remain: the so-called tariff spikes, especially in politically sensitive products. Success in the reduction of traditional trade restrictions has also been met with a proliferation of nontraditional trade restrictions that create tensions between trading partners.

3. The negotiations also brought agriculture under the increased discipline of international trade agreements. Agriculture remains one of the most controversial trade issues among both developed and developing countries. As a practical matter, trade liberalization in this sector was limited, but it did create a framework for future negotiations. Specific issues included rules regarding food safety and regulations as they apply to imports, state subsidies, market access, and the impact of liberalization on the least developed countries in the WTO. For political reasons, many developed countries continue to subsidize and protect agriculture heavily, and there are strong farm lobbies to support the status quo. For many developed and developing countries with the potential to export agricultural goods, it has been extremely difficult to penetrate protected markets, and the spillover of subsidized agricultural production into export markets has often suppressed prices and damaged farmers in importing countries.

4. The other major sectoral agreement in goods set out to liberalize trade in textiles and apparel. Previous international agreements had removed these goods from GATT disciplines and had established a global network of highly restrictive and detailed quotas, the Multifiber Agreement (MFA). Many developing countries were adamant in demanding a phase-out of these quantitative restrictions. The resulting timetable called for trade liberalization over a ten-year period, but most of the improvement in market access is backloaded in the last year. In addition, the document suggested possible loopholes that could weaken the liberalizing measures, and protectionist textile/apparel lobbies remain strong in many developed countries, while tariffs on many of these products remain high.

5. The WTO established a new Dispute Settlement Understanding (DSU) with greater power than its predecessor under the GATT. It has become a major lightning rod for WTO protest. Decisions of dispute settlement panels under the new DSU can no longer be vetoed by one of the parties, as was the case under the GATT. At the same time, such decisions have raised questions regarding the reach of such judgments into a WTO member country's trade policies and laws. A country found to have laws or practices inconsistent with WTO rules is in principle required either to change them to ensure WTO compliance, to offer compensating measures, or else to face possible retaliation, as authorized by the terms of the DSU. The new DSU has led to vehement protests that it violates national sovereignty. Environmental groups claim that it undermines legitimate trade measures to protect the environment.

6. The other major lightning rod for protest has been the agreement on trade-related intellectual property rights (TRIPs), which makes compliance with international standards on patent protection and copyrights a requirement for membership in the WTO. This part of the WTO agreement received strong lobbying support from the pharmaceutical and entertainment industries, which suffer most from patent violations and sales of counterfeit goods. Yet, complying with the TRIPs provisions has been expensive, especially for poorer countries with inadequate inspection and enforcement infrastructures. Developing countries will also pay more for goods with intellectual property content, a transfer of wealth from the poorer to the richer countries.

7. The WTO agreements included reforms of rules that regulate national trade restrictions covered by unfair trade and safeguard laws, but these issues have continued to generate controversy. WTO provisions regarding antidumping and countervailing duty (antisubsidy) laws introduced some new rules and clarity in how member countries could implement such laws, without changing much in terms of their basic scope. These laws are the source of many trade disputes. In addition, the WTO agreement stipulated a phase-out of the use of negotiated, "voluntary" trade restraints, which had become a popular way of achieving trade restrictions outside the existing rules. Yet the political desire to have recourse to some sort of contingency trade restrictions is still strong in many WTO member countries.

8. The General Agreement on Trade in Services (GATS) extends significant multilateral trade disciplines for the first time into the services sector. Financial services, insurance, and telecommunications industries in developed countries were strong supporters of the GATS. In general, services trade is growing more rapidly than merchandise trade, so this agreement is significant even though it only established a preliminary framework and commitments for liberalization in further negotiations. Aside from fears among smaller and competitively weaker service providers in some countries, some WTO critics opposed the possible extension of trade disciplines into critical public and infrastructure services.

9. The Uruguay Round agreement contained provisions for numerous other aspects of trade policy, including import licensing, rules of origin, preshipment inspection, customs valuation, and technical barriers to trade. In addition, it established a specific goal to improve the coherence of global economic policy, particularly with regard to the coordination of policies and activities between the WTO and the other Bretton Woods institutions, the International Monetary Fund and the World Bank.

Taken together, the outcomes listed here indicate an emerging WTO agenda to provide a global systemic framework for trade policy and trade-related activities and to establish holistic institutional links among trade, finance, and development. For those who have lamented the lack of coordination in international economic policymaking in the past, these are welcome steps. For others, who fear the consequences of globalization, the WTO is regarded as the embodiment of a bad idea.

| Seattle and the Seeds of Protest

The long pattern of sleepy receptions to the wearisome meetings of trade diplomats was to change radically in Seattle. Months in advance of the meeting, protest groups had begun organizing for a massive "mobilization against globalization," making arrangements for thousands to descend on Seattle. Some groups even held training sessions in the arts of street protest, including techniques for climbing the external walls of buildings (to erect protest banners), the proper method of chaining oneself to doors and railings, and strategies to maximize photo opportunities for the press (Helen Cooper, "Will Human Chains and Zapatistas Greet the WTO in Seattle?" *Wall Street Journal*, July 16, 1999, p. 1). By the time the meeting began on November 30, 1999, an estimated 40,000 to 50,000 protesters were in place to express their discontent with the WTO and globalization.

Numerous and diverse groups marched to protest the WTO for equally numerous and diverse reasons. At times, the protests disrupted the conference itself, shutting down the plenary session on the meeting's opening day, for example. Sometimes the protests erupted into rioting by small groups of anarchists, with estimated property damage of $3 million. It is tempting for some to conclude that the problem was one of insufficient security planning by the local police force, which failed to recognize the size and potential disruption of the protests and then overreacted when the situation began to get out of control. Many WTO delegates and conference observers were convinced, for example, that a more secure "protest-free zone," which could have been enforced by blocking off the conference area, would have prevented much of the disruption. The Seattle police chief did resign in the aftermath.

Yet the political significance of the protests themselves should not be underestimated. The conference had drawn an unusually large number of nongovernmental organizations (NGOs); there were more than 700 such groups officially listed in attendance, many of which came from foreign countries.[1] Not all of them were protest groups; several industry organizations with a stake in future trade negotiations also had a keen interest in the proceedings. Protest groups, however, especially labor unions and environmentalists, clearly dominated the scene.

Many interest groups in the United States and other rich economies were uneasy, despite the good economic times in general, about the impact of progressive globalization on their jobs, the environment, and the ability of their elected governments to carry out policies tied to their personal welfare. Many in the less-developed world, on the other hand, were angry about being left out of the benefits of globalization, since the institutions that set the rules are still dominated by the rich countries. So, there were plenty of reasons, it seemed, to go to Seattle with a grudge, a score to settle. Seattle became a magnet for a wide spectrum of groups dissatisfied with the globalized economy.

The timing of the Seattle conference also contributed to the protests. China's application for entry as a regular member in the WTO was riding on an upcoming vote in the U.S. Congress. Some protesters felt that granting full WTO membership to China, which would thereby virtually guarantee it favorable market access to the United States and other countries, would cause the United States to forfeit its leverage with China on human rights and other issues. Others were simply afraid of the increased "unfair" import competition that would result, endangering jobs in import-competing industries.

A related set of issues centered on labor rights. The Clinton administration in the United States had been promising to raise labor standards as a trade issue, and proponents of this position saw Seattle as an opportunity to press their case further. Protests against sweatshop labor, child labor, and working conditions in many developing countries had galvanized many college students as well as traditional organized labor groups to protest against imports made under these conditions.

Anger among environmental groups against the WTO had also been simmering for several years, and the Seattle conference provided a geographically convenient location for protest, since those groups have a strong presence in the American Northwest. Active hot-button issues during the conference included controversies over trade in genetically modified foods, destruction of the Amazon rain forest and other ecologically sensitive areas by trade-related activities, and the right of U.S. environmental groups to be represented in government policy activities.

Finally, the upcoming U.S. presidential primary season made Seattle an irresistible venue for public demonstrations and political statements. It offered the opportunity not only for several interest groups to call attention to their causes as voter issues but also for political candidates and their supporters to make campaign speeches on trade-related issues. In a significant press interview in Seattle, which would cast a long shadow over the entire WTO meeting, President Bill Clinton expressed sympathy with the protesters, pushing his demand for introducing labor standards into future trade negotiations. Specifically, he called for "a working group on labor in the WTO and then that working groups should develop those core labor standards and then they ought to be part of every trade agreement. And ultimately, I would favor a system in which sanctions would come for violating any provision of a trade agreement."[2] Labor standards, enforced with trade sanctions, had become an important issue for the core labor constituency of Democratic presidential candidate Al Gore. But they had also become a controversial issue for many WTO members, especially developing countries, which feared that they represented an attempt to justify more trade restrictions against poor countries. Many observers regard Clinton's statements as a key element in the collapse of the talks (see Ostry 2001).

There was, therefore, ample evidence that the public's attention could be captured in Seattle. The protests would be loud and visible, the issues would be passionate, the candidates would be listening (and talking), and the cameras would be rolling. It is not surprising that a large protest took place.

Who were the protesters? Among the largest organized groups were those representing environmental and labor interests, and there were anti-capitalists of various stripes, some of whom were organized enough to announce that the Seattle protests would be a "carnival against capitalism." In view of the well-known advance planning by the well-organized groups and the promise of a free-wheeling street party, with a dash of 1960s protest romanticism thrown in, it is also clear that Seattle attracted a small but highly visible anarchist element, all too eager to push the protest marches into riots and looting. Karl Marx would have called these hooligans the *lumpenproletariat* of the trade protests, with some strategic role to play in upsetting the existing order. For most of the more committed and peaceful protesters, however, the anarchists were both an embarrassment to clean up after and a distraction that drew media attention away from their messages. The broken glass and looting were the result of a small fringe element, which appeared to have come to Seattle mainly to raise hell. Altogether, about 600 protesters were arrested, apparently including some from the organized groups that were drawn into the street confrontations with police.

| Who Is "Seattle Man"?

The protests in Seattle were surprising not so much because of their manifestation of opposition to trade liberalization—this is nothing new—but rather because the focus of the protesters' fury seemed to be the WTO itself. A Web site set up to organize protests at the Seattle conference and elsewhere claimed, for example, that the WTO only serves the interests of multinational corporations, tramples over labor and human rights, destroys the environment, and increases inequality among nations. According to the protest group Global Exchange, the WTO allegedly violates the sovereign rights of nations, makes local development policies "illegal," and has a corrupt dispute settlement process. The U.S. decision to join the WTO was based on a congressional vote that was allegedly "undemocratic" because it restricted debate and bypassed the treaty ratification requirement of a two-thirds majority. Finally, some claimed that the WTO was "killing people" by denying medicines to victims of AIDS and other diseases in the developing world, a result of the Uruguay Round agreement on intellectual property.[3]

The vituperative attacks against the world trading system that had been so painstakingly constructed since 1947 seemed at first blush to be surprising in their suddenness: why protest the basic tenets of the trade rules now, after more than five decades of operation? While the WTO does extend trade policy rules into new areas not previously covered by its predecessor, the

GATT, the rancor over "faceless bureaucrats in Geneva," "undemocratic processes," and "violations of national sovereignty" targets some basic and long-standing principles of multilateral trade agreements.

Paul Krugman humorously dubbed the new species of antitrade protester "Seattle Man" (Krugman 2000), defined by the belief that globalization is evil and represents the way that multinational corporations will complete their exploitation of the world's workers. It may be useful, however, to take a more detailed view of the roots of the anti-WTO protest, since the motives for opposition to the system of liberal trading rules appear to come from different, although sometimes overlapping, sources.

| Globalization and the Age of Anxiety

It is indisputable that trade has grown rapidly in the postwar period and that globalization has progressed in many areas of economic life, not to mention social and political life. The growth in trade has indeed outstripped the growth in overall economic activity since the end of World War II, due to the continued integration of world and regional capital markets, increased direct foreign investment, the spread of technologies, lower tariffs, and lower transportation costs. As a result, global production patterns have shifted, based in part on changing comparative advantage (more on that in chapter 2) and more open markets. While the result is often one of increased specialization within industrial sectors, in which displaced production and workers tend to be reallocated within the firm or industry, there have been pressures on less competitive industries in many countries to downsize or even close their operations.

In this sense, the times and public attitudes toward trade have shifted since the founding of the GATT in 1947. During those heady days of postwar reconstruction and growing economic prosperity, GATT negotiations quietly but effectively achieved a broad and significant reduction in tariff and quota barriers to trade. Despite the protests of specific industries subjected to the adjustment pressures of import competition, the rising tide of broad economic growth made trade liberalization easy for most groups to accept as public policy. Beginning in the 1960s and 1970s, however, comparative advantage in sensitive industries, such as steel, textiles, apparel, footwear, and, later, automobiles, consumer electronics, and computer components, began to shift from advanced industrialized to developing countries. The ensuing economic disruption in established industries that came from increased imports undermined public confidence in a trading system that had previously been able to promote growth without extensive or painful adjustment measures. The age of economic optimism and anticipation had given way to the age of anxiety.

Traditional Protectionism: Jobs and Wages

The old pattern of protectionism typically joined the workers with the owners of companies threatened with import competition in their bids for tariffs and quotas. This sort of labor-capital coalition still holds for those industries where capital and labor are both immobile (that is, with no easy ways of adjusting to new competition), such as the apparel industry and, to some degree, the steel industry.

However, a further implication of globalization has been the increased mobility of physical capital across borders, with the rapid expansion in recent years of foreign direct investment (FDI). This development has given company owners a degree of flexibility not enjoyed by most workers in vulnerable industries. In many cases now, large portions of the production process can be moved offshore in response to competitive threats from imports. Without the support of a corporate ally, a labor union's chances for a successful protectionist campaign along narrow industry lines are significantly reduced. As a result, some unions have come to target the system itself—the WTO—as part of a strategy of forging a broader and more politically viable coalition against import competition.

Sovereignty

Rapid change triggered by globalization has also raised the issue of sovereignty and discontent with institutions deemed responsible for the loss of control over domestic affairs. In this regard, trade has provided some high-profile public issues in recent years, which have triggered passionate cries against globalization. Take, for example, the Asian financial crisis of 1997–1999, caused by a combination of excessive speculation, unstable capital markets, and mismanaged macroeconomic and regulatory policies in several Asian countries. Currency collapses led to drastic cutbacks in imports to these countries and some export surges from these countries. When steel imports from Japan and other countries surged in the United States in the wake of the crisis, however, it became a "trade problem," and WTO rules prohibiting unilateral trade restraints as a stabilization tool by governments shifted blame over to the system of trade rules itself.

Indeed, any perceived connection between increased imports and local job displacements or painful industrial adjustments often leads to calls for new trade restrictions and thereby a confrontation with the WTO rules, which prohibit or severely restrict such unilateral measures. Despite the extended boom in U.S. economic growth, fears about the uncertainties of progressive globalization continue and may even be growing in the face of increasing technological change and the threat of adjustment pressures on

many industries. Pat Buchanan, former presidential candidate for the Reform party in the United States, is a self-proclaimed "economic nationalist"
and opposes the WTO on the grounds that membership in it surrenders a
nation's sovereignty over its own economic policy:

> American sovereignty is being eroded. In 1994, for the first time, the
> U.S. joined a global institution, the World Trade Organization, where
> America has no veto power and the one-nation, one-vote rule applies.
> For America to continue down this road of global interdependence is
> a betrayal of our history and our heritage of liberty. What does it
> profit a man if he gain the whole world, and suffer the loss of his own
> country?[4]

| Environmental Concerns

Concerns that the WTO compromises national sovereignty have been ag-
gravated by some specific rulings by GATT and WTO dispute settlement
panels. In particular, some of these decisions have enraged environmental
groups. One particular GATT panel decision, for example, declared that a
U.S. trade sanction designed to protect dolphins was incompatible with
GATT obligations. Other cases have fueled the anti-WTO fire. Some of
the controversial WTO dispute settlement panel decisions ruled that (1) U.S.
environmental standards discriminated against gasoline imports; (2) a European Union ban on imports of U.S.-made hormone-treated beef was unjus-
tified; and (3) U.S. efforts to protect sea turtles during shrimp harvesting
with trade measures did not adequately pursue negotiated and other nontrade measures. Thus, the WTO is typically caricatured as the destroyer of
the global commons and endangered species and as the defender of "Frankenfood." The discussion of these cases in chapter 6 will show that the details
of these cases cast WTO jurisprudence in a different light and indicate that
viable alternatives are available for countries to pursue environmental goals.

| Antitrade Ideology and Conspiracy Theories

Underlying many of the anti-WTO arguments is an ideological view that
regards market mechanisms with distrust. The association of the WTO with
trade liberalization, market opening, and globalization puts it at odds with
many who are skeptical about market mechanisms and who therefore advocate extensive government intervention to achieve social goals. In this regard, many ideological opponents of capitalism see the WTO as a threat to
their policy agendas. To them, the WTO itself symbolizes globalization,
which in turn means the downsizing of traditional, often unionized indus-

tries and a weakening of their political base. The WTO also means an outrageous set of rules preventing environmental and food regulation, which enhances the power of multinational corporations, the principal agents of global capitalism and the enemies of workers' rights and social democracy. Consider this account of the WTO by the Industrial Workers of the World (IWW), an anticapitalist workers' organization:

> The World Trade Organization is a "union" of the largest corporations and most powerful nations in the world that uses solidarity between the rich to crush workers' rights, social well-being and the environment. The WTO member nations use their enforcement power on "free trade" agreements by collectively withholding their resources [capital?] to enforce their will on the entire planet and over every national government—thus creating the first undeniable global government in history. . . . Since the WTO was created in 1995 it has made over 100 judgments, all of which have been antiworker, antienvironment, pro–maximum profit.[5]

The vilification of multinational corporations as conspirators in the manipulation of international economic institutions is a pivotal element of the protest strategy of many anti-WTO groups. They deny the mainstream economic view that globalization is essentially an autonomous market-driven process, in which advances in technology, communications, and competition have unified world financial and product markets and improved global welfare, not just for multinationals but for consumers and workers as well. In contrast, the conspiracy view is that multinational corporations not only destroy jobs, the environment, human rights, and labor rights, but also have the WTO in their pockets. Public Citizen's Trade Watch, founded by Ralph Nader, champions this view. Its director, Lori Wallach, put the argument boldly in a letter to the *Wall Street Journal*:

> [Globalization] is controlled by secretive and publicly unaccountable, intergovernmental bureaucracies such as the WTO and IMF and by the business interests who designed and now influence these imbalanced institutions. We need trade that upholds the principles of democracy, that respects human rights and that protects public health, safety and the environment. We need a new set of trade rules that does not put corporate profits over all other concerns. (Wallach 2000)

Politically, it seems important to the more extreme anti-WTO critics to dramatize the issue of globalization as a grand morality play acted out on world markets. The forces of good—environmentalists, labor, the poor—must confront the forces of evil, which includes multinational corporations and institutions that do their bidding that manipulate the rules and micromanage the process of globalization itself to their advantage.

The Information Gap

Compounding this animosity is the fact that the organization and structure of the WTO are little known outside a small group of government, business, and academic specialists in trade. The small staff of the WTO has neither the capacity nor the resources to undertake a massive public relations campaign to explain itself or the benefits of an open trading system to the global public, notwithstanding its recent efforts to improve its Web site information pages. One gets the feeling that many protesters envisage the WTO headquarters as an intimidating tower of doom populated by hooded henchmen conspiring to extend the global reach of their evil empire, controlled by mysterious and obscure Darth Vader–type megalomaniacs. In truth, the WTO building is, by the standards of international organizations, a modest structure in the former home of the International Labour Organization; it has a staff of some 600, with little real power over WTO members' trade policies.

Developing Countries and Internal Strains in the WTO

Finally, there are some institutional features of the WTO that have led to resentment and mistrust of another sort. The WTO, as will be shown in chapter 4, has an official one-country, one-vote decision-making structure, but in reality, most significant negotiating activities take place behind the scenes, and larger, usually richer countries broker deals on the most important issues. Support from developing countries is certainly needed for a successful conclusion to a broader trade round, but the internal governance system may exclude many developing countries from important bargaining sessions. These so-called green-room discussions gather an inner circle of perhaps four or five to thirty WTO members. Most of these are the larger and wealthier countries, although developing countries, especially India and Brazil, have played an increasing role since the 1990s. Still, the green-room system does not provide equal and systematic representation for many developing countries in important WTO negotiations.

This situation has also led to suspicions harbored by some developing countries that the governments of richer countries are using the WTO system to feather their own political nests at home while at the same time treating developing-country issues with benign neglect, if not hostility. For example, demands by rich countries for environmental and labor standards in trade agreements play well to a home audience, especially among interest groups worried about import competition. At the same time, issues of crucial importance to many developing countries, such as textiles, intellectual property, and agriculture, often appear to get short shrift. These concerns have crystallized into a general developing-country critique of the internal WTO governance system. To this concern one could add a complaint by many environmental and labor-oriented nongovernmental organizations (NGOs) of an alleged lack of openness in WTO dispute panel proceedings.

The developing countries do not speak with one voice in their criticisms of, and protests against, the WTO. Several NGOs in these countries have their own concerns about WTO impingement on national sovereignty, the vulnerability of local industries to import competition, the power of multinational corporations, and the negative impact of WTO-administered intellectual property protection, for example. In this regard, their protests mirror those of their anti-WTO counterparts in the developed world. However, the agenda of the developing countries cannot always be easily aligned with "first world" anti-WTO protests. It is difficult, for example, to argue that the WTO displaces jobs in industrialized countries without acknowledging that it also creates new job opportunities in developing countries. (The discussion in chapter 2 will also show that trade creates new job opportunities in the importing countries as well.) With the jobs issue in the background, it is not surprising that calls for environmental and labor standards, enforced by trade sanctions, are conspicuously absent from developing-country criticisms of the WTO. One group of prominent Third World academics and NGOs has even issued a statement denouncing the linkage between environmental and labor standards and trade.[6] The issue of labor and environmental standards is perhaps the most significant fault line running between current developed and developing country protests against the WTO.

| ## The Trouble inside the Meeting

What is perhaps less well known about the Seattle ministerial conference is the fact that the meeting would have been declared a failure even if no protesters had shown up. The main purpose of the meeting—to launch a new round of multilateral trade negotiations—required some basic agreements among WTO members about what would be negotiated, and there was no clear consensus before the meeting on what the agenda should be. The United States wanted to keep the new trade round's agenda modest, focusing on services and agriculture and avoiding sensitive issues, such as antidumping and maritime shipping. Japan and Europe wanted more comprehensive talks, including competition policy, but wanted to put any agricultural talks within a multidimensional framework that would justify continued protectionism and government support in this sector. The developed countries as a group were also advancing plans for environmental and labor standards, which developing countries within the WTO opposed. The developing countries, for their part, had other issues in mind, including WTO internal governance, accelerated implementation of the elimination of the Multifiber Agreement (MFA), and generally increased access to developed-country markets for their goods.

And yet there were connections between the protests outside and the trouble inside. Increased trade had displaced or threatened to displace workers in politically sensitive sectors in developed countries, such as agriculture, steel, textiles, and clothing. Protests from labor unions were joined by protests from environmentalists and other activists. The common denominator was the fear of uncontrolled imports from countries characterized by lower labor costs and more lax environmental protection. In response to these political pressures, many developed-country governments had in recent years attempted to introduce labor and environmental standards as legitimate trade policy issues in the negotiations. At times, their seemingly heavy-handed methods of dominating the WTO agenda had alienated some developing country members.

Who's Afraid of the WTO?

Criticism of the WTO ranges from outright opposition to its existence to recommendations for its internal reform. Here is a summary of the main categories of charges leveled against the WTO:[7]

1. The WTO system prevents governments from protecting the interests of working people displaced by import competition.
2. The WTO system favors open markets (capitalism, profits, the interests of multinational corporations) over environmental protection, labor standards, and human rights.
3. The WTO system tramples upon its members' sovereignty.
4. The WTO is undemocratic (or worse, antidemocratic) in its control over national trade policies.
5. The WTO system of internal governance tends to concentrate power among a small group of developed countries, to the detriment of less developed country interests.

In some ways, the most politically influential groups critical of the WTO remain the traditional, but continually renewed, collection of old-line protectionists, those engaged in largely rearguard actions to protect their wages, jobs, or profits in declining industries. Their complaints focus on the first category above, which is one of the oldest arguments against free trade. The counterarguments have remained constant over the years and are based on the gains from trade and the desirability of alternative measures to address the adjustment problems that often accompany import competition. Chapters 2 and 3 will elaborate on these issues.

The most prominent exponents of this position include the United Steel Workers and the United Auto Workers in the United States and farmers in certain highly protected agricultural markets in Europe and Japan. For protectionist interests, the WTO is a threat because of the adjustment problem of trade, to be discussed in chapter 3. The real culprit for them is globalization and the increased import competition that comes with it, but that is largely beyond their control. They target the WTO because the WTO rules make government actions to suppress import competition more difficult.

The new anti-WTO groups are led by environmental activists (category 2), who see the WTO as a major enemy of environmental protection. Most of these organizations, such as Greenpeace and the Sierra Club, are based in the United States and Europe. In particular, they support measures to establish standards for pollution, species preservation, biotechnology, and other issues that often involve trade restrictions as enforcement measures. Other groups favoring international standards on human rights and labor rights similarly favor the use of trade measures to compel compliance. Their opposition to the WTO is based on that organization's insistence on open trading rules that limit member countries' discretion in restricting imports as a tool to force compliance with these nontrade goals. For example, some WTO dispute settlement rulings have declared some national environmental protection laws to be "WTO-inconsistent." In addition, some human rights groups attempted to prevent China from joining the WTO. (China later entered the WTO after a bitter legislative fight in the U.S. Congress in 2000.) Negotiations within the WTO to establish environmental and labor standards have stalled, a situation that will receive further treatment in chapters 6 and 7. These factors have created extreme frustration among activists in these areas.

The lines between the old-line protectionist groups and the new activists in favor of socially motivated trade restrictions are sometimes blurred. This in itself is a challenge for the WTO system. Many anti-WTO protesters have formed an alliance of sorts that puts "protect our jobs from imports," "protect our environment from free trade," "support human rights with trade restrictions," and "give Third World workers a fair wage, enforced with trade restrictions" under the same tent. This broad-based "teamsters and turtles" approach to anti-WTO protest has been pursued most prominently by Public Citizen's Trade Watch, which played a large role in organizing the Seattle demonstrations and coordinates antitrade lobbying efforts in Washington, D.C.

Economic nationalists and isolationists, such as Pat Buchanan and Ross Perot, oppose the WTO largely on sovereignty grounds (categories 3 and 4), declaring that the United States, for example, should be free to re-impose a system of high tariffs (from the 1800s) to safeguard domestic prosperity and stability. They also believe that the United States should not have to comply with any WTO dispute settlement ruling that finds it at fault. The major crossover link for this stream of anti-WTO protest occurs on the traditional protectionist issue of jobs. Such isolationist sentiment also exists in other countries, particularly in France and Japan. Public support for this view appears to ebb and flow with perceptions of foreign threats to the national economy. Chapter 5 will examine the general issue of sovereignty as it pertains to trade policy.

Economic nationalism also has a curious link to Naderite and other groups, which oppose any WTO rulings that prevent unilateral trade restrictions for environmental and other social purposes. The irony of this position is that the ends are typically international—improve the global commons, human rights, worker standards—but the means are national in that they depend on local lobbying and sovereign control over trade policy for success.

The claim that the WTO is undemocratic often appears with some of the other accusations in this list. The WTO is characterized as an undemocratic institution staffed by unelected "faceless bureaucrats" and driven by an insular "neoliberal elite," who decide the fate of millions with decisions based on a blind adherence to pro-trade rules. According to this argument, the WTO destroys the freedom of a country to determine its own economic fate or to implement trade restrictions based on its judgments of foreign countries' environmental, labor, and human rights policies. This allegation is based on a widespread misunderstanding of the structure of the WTO and the costs and benefits of economic sovereignty in a global economy, the subjects of chapters 4 and 5.

Finally, there are complaints about the internal governance of the WTO, which came painfully to light at the Seattle ministerial meeting (category 5). This criticism comes from the governments of many developing countries, although it has not gone unnoticed among nongovernmental organizations such as Third World Network (TWN). As noted earlier, the use of green-room negotiations has tended to exclude participation by many developing countries. They have a right to be suspicious about this system, which has opened up the charge that the WTO has dealt mainly with trade issues of interest to the rich countries, an issue discussed in chapter 8. Efforts by the developed countries to push for environmental and labor standards in new trade agreements has reinforced these concerns.

Other protest groups participate at the margins of the political debate over the WTO, although they attempt to grab the coattails occasionally of other issues described above. They often attach themselves to environmental, labor, human rights, or developing-country issues. More extreme ideologues include neo-Luddite groups that oppose not only trade but new technologies and economic growth, anticapitalists of various stripes, and scattered anarchists, who are generally interested in tearing down any and all market-oriented economic institutions and having some fun while they do it.

It is important to identify the disparate sources of protest against the WTO because they each imply a different sort of political response. Thus, displaced workers' opposition to the WTO, for example, might diminish if retraining, transfer payments, or other adjustment assistance became available to them. Environmental and labor rights opponents might be willing to consider alternatives other than unilateral trade restrictions to pursue their goals. In general, the numerous types of WTO opponents are unlikely to speak with one voice if various alternatives are found to address their concerns. As the following chapters will show, new global institutional developments in particular can play a key role in reducing opposition to the global trading system, and thereby strengthening it.

| A Black Eye?

What really happened in Seattle, which began a series of anti-WTO, anti-globalization demonstrations at international trade and financial meetings? Clearly, the protesters got center stage and showed the world that they were very upset with this previously obscure institution called the WTO. By drawing attention to the Seattle ministerial meeting, they also perhaps inadvertently brought to light some internal difficulties in the WTO, whose largest members failed to complete the necessary preparations for a successful agreement to move forward with new trade negotiations. Representatives from many smaller member countries took the opportunity to criticize the WTO's decision-making structure. In that sense, the WTO got a public relations black eye, a real shiner at that.

Yet if the protesters believe their own rhetoric, then they have a difficult task ahead of them. Despite all of the attention-grabbing demonstrations, there is no indication that the true propelling forces of globalization—competition, communications, technology—will abate simply because the world saw the WTO stumble through a poorly planned ministerial meeting. In the wake of the Seattle protests, most WTO member countries agreed to redouble their efforts to launch new trade talks, which began at the November 2001 WTO ministerial meeting in Doha, Qatar.

It is therefore doubtful that the protests in Seattle or at other antiglobalization rallies have had any direct impact on WTO policies or negotiations, although they have had some influence through national delegations. Sylvia Ostry, in a study of NGOs and their influence on global economic institutions, does detect some direct influence of these groups, for example, on the World Bank, whose governing board functions as an executive committee and therefore has more direct control over the organization's operations.[8] In contrast, the structure of WTO rulemaking, which is dependent on consensus-based approval by the member governments, is much more difficult for the NGOs to penetrate. Their only available channel of influence is lobbying at the national level. Traces of these influences are in fact visible in the WTO, which established a Committee on Trade and the Environment (CTE) in response to pressure from the United States and the European Union in the Uruguay Round. It is telling, however, that the CTE has been ineffectual as a forum for actual WTO policy reform.

Indeed, the national political agenda of the more extreme anti-WTO groups has been to cripple the long-standing support for trade liberalization in the United States, Europe, and Japan especially. There is, to be sure, the danger that the liberal trade coalition in these countries will weaken under the political pressure of lobbies favoring increased trade restrictions. Government support is essential to the viability of the global trading system. Yet the motivations that drive international commerce remain. In the meantime, undermining the WTO system will result in missed opportunities for growth and economic betterment, and in the developing world especially, this would be a tragedy.

It is in the end best to recognize the black eye that the WTO received as a wake-up call for those who favor trade liberalization. New efforts are required to shore up public support for a trading system that has delivered decades of prosperity but still has much work left to do. For those who oppose the WTO, there should also be a wake-up call: globalization is a fact of life, and it is here to stay. Most of the world believes strongly enough in the merits of trade to support the WTO. How can the world be made better for the environment, for workers, and for human rights—all of which benefit ultimately from economic growth—if opponents continue to undermine the trading system that has proven to be the best global engine of growth? These issues will be the subject of the following pages.

2

Why Countries Trade (and Join the WTO)

Few people deny that there are benefits from trade. Trade across borders has occurred throughout human history, and to the extent that it is an international extension of trading within borders, it represents a traditional and basic form of commercial interaction. Even anti-WTO activists claim, for the most part, that they are not against trade itself, but rather against the WTO trade rules, which they regard as unacceptably pro-business, pro–multinational corporation, antienvironment, antilabor, or anti–human rights.

Their position implies, however, that some types or categories of trade should be restricted in service to the public interest, or to a political or ideological agenda. If there are gains from *some* trade, as most people believe, then at what point does increased trade become a problem? The relevant question regarding the gains from trade therefore becomes: how much should nations trade? Or rather, in terms of national trade policies and the world trading system: why, how, and when should nations restrict trade?

The general answer from economists is that free trade should be the rule, with very few exceptions. The WTO system rests on the ideal of free trade, but as a practical arrangement among nations, the important

33

point is to follow certain rules about trade policy. The principle underlying most WTO agreements is that more trade (that is, trade liberalization) is better than less trade, but that if a member country does have trade restrictions, it should generally stick to tariffs, and it should not increase trade restrictions unless certain conditions apply.

This chapter will focus on the basic arguments for "free trade" and what they mean for the WTO. The first conclusions we will be able to draw is that most countries recognize that trade improves their overall economic welfare. Second, the political forces that favor trade restrictions are strong and difficult for governments to resist. Finally, we will show that a global trading system allows governments to overcome the political opposition to trade liberalization and to garner the gains from trade. This is where the value of the WTO system becomes clear.

For the present discussion, we will refer to the opposite of free trade as "restricted trade" rather than "protectionism," since the latter term carries negative and insulting connotations for some anti-WTO groups. Protectionism implies in some people's minds craven self-interest, as when a tariff is motivated merely by the desire to raise import prices to boost profits or wages in a particular protected domestic industry. In contrast, these same observers might define "trade with a human face" or "trade rules to protect the environment (workers' rights, human rights, and so on)" as a set of policies that restricts trade for some higher purpose.

It is important to note in this connection that trade restrictions do indeed tend to raise import prices and increase profits or wages in domestic industries that compete with restricted imports, regardless of the motives behind the policy. Rather than quibble with motives, however, we will set aside the partisan issue for now and assume a neutral stance on the moral purity of the arguments. The task at hand is to identify the benefits from trade, possible arguments for restricting trade, and the purpose of the WTO in establishing a workable global trading system.

The Simple Economics of Trade

The question of why countries trade can be utterly obvious or tremendously arcane. The obvious approach is to look at the decision of a consumer who buys an imported item that is either cheaper than its domestic equivalent or not available from domestic sources at all. The central truth that underlies this transaction is that trade is beneficial to consumers in the importing country because it allows them to enjoy lower prices and more variety in what they consume.

The editorial cartoon "Seattle Coffee" captures both the idea of the gains from trade and the irony of antiglobalization protests. A group of Seattle anti-WTO protesters, the words "Stop Globalization" emblazoned on their T-shirts, are inside a café, taking a break from the street demonstrations raging outside; a brick is about to come through the window. The waiter calmly takes their orders: exotic coffees from around the world, the very benefits of the globalization they are protesting. In an added note of irony, the cartoonist (or perhaps the character he is lampooning) has evidently forgotten that the order for Colombian latte, Italian cappuccino, and Ugandan regular could not also legally have included Cuban espresso, as shown, due to the long-standing U.S. embargo on all Cuban goods. Perhaps globalization has not gone far enough to suit these protesters.

But now we switch to another side of the trade phenomenon. The domestic consumer's decision to purchase the imported item may in some cases reduce the demand for the domestically produced version of that item. This economic effect, in turn, may reduce the demand for workers in that domestic import-competing industry, causing layoffs, or it may even cause entire firms to shut down, perhaps in extreme cases closing most or all of the entire domestic industry. Where are the gains from trade now? It may seem that the importing country loses in terms of reduced output and employment in the declining industry. But consider also the case where the imported good is an intermediate product and the consumer is another U.S. firm that uses the import in production. Now, the losses of the declining industry are offset in part by the gains to the U.S. firm using the imported product, which may be able to expand output and employment.

Switch yet again to another group of producers in the domestic economy, those who have found export markets for their products. Just as the consumers described above benefit from a new consumption opportunity from imports, so also do the providers of those goods benefit from the new selling opportunity from exports. In this case, we consider domestic firms selling to foreign customers. For them, there are also clear gains from trade.

The question now is to see if the "winners" from trade gain more than the "losers" lose. If so, then we can say that the country as a whole gains from trade. If there is not a reasonably straightforward answer to this question, then we would expect trade policy to be nothing more or less than a battle between special interests. For then the determining factor would always be who has the stronger political support, the winners from trade or the losers from trade (that is, the winners from trade restrictions).

From the perspective of economic theory, there is usually a straightforward answer to the question: the gains outweigh the losses, and both countries involved in the exchange of imports and exports will benefit from trade. David Ricardo, an English economist of the nineteenth century, provided the simplest form of this proposition, which became known as the *theory of comparative advantage*. Essentially, it states that a country gains from trade by (1) specializing its production in goods and services that are less expensive for it to produce, compared to its trading partner, and (2) exporting some of those items in exchange for imports of goods and services that its trading partner can produce less expensively. Trade improves overall economic welfare because it improves economic efficiency; specialization and exchange allow countries to use their limited resources for maximum economic value.

The Ricardian demonstration of the gains from trade is elegant in its simplicity, mathematical rigor, and sweeping policy conclusions: a country will gain by adhering to a policy of free trade and allowing its industries to specialize according to global market forces, even if other countries do not. This model and its extensions and refinements still provide the core of international trade theory today.[1]

There are some flies in the ointment, however. One problem is that the theory's conclusions depend on a number of assumptions about the economy. Of particular importance are the assumptions that factors of production are mobile and are always fully employed. This means that when trade opens up and the country begins to specialize its production, capital and labor can move from the declining industries to the booming industries and thereby maintain full employment of resources.[2] Workers and factory owners for whom it is difficult to transfer their labor and capital, respectively, from declining to booming industries would therefore have an incentive to oppose trade liberalization.

Subsequent developments of the basic theory also showed mathematically what was already known intuitively: while the country as a whole tends to gain from trade, some groups are winners while others tend to lose, even when all the underlying assumptions of the model are fulfilled. In particular, after trade opens up, those factors of production used most intensively in the booming industry will gain, while their counterparts in the declining industry will lose.[3] So if trade-induced specialization causes the capital- and land-intensive farming industry in the United States to boom, for example, and the labor-intensive apparel industry to decline, then the owners of capital and land would gain, while labor would lose, according to the theory. Trade may also induce specialization within companies that can outsource parts of their production process to foreign subsidiaries, which may impose losses on domestic workers whose jobs are tied to the outsourced activities.[4]

Already, even economically enlightened politicians are beginning to squirm. The utilitarian logic of free trade will be difficult to sell politically if trade-related adjustment is disruptive to certain sectors of the economy. The losers are likely to know in advance what awaits them under free trade, since one can often reliably predict that cheaper imports will displace competing domestic products in an open market. These groups are generally easy to organize in a campaign against free trade. The winners, on the other hand, may be more difficult to identify and mobilize in favor of free trade. Some industries, to be sure, will be able to identify in advance their export market potential under free trade. However, opening up an economy to trade also typically leads to new and often unpredictable market opportunities for entrepreneurs. A group could very well be a major winner from trade but may not know it with much certainty in advance. Finally, the other clear winners will be domestic consumers, who, as shown above, will enjoy lower prices and more choices in their consumption. Yet these gains are less concentrated than the losses to specific workers and import-competing industries. The broad mass of consumers, each of whom gains perhaps a small amount from trade, is much less likely to stage a march on Congress or Parliament to demand the gains from trade.

At this point, the economic theory of free trade would not seem to be faring well with the politicians. Arcane mathematical models of economic efficiency have never gone over well with them, and all the goodies seem to depend on a long list of assumptions. During times of intense trade policy debate, economist jokes circulate freely. The only imports that might find political favor for sure would involve noncontroversial products for which there is no domestic import-competing industry and thus no active antitrade lobby.

| *Building a Political Case for Trade Liberalization*

If the country as a whole would indeed be better off under trade liberalization, perhaps we are not giving the politicians enough credit for seeing the big picture. The key to translating the theoretical gains from trade into political reality is in one sense an issue of overcoming special interest opposition to trade, perhaps through some form of compensation or offsetting benefit for those whose economic welfare may decline from trade. This should be theoretically possible if overall economic welfare rises from freer trade. But the point is that the basic gains-from-trade theory alone may not be enough to persuade politicians to embrace it.

Luckily, free trade has more ammunition in its political arsenal than just the comparative advantage model. Additional arguments derive from other economic factors, such as increased competition and technological dissemination. Yet some of the most compelling arguments for trade are political: trade is in the national interest because it furthers a country's political goals at home and its diplomatic goals in the international arena. For example, some countries, notably the United States, Germany, Italy, and the United Kingdom, achieved political unification at least in part through internal economic consolidation. Formerly independent subregions, states, provinces, territories, or principalities, often with their own tariffs, were joined together to form a country that also became, through sovereign control, a free-trade area. The expansion of internal markets and exchange tended to spur or reinforce economic growth through specialization, the spread of technology, and economies of scale. Many policymakers recognized the logic of extending these enlarged domestic markets abroad, for even greater economic gain and the associated political gains at home.

This argument for increased trade points to broader connections between trade and economic growth. Many policymakers in countries with a tradition of trade know, perhaps instinctively, that trade offers a way of being connected to the newest products and technologies and the best business practices in the world market. Staying out of the world market with high tariffs and other trade restrictions runs the danger of missing out on important developments. More recent economic research has also begun to identify the causal links between trade and economic growth, although they are difficult to document precisely. The likely growth catalysts triggered by trade include the exposure to world-class competition, which tends to spur efficiency and innovation in itself, the incentives of new export market development, and the access to new technologies.

A related and less convincing economic argument—but a more compelling political argument—for trade liberalization lies in the goal of expanding the reach of politically prominent domestic export industries. Especially with regard to large domestic industries with high levels of employment and high political profiles at home, governments may take the opportunity to enhance the strength of their "national champions" by giving them larger markets abroad. This argument becomes even more appealing when applied to smaller industrialized countries, whose limited domestic markets constrain its firms' abilities to exploit economies of scale. In order to gain market access abroad, of course, the country must "pay" for it by granting reciprocal market access for imports. This negotiating principle became a crucial element of the GATT/WTO system.

The at-times obsessive concern for export industries has its roots in the mercantilist philosophy that free trade economists such as Adam Smith and David Ricardo fought hard against in the eighteenth and nineteenth centuries. The mercantilist policy prescription was that exports should be maximized and imports minimized, in order to maximize the balance-of-payments-driven inflow of silver and gold into the national economy. It is ironic that elements of this mercantilist approach to trade would later be harnessed for the purpose of multilateral trade liberalization, as tariff reductions became viewed as concessions, instead of the pure gains to the country's well-being that the economic theory implies.

Another overtly political argument in favor of global trade liberalization emerged after World War II. During this time, when many war-ravaged countries were trying to recover and some former colonies were gaining independence, the United States and its major allies saw the advantages of a stable, market-oriented trading system based on expanding world markets. Beyond the simple domestic economic gains from trade, the greater systemic benefit would be a prosperous global community of trading partners. This was also the period of heightened tension between the two superpowers, the United States and the Soviet Union. A trade pact linking market economies and promoting economic growth and political stability would therefore also act as a bulwark against communism.

It is tempting to take the cynical view that the United States came to support multilateral trade liberalization merely as a selfish attempt to consolidate its position as a military and economic superpower. The alleged plan was to spread the doctrine of capitalism, increase interdependence among trading nations, and extend the global reach of its multinational corporations. The political/economic theory behind the support for a global trading system was that as countries with market economies increased trade with each other, the more prosperous they would become and the less likely they would be to start wars with each other and civil wars leading to communist regimes. Globalization, in other words, would create levels of prosperity that would make communism obsolete and war prohibitively expensive. Simultaneously, American firms would profit. The leader of the world order would clearly be the United States. Thus the United States and its allies had yet another argument for trade liberalization.

Even if one takes the cynical view, however, it is difficult to avoid the conclusion that the plan had a lot going for it as both geopolitical strategy and economic policy. Economic theory shows that gains from trade accrue to all trading partners, and experience has supported this conclusion. After all, why should the smaller, weaker countries begrudge the benefits of trade to the big, dominant countries if they also gain? More trade and interdependence, if it occurred, would promote prosperity and stability within countries and peace among countries linked economically. A market-oriented trading system would show the superiority of the capitalist over the communist economic model.

This discussion has shown that the arguments in favor of liberalizing trade include both economic and political elements. Trade policy and its link to the WTO is therefore a component not only of economic policy, but of domestic political strategy and of foreign policy. The motives have not always been pure or altruistic. Yet the economic analysis allows us to draw three major conclusions about the gains from trade and the motivation for founding the WTO. First, the basic argument in favor of trade rests on the economic benefits it brings to all countries that participate in trade. Second, there are political benefits that flow from the economic gains, not only at home but also in relations with other countries and, ultimately, in establishing a stable global environment. Finally, countries could increase the gains from trade and also make them easier to achieve at home if they could conclude reciprocal trade agreements. To take this last point to its logical conclusion, there would be a systemic advantage in organizing a global institution devoted to trade, which would make it easier for governments to negotiate trade liberalization multilaterally.

| Turning the Gains from Trade into Policy

The institutional building blocks of the WTO come directly from the gains-from-trade considerations discussed above. If countries consider trade liberalization to be a worthwhile goal, then they must address the root problem of why countries often impede trade and devise a political formula to encourage countries to remove these restrictions.

Consider a firm that could potentially export its product to foreign markets. In order to pursue an export strategy, extensive investments are often required. The firm may need to build additional plant capacity or retool some of its production to meet foreign specifications or regulations. The firm must procure shipping and handling facilities, purchase insurance, and find a foreign distributor. It may need foreign marketing and legal services and may even need to establish a foreign office to handle local customer, regulatory, and logistics problems. The potential exporter must in many cases also invest in relationships with its foreign customers, business partners, agents, and vendors. This last expense is often difficult to quantify because it typically involves the value of the managers' time in addition to financial outlays, which could otherwise be used to pursue domestic market opportunities.

The same sort of investments would apply in principle to a firm considering an importing operation, either as a distributor, partner, or long-term client. The point is that international trade typically involves transactions that involve considerable sunk costs to be shared between the buyers and sellers. With these investments come risk. The investments will have value to the extent that the international transaction can take place without unexpected interruptions or delays. As in any business operation, there are many different sources of risk, many of which apply more or less to domestic trade as well, such as the risk of default by the customer, shipping delays, and strikes.

Of special concern to the firm trading across borders, however, is the risk of market closure through changes in tariff levels, regulatory regimes, and bureaucratic behavior by governments. While many types of risk in business can be reduced or eliminated through insurance and hedging contracts, there is no reliable, effective way for individual firms to avoid the political risk of a change in trade policy or administration.[5]

One might offer the counterargument that large firms, especially multinational corporations, do this all the time, through lobbying, if not bribery. Lobbying is certainly the traditional way of achieving influence on public policy, and many firms do it, either individually (if they are large enough) or collectively through industry associations. Yet we must also acknowledge that the payoff for lobbying in a foreign country for access to its market is much less certain than on one's home turf. In addition, this activity occurs at least as much among domestic firms seeking trade restrictions on their competition as it does among those firms favoring open markets. It also applies to other lobbies with an ax to grind over trade policy, such as environmental groups and trade unions. In view of these countervailing forces, even the large firms would agree that lobbying does not offer a reliable way to eliminate the political risk of unexpected market closures or barriers. Certainly, smaller firms have even less certainty of market access.

From the perspective of firms engaging in international trade, the mischief that can occur through changes in trade policy poses a serious threat to the profitability of foreign commerce in general, especially in view of the sunk costs invested in the international operation. The uncertainty associated with foreign market access under these circumstances would be in many cases sufficient to discourage the export or import activity altogether. But that would mean that gains from trade are also lost.

In formulating trade policy, governments therefore typically find themselves on the horns of a dilemma. The right thing to do economically would be to agree to lower tariffs, whether or not other countries did the same thing, and thereby capture some of the gains from trade. At the same time, domestic industries that would potentially suffer from increased import competition would strongly oppose such a policy. Political support for trade liberalization sufficient to overcome the opposition would often be difficult to muster. Each government knows that its foreign counterparts have the same political problem, so everyone is afraid to take the first step.

The GATT/WTO system offered governments an effective and politically ingenious way out of the trade policy dilemma. The multilateral trade policy rules and negotiations include the following four important principles:

1. nondiscrimination among members ("most-favored nation" treatment), so that any country lowering its tariff on goods from one country must extend the same tariff cut to all members of the agreement;
2. national treatment of imported goods, so that member countries must treat imported items the same as domestically produced items;
3. tariff binding, which required countries to fix their tariffs at the negotiated rates with no possibility of unilateral increases above the bound level;[6] and
4. reciprocity in trade negotiations, which requires that all countries come to the table ready to offer improved terms of market access to the others.

The WTO rules of nondiscrimination, national treatment, tariff binding, and reciprocity in negotiations gave governments the framework they needed to turn the gains from trade into policy. Specifically, the rules allowed each country to play its most effective pro-trade card at home: securing market access for their exporters. The price of such access, of course, was that each country also had to make concessions in the form of reciprocal market access for imports, but then *all other members had to do the same thing*. Typically, a government would be able to trumpet the "victory" of prying open foreign markets while minimizing the "concessions" of lower domestic tariffs. The nondiscrimination, national treatment, and tariff-binding provisions would prevent member countries from cheating or backsliding on their trade liberalization commitments.

From an economic point of view, this is a trick, but one that works. The gains from trade come as much from increased imports as they do from exports, and countries would benefit from unilaterally opening their markets to trade. Yet, the WTO's negotiating focus on exports, with import market access defined as a concession, manages through its multilateral application to accomplish generalized trade liberalization. If, as a result, all member countries lower tariffs, then all will export more, all will import more, and all will gain from trade.

This combination of negotiating principles creates what can be called the *basic value proposition* of the WTO, the underlying economic benefit it provides to promote the gains from trade. The WTO principles, which impose the sort of trade policy discipline on governments that they actually need to negotiate for more open trade, are also exactly what exporters and importers need to reduce the risk of international business. The systemwide commitments by governments to abide by market access rules significantly reduce the risk of being cut out of foreign markets and thereby increase the value of investments in trade activities.

This point is crucial because it is ultimately the glue that holds the WTO membership together. It is the principal thing of value gained from WTO membership and the primary reason that nearly every country in the world is either in it or else wants—sincerely, enthusiastically, or desperately—to join. The gains from trade will be realized if trade takes place, and trade will take place if the benefits of export/import activities exceed the costs. Risks play a major role in anticipated costs, and government-induced market access barriers are the one significant source of risk that can be reduced through international agreements. Take away the market access assurances of the WTO, and you take away the biggest single reason for being a member.

It is important to keep this point in mind when considering proposals to load up the WTO with new obligations in nontrade areas. Subsequent chapters will examine the implications of introducing new requirements for market access, such as compliance with environmental rules, labor standards, or human rights standards, for this basic pact.

In Case of Unavoidable Trade Restrictions

The discussion so far has emphasized the economic arguments in favor of trade, and how the WTO helps to provide a political framework for turning the gains from trade into reality. At the same time, no government, either member or nonmember of the WTO, has adopted a policy of absolute free trade. Does economic theory allow for exceptions to the rule that free trade is the best policy? How does the WTO system treat departures from free trade?

Economic theory is stingy with exceptions to free trade. In order to have a good economic argument in favor of a trade restriction, you usually need to show that markets are not working properly somehow, that, for example, the economic benefits to the country would be greater if there were a tariff. One possibility is that the importing country is so big and has so much bargaining power on world markets that it can actually cause the net price received by the exporter to fall substantially by restricting trade. For such large countries, the tariff can theoretically be calibrated selfishly to maximize its own economic welfare. This is called the *optimum tariff*. It assumes a number of restrictive conditions, including the lack of foreign retaliation and no negative side effects from protecting the domestic industry.

Most other examples of economically justifiable trade restrictions are surrounded by even more special conditions and caveats. The "infant industry" argument for protection is based on the assumption that a start-up industry may increase its contribution to a country's gross domestic product (GDP) if it receives protection in its early years, so that imports from more mature competitors will not strangle the infant in its crib, so to speak. Yet the conditions for imposing a beneficial trade restriction in this case are pretty severe, usually requiring the presence of imperfect capital markets, which should otherwise be able to sustain a fragile but viable infant during its early years, in anticipation of net economic gains later on.

More recently, a group of new protectionist approaches to trade policy has extended economic theory to identify potential gains from imposing trade restrictions. The economic models usually involve large oligopolistic or monopolistic domestic firms that can snatch additional profits from foreign rivals or exploit economies of scale with the help of strategically timed and calibrated tariffs, quotas, or subsidies. While these new theories have advanced our understanding of the implications of trade policy under conditions of imperfect competition, they have had little practical applicability to trade policy, due to the restrictive conditions for their validity, the information required to make them work, and the problem of foreign retaliation.

The new protectionist theories represent in general an interesting set of parlor games for smart people, but provide little practical help to the trade negotiator or trade policymaker. This has not stopped some politicians from embracing what they consider to be newfound economic support for trade restrictions in general. At last, they say, economists finally acknowledge that tariffs and quotas can be good. Many economists associated with the new theories found themselves attaching policy disclaimers to their work, horrified at the prospect of having their names attached to protectionist trade policies.[7]

It is interesting to note that the WTO, for its part, does not acknowledge any economic justification for trade restrictions. Certainly, to the extent that economic theory suggests the possibility of welfare-improving trade restrictions, they would not fit at all into the WTO system. The optimum tariff argument, for example, suggests that large countries would benefit by raising or keeping high tariffs, while small countries would not. Also, a change in market conditions would imply a possible change, including an increase, in the optimum tariff. Yet the WTO system depends on broad, across-the-board tariff cuts in trade negotiations. Other economic theories suggest the possible benefits of strategic tariffs or quotas, but these would often conflict with WTO obligations regarding either the level of the tariff or the use of quotas, which in general is not allowed, according to WTO rules.

On the other hand, the WTO agreement is not a free-trade document, and it operates under the assumption that sovereign governments control their trade policies. It also acknowledges as a practical matter that trade restrictions will continue in some form in the foreseeable future. The WTO's attitude toward trade restrictions is to subject them to the discipline of binding rules, so that they cannot be arbitrarily raised or applied without explicit justification. In other words, the WTO rules start from the assumption of an imperfect world of countries imposing trade restrictions, and then set out to liberalize trade at the margin, that is, through incremental tariff cuts.

Membership in the WTO begins with a country's depositing its schedule of tariffs and other trade restrictions with the WTO Secretariat. A WTO member may in some cases choose not to place certain categories of goods or services subject to trade restrictions on the table for negotiation, for internal political or other reasons. Many signatories to the original GATT agreement kept much of their agricultural and, later, textile/clothing trade restrictions off the normal trade-negotiating table. The WTO rules therefore do not force free trade across the board on all members. Trade liberalization is the result of a process of negotiation and compromise, which may exclude some items from the discussion and thereby reduce the country's bargaining chips.

The way the WTO handles "acceptable" increases in trade restrictions is to identify the appropriate uses of tariffs and, occasionally, quotas and the rules for their legitimate use. The main categories are

- antidumping and countervailing duties, which are allowed to restrict "unfair" trade that benefits from prices set below "fair value" or that enjoy an "actionable" domestic subsidy that distorts trade;[8]
- emergency protection under the "escape clause" against surges in politically sensitive imports that cause "serious injury" to a domestic industry, allowing temporary trade restrictions that must follow certain rules and timetables;
- trade restrictions to protect the balance of payments under strict conditions and time limits;
- general exceptions allowing trade restrictions for a variety of reasons, including measures taken against imports made with prison labor and measures to protect human, animal, and plant life, health, public morals, national historic and artistic treasures, exhaustible domestic natural resources, and certain strictly defined market conditions;
- national security exemptions, which allow wide-ranging trade restrictions for this purpose; and

- approved retaliatory measures, which are permitted when a WTO member fails to comply with the ruling of a dispute settlement panel.

The important point to remember is that the WTO agreements and rules are the result of extensive compromise that came out of long and hard negotiations. It should therefore not be surprising that the system was set up to accommodate numerous reasons for trade restrictions, measures that were needed to secure political coalitions at home in support of ratifying the WTO.

Significantly, none of the stated rules allowing new trade restrictions under the WTO finds any strong support in economic theory. Economists have been particularly critical of the rules for antidumping duties, which are arguably subject to considerable protectionist abuse. Most of these exceptions give governments permission to impose trade restrictions for political purposes, and the WTO rules are attached as a method of establishing proper thresholds, conditions, and rules to make their use predictable, limited, and transparent. To the extent that the rules circumscribe the use of such trade restrictions and allow the general market access guarantees to remain basically undisturbed, we can regard them as useful safety valves for channeling otherwise dangerous protectionist pressures.

At the same time, it should also be clear that any such WTO-approved trade restrictions typically diminish the gains from trade. Economic theory is quite good at identifying the stakes involved in raising tariffs: who loses, who gains, and the costs to the world economy. If the cost is not great, then one might judge the rules to be beneficial, compared with the alternative of letting unchecked protectionism take its course. A real problem would arise, however, if WTO-approved trade restrictions began to undercut the gains from trade more extensively, or if they began to undermine the basic market-access expectations set up by the fundamental value proposition of the WTO. This point will be important to recall in the subsequent discussion of proposed WTO sanctions for purposes of protecting the environment and labor standards, for example.

| *Trade Is Good. Any Questions?*

This chapter has shown how governments desire the proven benefits of trade but often find them difficult to capture because of political opposition at home. The WTO gets around this problem by committing its members to reciprocity in trade negotiations and a set of rules in the conduct of their trade policies. Governments can then bring home the bacon in terms of foreign market access for their exporters, while at the same time justifying the concessions of lowering domestic tariffs and other trade barriers as the necessary price to pay. And besides, everyone else must make concessions, too. The WTO clears the path, and economic theory delivers the goods: all participating countries in the trade agreement gain, and all the governments can declare victory, rightfully so.

A global trading system thus has the characteristics of a classic public good, in that it overcomes a political failure, in contrast to a traditional notion of an economic market failure. The system and the benefits of its cooperative outcomes would probably be impossible if they relied on individual participants acting independently within their own political constraints. Any single member's benefit from it does not diminish the benefits of other countries—instead, the joint benefits tend to rise as participation and trade liberalization expand. When all members play by the collective rules, all members become better off.[9]

The gains from trade can be achieved through the fundamental value proposition of the WTO. Locking in lower tariffs and guaranteed terms of market access through trade policy commitments are the keys to understanding the value of WTO membership. It is through these constraints on government action that private economic actors can reduce the risks of international trade and profit from their investments in trade-specific assets. This is important because the gains from trade rely on making possible these private transactions.

Despite the apparent significance of the role of the WTO as an institution in motivating trade liberalization, the benefits of trade themselves raise the question of just how important the WTO really is. In a provocative article, Andrew Rose (2002) provides a statistical study that suggests that trade patterns and trade policies have not been affected by the existence of GATT or the WTO. The logic of the underlying hypothesis is that countries will want to trade anyway and that geography, income, and other economic factors ultimately determine trade patterns.[10] According to this theory, if there were not a WTO, countries would have found a way to open trade anyway, which means that the current WTO system is just an irrelevant, empty shell within which fundamental economic factors drive international trade.

It is of course impossible to test this hypothesis, since no one can go back and reconstruct the world since 1947 to see what trade would have been like without the GATT and WTO. However, it is perhaps too optimistic to assume that trade policy without such an institutional framework would have followed such rational economic patterns. After all, the global collapse of trade and the descent into protectionism in the 1930s defied market-driven rationality and inflicted a terrible cost on the world economy. Institutional arrangements such as the WTO may in the end serve primarily to overcome the human foibles, suspicions, and mercantilist reflexes of governments conducting trade policy unilaterally, so that the market-driven factors can have a chance to work. Maybe governments would have found some way to get to the same outcome, but those who make trade policy, perhaps even more than academic economists, are likely to shudder at the prospect for global trade without the WTO.

The WTO therefore offers its members a simple proposition: join the trading club, follow the rules, and everyone benefits. It is a simple enough and attractive enough concept that nearly all countries are in it or else want to be. The key to its continued success and to progress toward building the global economic foundation for other goals among the community of nations is to *keep* it simple.

3

The Adjustment Problem and Protectionism

The previous chapter described an important motivating force behind the founding of the GATT/WTO system: giving governments the ability to overcome political opposition to trade liberalization from industries facing adjustment problems. For all the new challenges facing the world trading system, the long-standing and fundamental problem of industrial adjustment to international trade remains the principal barrier to trade liberalization. Since the WTO establishes the rules for trade policies among its member countries and provides the forum for trade negotiations, many such protectionist groups have targeted the WTO as the cause of deindustrialization and lost jobs.

The adjustment problem is the most politically charged element of the debate over trade policy. However one feels about the rain forest, or butter-flies, or someone else's minimum wage or human rights, it is the fate of one's own job that will excite the most passion in a discussion of public policy on trade. The economics of trade show that jobs are at stake on both sides of the issue, and the high emotional pitch has inspired political carica-tures both pro- and anti-WTO. One typical pro-WTO political cartoon, for example, shows a confrontation between a trade diplomat and a group of protesters in Seattle. The diplomat, portfolio in hand, is calmly speaking about the "real world," a round globe pictured in his text balloon, while the wild-eyed protesters are screaming ignorant "flat-earth" slogans. This concise depiction of free trade versus protectionism as rationality versus irra-tionality, truth versus ignorance, is perhaps most appropriate in describing the small Luddite antitrade groups, who see technological and other labor-saving change in general as undesirable. While it captures the element of fear among many of embarking on the uncharted oceans of globalization, it does not do justice to the larger and politically more influential WTO critics, who know the simple political calculus of trade adjustment only too well.

In contrast, one particularly mordant anti-WTO cartoon shows a well-swept room marked "your workplace" with a broom labeled "globalization" and a dustpan marked "WTO" resting against the wall next to a dustbin marked "jobs." The simple message is that the WTO works hand in hand with the economic forces of globalization to eliminate "your job." This symbolic demonization of the WTO as the casual eliminator of jobs is per-haps the best representation of politically potent antitrade sentiment in in-dustrialized economies. Global corporate greed, it seems, is tidy, efficient, and ruthless. The WTO, in this compact morality tale, is its tool. Fairly or unfairly, this cartoon aptly illustrates the political context of the debate over trade and adjustment.

Adjustment Is a Central Issue

Adjustment costs typically represent the downside of the pocketbook issue of international trade. It is important to acknowledge at the outset of this discussion that some workers will lose from more international trade. Those with less education and low skill levels who work in industries that use unskilled labor intensively in the production of tradable manufactured goods are especially vulnerable to import competition. They are also less likely to land on their feet and find alternative job opportunities. The position taken in this chapter will be that securing political support for trade liberalization will require policies that facilitate the adjustment process and provide an adequate safety net for those who might ultimately lose from the process. At the same time, it will be shown that trade is typically not the main cause of job displacement; technology is typically a more important factor.

Adjustment assistance, if it is used at all, should in principle therefore be extended to all workers displaced by market forces. Finally, the gains from trade and global engagement are so valuable to the national economy that the benefits far exceed the costs of adjustment, which points to the importance of well-designed and efficient adjustment policies and incentives.

As noted in the previous chapter, the firms and workers exposed to import competition are generally more likely to take political action *against* trade than the beneficiaries of trade are likely to take action *for* it. At the same time, many of the arguments of environmentalists and labor and human rights activists feed into the protectionist arguments as well. This is a sensitive issue among social critics of the WTO, who claim to have no protectionist ax to grind. Yet one can see the logical connections between them. Consider an argument that some developing countries have "inadequate" environmental protection policies. Import-competing industries in developed countries will often cite the lack of environmental controls as an "unfair" trade advantage and propose an eco-dumping tariff to restrict imports from those countries.

Labor standards have an even more direct connection to protectionist arguments. Allegations that less developed countries lack an adequate minimum wage, child labor laws, or the right for workers to form labor unions translate quickly into an argument that labor is made unfairly cheap in those countries. It is not difficult to recognize the interest of labor unions in developed countries in lobbying for trade restrictions to enforce labor standards and presumably level the playing field for politically sensitive traded goods. Human rights issues are also often connected with labor standards, to the extent that their supporters regard labor rights as human rights. In addition, repressive human rights policies and practices often correlate closely with low labor standards, adding fuel to the protectionist fires against imports of labor-intensive products from countries with poor human rights records.

Proposals to establish global standards in environmental, labor, and human rights protection, independent of traditional import protection, are worthy of a separate discussion, and subsequent chapters will address these issues. For the present discussion, it is extremely important to conduct a political reality check whenever words like *standards, compliance,* and *enforcement* get hooked up with the words *trade sanctions.*

The simple truth is that nearly every nontrade argument for trade restrictions has a protectionist argument lurking behind it, if not by design then by coincidence of interests. Differences in countries' endowments of labor, capital, and land, as well as their levels of economic and political development, imply patterns of comparative advantage that give rise to trade opportunities. Attempts to harmonize policies and behavior among the many disparate countries of the world will thus invariably generate conflicts over trade. Even if there is genuinely no protectionist sentiment behind a proposal to regulate trade for social purposes, it will always spark the suspicion of hidden protectionism. This attitude follows from the fact that whenever trade is restricted, there are losers and winners, as the earlier gains-from-trade discussion illustrated. The political economy of trade restrictions always brings us back to protectionism motivated by the adjustment problem.

Ultimately, the adjustment problem is a domestic issue for countries engaging in trade, regardless of the international negotiations and agreements that create the conditions for increased import competition. It is up to individual countries to create the economic environment in which capital, labor, and other resources can move from one sector to another when economic change calls for it, whether that change derives from trade, technology, or other sources. Yet the political viability of the WTO system is so closely tied with effective management of the adjustment problem among its members that the issue deserves special attention in any discussion of the WTO.

The following sections will focus on the role of adjustment in general in a growing economy, the cost of adjusting to trade, and the cost of *not* adjusting to trade. Some tentative conclusions regarding possible domestic policy (not trade policy) solutions are also offered. The chapter concludes with a brief analysis of the role of political cartoons in the public debate over trade adjustment and the WTO.

| *The Adjustment Issue in Perspective*

All economic systems must accommodate change if the goal of continuously improving the standard of living for its participants is to be realized. This is how a country progresses from an economy producing buggy whips and slide rules to one producing sophisticated scientific instruments and computer software. It is also why centrally controlled communist economic systems tend to collapse and why overregulated economies that freeze out market signals tend to stagnate. The key element of market signaling is a well-tuned price system, which transmits crucial information about all the resources and outputs that make an economy run. Prices indicate what is scarce and what is in oversupply, what consumers want to buy, and which investments are most cost effective. Ultimately, the price system determines how companies should run their operations to make profits and remain competitive and how consumers use their incomes to make consumption choices.

Openness to trade is an important part of such a well-adjusted economy. It is not always the most important element, but in many ways it is an indicator of the presence of effective market-based incentives that drive the adjustment process. These channels of adjustment must function effectively in order to prevent a clogging of the economic arteries. In this regard, government policies that suppress price signals in product and labor markets (such as trade restrictions) work against adjustment.

Economic adjustment is an ongoing and continuous process in all markets, in all countries, and it comes in many different forms. Any significant change in the underlying conditions of supply and demand will initiate market-driven adjustments. Technological change is probably the most important and pervasive adjustment force in today's economy. In addition, changes in tastes, demographics, availability of inputs, and competitive conditions, as well as expectations regarding all of these factors, can trigger the forces of economic adjustment.

It is important to remember that adjustment typically calls for economic resources—capital, labor, land, and natural resources—to move from one activity to another. Jobs are lost in some sectors of the economy and jobs are gained in others; some industries contract while others expand; firms switch from making one set of products to making another. Adjustment is one way of describing the churning that occurs in any economy buffeted by the winds of change. It is also typically an important element of how an economy grows.

But bad news receives more attention than good news, and the disruption created by adjustment often gains a politically potent voice in public policy. The focus of any policy discussion regarding adjustment therefore remains primarily on those participants in the market whose assets lose value. This description of loss applies not only to the owners of physical capital (machinery, buildings, and so on), whose assets lose value because market demand has shifted away from the firm's output. More important politically is the loss of value in human capital, as represented by the skills, education, and experience of workers used to make that output. Often, the displaced worker has low skill levels whose value declines further when competition lowers the price of the output she produces.

The adjustment process poses challenges to the various economic participants in the market. When the firm can no longer make a profit on the output it has been producing, management and the owners of the firm must make a decision on how to respond. The decision may be relatively easy and simple, as for example when the business can adjust effectively by switching resources internally and moving to production of a different product line. Or it may involve hard decisions and complicated implementation, as when it must make massive new capital or technology investments in order to keep the firm competitive or relocate to areas domestically or internationally where resource costs are lower. The final, extreme example of adjustment in a declining industry occurs when entire firms must be liquidated, which often involves large financial losses to the owners of the firm and massive layoffs of its workers.

For workers, the adjustment process may also be easy or difficult, depending on the circumstances. Internal reassignment within the firm is an example of low-level disruption. Having to relocate to another region in order to keep the job, if this is a possibility, is obviously more difficult. Things can get even more burdensome when the original job is gone for good and a new job search is required, especially if it also involves relocation. At the same time, the displaced worker must often consider further investments in retraining and education. An internal reassignment will often mean that the firm takes on this expense as it prepares the worker for a new job. If the worker is let go, he may need to consider going back to school or otherwise acquire new skills or training as part of a strategy for finding a new job. Such an investment will usually make more sense for a twenty-five-year-old than for a fifty-five-year-old worker.

In declining industries, all of the players want to protect the value of their assets, and that is what typically leads to protectionist lobbying. For the owners of the firm, physical capital may be mobile in the sense that the firm can relocate its operations to another site without prohibitive cost and thus without calls for government intervention. In such cases, the ability to relocate maintains the value of the firm's capital (although the workers may lose, if they cannot relocate). On the other hand, new competition or other market disturbances may make the capital effectively outdated, obsolete, or otherwise unprofitable to use, drastically lowering its market value. For this firm, the incentive to lobby for import protection is much higher, because eliminating the competition would tend to raise the product price and thereby increase the value of physical assets used to make the product.

Many firms in this position will fight particularly hard to protect their capital asset values through government intervention. The owners of capital are often unable to upgrade physical capital in the same way that workers can upgrade their human capital by going back to school and then finding employment elsewhere. Physical capital is often very specific in its use, and once rendered obsolete, the owners' only alternative is to junk the equipment and take the loss, which is often substantial.

Workers also have capital investments, usually in the form of homes, as well as in their own human capital (the value of their skills). They will tend to have an easier time with the adjustment process if they are mobile, young, and open to more education or training. A factor such as home ownership in an area where selling the home may be difficult detracts from mobility; this factor is often tied to the adjustment problem itself, to the extent that property values may be driven down by plant closings. Relocation could therefore involve a substantial capital loss for such a displaced worker. Mobility may also be lower if the worker has few skills to offer and has poor prospects for retraining. A worker is also more reluctant to move if alternative employment opportunities are unattractive; this will be especially true if the lost job was relatively high paying (with a union-scale wage, for example) compared with other job possibilities.

It is worth noting in this context that unions that represent workers facing adjustment pressures also have a stake in the outcome, since job displacements will cause them to lose even if the downsized worker does not. Specifically, lower employment in the unionized industry will diminish union ranks, union dues, and along with it, union influence and power.

Successful economic adjustment for the worker—reemployment in another job with higher wages and benefits, for example—still spells losses for the union now depleted of another member. It is often less likely that the new job in a growing sector of the economy will be unionized. The unions, for their part, tend to argue vehemently that their members' wages and benefits would be difficult to match at alternative jobs. The validity of this claim will depend on the ability of the union to raise wage rates for its members above the level that workers can expect elsewhere.

Here is a typical scenario for industrial lobbying for trade restrictions driven by the high private cost of adjustment to import competition. The firm has extensive capital investments that are difficult to move or liquidate without large capital losses. The workers are either unionized (facing large prospective wage losses), low skilled, or older (few alternative job prospects). The plants are typically located in either depressed areas or in areas that would become more depressed if the plant closed down (high relocation costs). The industry association and the workers will walk hand in hand to Washington to lobby for protection. They will also speak out against the WTO, whose rules limit the ability of the government to grant protection.

Yet the asset protection stakes may vary considerably between the two groups when the effects of protection are measured. If physical capital is immobile and subject to a sharp decline in value when the product price falls, the owners of capital may have more to gain from protection than the workers. If, on the other hand, the firm has an easier time adjusting than the workers, as for example when outsourcing is possible, then the workers will probably have to fight their protectionist battle alone. Given the added difficulty of lobbying for protection directly without industry support, this may be why unions have turned recently to attacks on the WTO and trade treaties themselves.

The foregoing profile of the adjustment problem suggests, first of all, that it is important to identify the source of the adjustment pressure, since trade may not be the only or even the major reason for it. In addition, there is a need to consider further the other side of the adjustment issue—the cost of *not* adjusting—and how protectionism may bring unexpected damage. The goal of public policy in dealing with adjustment should be to find a way to neutralize protectionist sentiment by addressing the true underlying problems of labor skills and mobility.

| *The Culprit: Technology or Trade?*

So far, the discussion of adjustment has established that there are many reasons one might lose a job—or find a new one. There has been much discussion in recent years among economists about the roles of trade, technology, and other factors in determining wage levels and employment patterns under conditions of increasing globalization. The effects of trade and technology are difficult to disentangle. Technology, for example, can improve production processes or introduce new products at home, leading to greater exports but also forcing obsolete domestic industries or firms to downsize or shut down. Technology can also spread to other countries through trade and investment, which in turn leads to exports from foreign countries, which could then displace domestic production in the domestic economy. New technology may also open up new trading opportunities within the firm. For example, improvements in information technology have increased the efficiency of international outsourcing along the value chain of companies' production processes. The increased trade occurs at the level of intermediate inputs. Trade and technology therefore often complement each other in the process of economic change.

It is useful in this regard to consider trade as a form of technological advancement. Suppose you own a business that produces widgets and your competitors discover a new method of producing an important input (call it a doohickey) that goes into widget production. The new method will also require you to adopt the new technology in order to remain competitive. You will need fewer workers and you will have lower expenses, but this is part of the adjustment you need to make in order to stay in business as a result of new labor-saving technology. Now suppose that, instead of the new technology, you discover that foreign suppliers can provide you and your competitors with the same doohickey at a lower cost. Again, you need fewer workers to make widgets if you outsource the doohickeys, and the adjustment is again necessary in order to remain competitive. There is little difference economically between the two examples of cost-saving adjustment.

Efforts to sort out the trade effects from the technology effects in labor markets are challenging from the point of view of economic theory but probably less interesting to the laid-off worker. Do you really care if you lost your job due to 60 percent technology and 40 percent import competition? Or was it 90 percent technology and 10 percent trade?

The state of economic research on this question tends to give more weight to technology than to trade in such issues as greater wage inequality and the recent trend toward lower average real wages in many industrialized countries. Other factors, such as labor institutions, have also played a role. The underlying problem in industrialized countries boils down to the fact that changing economic forces cause the demand for certain—usually low-skilled—types of labor to decline. The general trend in advanced economies has been to generate fewer low-skilled and more high-skilled jobs. Difficulties obviously arise when low-skilled jobs disappear (because of technology, trade, or whatever other reasons) and displaced workers do not have the requisite skills to move easily into the new high-skilled jobs as the economic structure changes.

Many trade economists continue to focus on the role of trade in driving these labor market outcomes because the political acceptability of trade agreements may depend on making sure that globalization does not create terrible economic disruption and income inequality within countries. For this reason, the WTO members, all of whom have a stake in the continuing viability of the global trading system, must pay attention to the adjustment issue.

This observation restates the political aspect of trade policy, one that we already know: economic change, whether in the form of technology, trade competition, or other factors, can be disruptive. At the same time, the forces of economic change are widely recognized as holding the key to economic growth. Managing trade policy in this context can be tricky, but it should not be. The gains from trade (and from technology) are real and work together. The focus should be on avoiding the cost of *not* adjusting.

| *More on Winners and Losers*

Economic theory states that factors of production tied to the import-competing industry tend to lose from free trade, while consumers and production factors tied to export industries tend to gain. A popular anti-WTO stream of thought stylizes the winners and losers scenario as follows: big corporations get most of the gains, while workers (often defined to include anyone with a job connected to the global economy) bear most of the cost. This approach also tends to minimize consumer gains: consumers are either counted among the losing workers, or are duped by low-priced but shoddy goods foisted upon them by trade, or suffer from the environmental degradation caused by trade, or do not get anything more from trade than they would by buying similar domestically produced goods.

It is unlikely, however, that consumers are as stupid as this. The presence of international trade increases the variety of products available and typically lowers their prices. The lower prices will filter through to domestically produced goods as well because of competition from imports. When one considers the role of many imported items in consumer budgets in developed countries, including automobiles, clothing, footwear, electronic appliances, and foodstuffs, the impact of trade on the standard of living can be substantial. Even in today's post-Uruguay era of reduced trade protection, the United States would stand to gain an estimated $12.4 billion in economic welfare annually if it eliminated all remaining tariffs and quota restraints on imports.[1]

In addition, one must also consider many domestic industries as consumers of imported intermediate-input goods, such as steel, chemicals, textiles, and other industrial components used in making final products. Producers of the final manufactured good benefit from both the increased availability and quality of imported inputs and their lower prices. These domestic industries are also often able to expand the markets for their final goods both domestically and abroad as a result of the imported inputs.

The supposed curse of low-priced, shoddy imported goods is an old protectionist canard that is particularly insulting to consumers. Imported goods are subject to the same product standards as domestically produced goods, as explicitly stated in the national treatment principle of the WTO. The availability of cheaper goods gives consumers greater choice, and if those products are also of lower quality, it is up to the consumer to purchase them or reject them. It is furthermore at least as likely that imports enter the market to compete at the other end of the quality spectrum, providing higher quality products or special differentiated features.

While workers in some import-competing industries may lose—or at least suffer an adjustment cost—from trade, there are many other workers who gain substantially from trade and from globalization in general. Just as trade decreases the demand for some types of labor, it increases the demand for others. In developed countries, workers with higher education and special skills tend to benefit most from globalization, a factor that will play a role in recommendations for improving the plight of workers caught in declining industries (not just because of trade).

Protection may even damage the workers it is intended to help. By sheltering a domestic industry from competition, protectionist policies create perverse incentives for investment and employment. Consider a young worker hired by a steel company that was able to charge higher prices because of tariffs and quotas in the late 1960s. Experience has shown that protection does not solve the underlying adjustment problem of uncompetitive firms but only postpones the day of reckoning. In the meantime, the worker has made investments in her career, perhaps purchased a home in the area, and forgone other job and training possibilities.

When, despite continued protectionist measures, the roof finally caved in during the early 1980s, the steel firms finally did what they should have done earlier: they modernized, closed unproductive plants, improved their management practices, and downsized their workforce (a process that had actually begun in the 1970s). After ten or fifteen years of employment in a protected industry, many steel workers were then left with limited skills, home mortgages, families to support, and no job in the middle of a recession. Can one still argue that the protection served the interests of these workers?[2]

Consider also the role of the winners from trade liberalization: multinationals. It would be ridiculous to argue that multinational corporations do not benefit from trade; that is one big reason they are multinationals. They are not the only winners, however. In addition to the consumers and workers gaining from trade, other agents of and participants in trade gain by virtue of the reduced uncertainty of arbitrary market closure, which follows from the fundamental value proposition of the WTO. Multinational corporations (MNCs) are the most prominent examples of these agents, but they also include small- and medium-sized importers, exporters, and firms with a stake in international trade. It is also important to understand that the fact that such agents are willing to engage in the trade transaction allows workers and consumers along the value chain of the market to benefit as well.

It is therefore politically disingenuous to argue, as some of the more extreme critics of the WTO do, that MNCs "control" or have "captured" that organization. MNCs typically lobby in their own self-interest in favor of trade liberalization, intellectual property protection, and the removal of foreign investment regulations. Other groups lobby their pro- or antitrade positions as well. In the end, however, it is governments that do the negotiating at the trade talks, and they must represent the best overall and general interests, as they see it, of the countries they represent. Economic theory and revealed political practice converge to support the market-opening measures of WTO negotiations, based on national interests.

| Protectionism, Poor Consumers, and Corporate Welfare

The debate over trade policy is often presented as a sort of morality play, in which wealthy export-oriented corporations are pitted against workers in threatened industries fighting for a living wage. The political economy of trade protection suggests some unexpected results regarding the distribution of the costs and benefits of trade, however. As noted above, many domestic companies are importers of intermediate goods used as inputs; tariffs and other trade restrictions would tend to raise costs and lower profits for these domestic firms, possibly leading to layoffs. The jobs issue may therefore cut both ways when the government restricts imports.

The impact of tariffs may be even more perverse in terms of income distribution among rich and poor. William Cline (1997) studied the impact of protective tariffs and quotas in the U.S. textile and apparel industry on the economic welfare of different income groups, from the upper quintile of annual income to the lowest. As the gains-from-trade theory predicts, the country as a whole loses from the trade restrictions. But the surprising result is that the only income group that actually increases its economic welfare from protection are the wealthy, based on the gains of stockholders in protected companies. The poorest income groups suffer net economic losses from the tariffs and quotas, even when the increased wages of textile and apparel workers are taken into account. In general, protection in this case tends to have a regressive distributional effect on economic welfare.

Some straightforward economic reasoning shows the reasons that this is so. The trade restrictions force the prices of imports to rise, which allows the producers of domestic import-competing goods—in this case, American-made textiles and clothing—to raise their prices as well. The next step is to consider who will pocket the extra profits in the domestic industry: the workers or the owners of the company's capital (the stockholders). Generally, the extra profits are shared, but how big the slice is for each group depends on their relative bargaining power. Cline's study suggests that, in this case, the stockholders, relatively small in number but concentrated in the upper income brackets, got a larger share of the extra profits than did the more numerous workers.

Add to this factor the impact on consumer prices of clothing. Keep in mind that textiles and apparel are necessity goods and that imports of cheaper clothing are the ones most often targeted for protection, since their lower prices tend to pose the greatest threat to domestic firms. As a proportion of income, the higher prices of clothing and related items hit the poor much harder, since clothing is a greater proportion of their total expenditures and since the cheaper imported grades of clothing subject to tariffs will experience the greatest relative increases in price. The protection-induced losses to consumers in the lower income groups more than offsets any protection-induced wage increases received by the industry's workers.

In other protected industries, the workers (especially those with higher skills) have more bargaining power and would be able to claim a larger share of the profits generated by the trade restrictions. However, the pattern of hitting poorer consumers with the consumption losses is common among protected goods, since cheaper, commodity-grade items most often become the targets of protectionist campaigns. When quotas restricting Japanese automobile imports to the United States and later to the European Union countries were negotiated in the 1980s, the models restricted most heavily (and whose prices rose most in relative terms) were the smaller subcompacts popular among lower-income consumers. Other common trade restrictions that tend to discriminate against the poor include those levied on food, footwear, children's toys, and consumer electronics.

At its worst, then, protectionism is a particularly perverse example of corporate welfare. Not only does the larger share of extra profits from protection go to the owners of capital rather than to the workers, but the deficient business practices of the firm's management are bailed out at public expense. It is important to note in this regard that adjustment pressures may come from a legacy of protection itself. The underlying problem, in other words, may be the firm's poor management or ill-advised investment decisions from earlier periods of shelter from import competition. In industries with a history of import protection, these problems may sometimes be linked with disincentives to adjust to the forces of economic change. After all, if an industry is being protected from import competition, individual firms that otherwise would have to adopt the latest and most efficient technologies, production techniques, and management practices may find it unnecessary to do so—at least in the short run. Jagdish Bhagwati has called this the "goofing off" effect of protectionism, which in turn can create new adjustment problems later on (Bhagwati 1988, p. 105).

Adjustment is admittedly an antiseptic term for situations that create possibly serious hardship for individuals. There are of course all the caveats and mitigating circumstances discussed earlier. Trade is but one of many sources of adjustment pressure, and the costs of adjustment may not always be severe. Yet the haunting scenario of job displacement, steep wage losses, and the burdens of relocation are all too real during times of rapid economic change. If a dominant employer in a town or region closes its gates, the upheaval may encompass entire communities. Economic catastrophe typically brings with it psychological and social catastrophe as well. Such situations are all the more troubling as public policy issues because they often affect society's most vulnerable workers: those low-skilled, low-wage laborers with few attractive alternatives in an increasingly high-skilled economy.

At the same time, intervention by the government to prevent the adjustment pressures from materializing is usually worse. Restrictive trade policies are blunt instruments that often lead to undesired outcomes. The protection may end up bailing out the managers and stockholders of the firm more than the workers. The underlying economic changes that drive the adjustment process cannot be suppressed indefinitely, and the cost of delaying the needed reallocation of the economy's resources is probably much higher than the cost of adjusting right away. The government of France found this out the hard way when it imposed trade restrictions on imported steel throughout the 1970s and early 1980s in an effort to maintain the industrial structure of its Alsace-Lorraine region. When the retirement of the old, antiquated, state-owned steel mills of that region could no longer be delayed, displaced steel workers rioted.

The blurred lines between the sources of adjustment pressures, especially between technology and trade, make the use of trade restrictions to resist adjustment particularly inappropriate. Any reforms of the WTO that would make it easier for governments to impose trade restrictions would be equally ill advised. In general, governments must find a delicate balance between aiding displaced workers and making sure the needed adjustment actually takes place, whatever its cause.

One reason that the WTO enters the adjustment debate is that it does allow for emergency tariffs for adjustment purposes when there is a surge of imports in a member country. These measures, contained in the escape clause, were part of the original political compromise needed to establish the GATT. There is no doubt that this and other types of safety valves will continue to be important as a way of maintaining the political consensus for trade liberalization. However, these measures have never proven to be effective in dealing with the adjustment problem, since they have merely delayed the day of economic reckoning for the affected industries. They have also rarely satisfied the protectionist interests they were meant to appease because of the conditions and compensation requirements for their use.[3] All of the extra hoops that governments must jump through were deemed necessary in order to prevent the basic value proposition of the WTO—and thereby the basic consensus holding its members together—from unraveling. The WTO has found, in other words, that it cannot effectively liberalize trade while at the same time solving the adjustment problems of its members. This task must remain primarily a domestic undertaking.

| Adjustment Policies and Assistance

Governments have the responsibility to make sure that the policy environment facilitates adjustment to trade. The most basic element is effective macroeconomic management of the economy. A stable, non-inflationary environment encourages investment, entrepreneurship, and economic growth. In addition, the education system must provide the necessary skills for job viability in a changing economy and labor laws and regulations that allow worker mobility and adaptation as job markets change. The easier it is for a displaced worker to find a new job, the less will be her trepidation about trade and the WTO. Other policy suggestions have included income-compensation transfers to displaced workers, general wage subsidies to all low-wage workers, retraining subsidies, and government-sponsored job information. All of these proposals involve considerable challenges in terms of policy design and effective incentive structure, not to mention cost to the public.

Regarding interventionist micropolicies to deal with adjustment, economists are divided. Certainly, the modest programs of trade adjustment assistance attempted over the years in the United States have failed to quell protectionist sentiment or alleviate the disruptions of adjustment. These programs have always suffered politically from the fact that they provide only partial coverage of lost wages, require proof that the job loss was due to imports, and create disincentives for reemployment. The approaches of several European countries to dealing with adjustment, through a combination of industrial subsidies and labor regulation, have not been successful either, since they have often led to elevated levels of unemployment.

Recent proposals to reform trade adjustment assistance (TAA) have shifted the focus to a general coverage of workers displaced for any reason. Kletzer and Litan (2001), for example, propose a wage and health insurance subsidy to cover net losses in wages once the displaced worker finds a new job. This sort of plan would cover the most serious losses of those who suffer job displacement, while requiring that the job adjustment take place before payments begin. Some of these reforms were incorporated into the U.S. Trade Adjustment Assistance Reform Act of 2002.[4]

In an age of fiscal conservatism, any unemployment compensation scheme must make sense in terms of its costs and benefits.[5] There are also political factors involved in such an analysis. But the critical consideration in this case is whether the additional worker protection is effective in promoting a political consensus for trade liberalization. Do the additional gains from trade outweigh the costs, budgetary and otherwise, of government subsidies to displaced workers, for example? Recent studies of political attitudes toward trade suggest that the benefits from such a safety net in terms of public acceptance may be quite high, at least in the United States.[6]

Realistically speaking, it is virtually impossible to protect everyone who might suffer a loss from open international trade, or from any other economic change. In particular, firms with fixed assets that suffer capital losses from increased import competition will probably continue to resist trade liberalization; apparel and steel companies in developed countries are the most prominent examples. Labor unions, as noted earlier, also often have strong economic incentives to pursue protectionist policies. They can be expected to continue their opposition to the WTO and to favor the inclusion of labor, environmental, and other standards that will protect existing jobs in sectors they represent.

In general, the adjustment problem has served as a potent rallying cry for trade restrictions, amplified by the protectionist furies of declining industries. Governments have often been timid in responding to this problem because either (1) adjustment policies require visible budget expenditures (while trade restrictions do not), or (2) the open acknowledgment of adjustment costs risks political accusations that the government is sitting by while foreign forces disrupt the economy.

Yet, in the end, policymakers can more effectively defuse the opposition to trade and the WTO by a combination of safety net policies and a public emphasis on the cost of *not* adjusting. A growing economy must constantly adjust, and avoiding adjustment due to import competition necessarily impairs the country's ability to gain from increased exports, exposure to new technologies, and access to more and better goods. A study by Lewis and Richardson (2001) compiled information on the benefits of "global engagement" by domestic firms in the United States and in other countries, either through entering export markets, adjusting to import competition, taking part in inbound or outbound foreign investment, or importing components and capital equipment. The evidence indicates that firms that establish such links with global markets tend to experience increased worker productivity and to pay higher wages. Aggregate gains to the U.S. standard of living from this type of globalization are estimated at 1–3 percent, with 0.5–2 percent faster annual growth in the standard of living.

Shifting the policy debate toward facilitating adjustment and away from quick-fix solutions based on blocking imports or changing WTO trade policy rules to make it easier for governments to implement such protection would therefore be a step in the right direction. If political forces opposing trade must be neutralized, efforts should focus on making the transfers in such a way as to address the broader underlying problem: getting actually or potentially redundant workers hooked up with the proper skills and training to make their services viable in the marketplace and strengthening incentives for firms to adjust to global market opportunities.

| *Overcoming the Caricature*

Let us come back to one of the political cartoons introduced at the beginning of the chapter and all of the frustration it represents. It is an interesting exercise to take this picture apart as a way of summarizing the political economy of trade and the WTO. Consider first the allegation that trade eliminates jobs. A pro-trade cartoon on this same theme could just as well show trade *creating* jobs, perhaps in the form of a globalization broom sweeping away inefficiency, high prices, monopoly practices, and obsolescence to reveal new doors of opportunity for economic growth and new jobs. A more balanced view, using different symbols, would show trade—along with technology, investment, changing tastes, and all other economic forces of change—transforming existing jobs into new jobs. The appropriate metaphor might be an adjustment machine that processes old jobs formed from old market conditions and old job requirements into new jobs and economic growth based on correspondingly new market conditions and job requirements. Most (if not all) new jobs will be higher paying than the old jobs. All economic forces, not just trade, are involved in the input-output processing of the machine. Education, worker training, job information, and government policies to promote (or hinder) adjustment also affect the functioning of the machine and play a large role in determining how quickly and smoothly the job transformation takes place.

The "jobs processor" presents of course a more complicated picture, defying the simple reductionist caricature of trade policy as having uniformly positive or negative effects on all individuals. It also confirms the difficulty that economists would have in pursuing careers as editorial cartoonists. An effective cartoon of this sort typically shows a clear winner or loser, hero or villain, buffoon or sage, saint or sinner, with the forces of good and evil lined up according to the intended political message. It is a form of blunt political discourse intended to portray the issue in terms of black and white; by definition, the message cannot be completely fair, no matter what side is taken.

The more difficult, sometimes tedious, and usually thankless but necessary task is therefore to ensure that both sides receive fair representation and to minimize the disinformation that often accompanies emotional debate. Portraying the WTO as a dustpan working with a globalization broom, for example, appeals to those groups convinced that international trade institutions are equal partners with global economic forces in "destroying jobs."

At the same time, the image reinforces the WTO's alleged role as a tool of capitalist or corporate manipulation in the world economy.

Yet these implicit messages wildly exaggerate the ability of the WTO itself, which is essentially a set of consensus-based agreements with no powers of legislation, to change the course of domestic economies. Anyone who thinks that eliminating or rewriting the WTO will somehow stem the tide of globalization is sorely deceived. Globalization is driven by rapidly advancing technology, communications, and competition. Individual governments can do little to affect cross-border movements in these forces. Even within their own borders, global market forces will eventually, inexorably, assert themselves. Governments, not corporations, founded the WTO to help them do what they know they should do: reduce trade barriers and take advantage of the economic benefits of increasingly interdependent markets.

Opposing globalization and the adjustment that goes with it through a strategy of opposing the WTO is, in the end, a rearguard action against structural economic change and a political bid to shift the burden of that change to others and to the economy as a whole. Do away with the WTO, and many governments will succumb to the protectionist influences that the WTO was intended to keep at bay. Trade flows will shrink. Most older import-competing industries will temporarily maintain employment levels, until market forces working around the trade restrictions allow consumers or downstream industries to find alternative products. Potential new and probably higher-paying jobs, especially in export industries, will not materialize, as other countries with more open trade policies develop them or export markets close their borders in retaliation. Or the new jobs too will have to wait for economic forces to make their end-run around the trade regulations. The result: many if not most "protected" workers will eventually lose their jobs anyway or suffer declining real wages, while the economy as a whole follows a longer, more painful adjustment path with stagnating innovation and economic growth.

Try this caricature: keep the same picture and just relabel everything. The room is "your national economy." The broom is "protectionist special interests." The dustpan is "trade restrictions." The dustbin is marked "new jobs" or, even better, "economic growth."

Those in favor of trade restrictions will surely protest that the pro-trade focus on new jobs and economic growth ignores the cost of adjustment imposed upon displaced workers. To this complaint, one might respond that the original cartoon ignored the cost of *not* adjusting. In the battle of competing caricatures, perhaps it would be best to present both pictures, side by side, two camps seeking to persuade, each providing its own view of the same phenomenon of globalization. Yet the more the arguments that highlight the benefits of trade liberalization enter the public debate alongside the protectionist views, the more individual citizens will have the information needed to draw informed conclusions themselves. Trade theory suggests that, for workers in a globalized economy, another room exists next door to the one marked "your [current] workplace," a room with new jobs, more consumer choices, better prices, and a higher standard of living. A balanced view will spread the word, so rarely articulated for broad public consumption, about how much protectionism hurts.

4

Whose Trade Organization?

Can it be that the economic affairs of sovereign nations are ruled by a secret cabal of unelected bureaucrats? Many protesters in Seattle and elsewhere have decried the "undemocratic" nature of the WTO, which is often described as "faceless bureaucrats" dishing out their brand of corporate, free trade justice without regard to the environment, human rights, labor conditions, or national sovereignty. A Seattle-inspired editorial cartoon offers the prevailing stereotype of WTO officials: arrogant, bullet-headed (bald again!) sourpusses in business suits with Chablis glasses, perched safely on the WTO balcony, shaking their fists at the masses of antiglobalization protesters below. One sneering bureaucrat announces the WTO response to the protesters: free speech is declared an illegal barrier to trade! Thus the WTO again steamrolls over any opposition to free trade, just as it allegedly regards environmental rules and human rights concerns as illegal barriers to trade.

This devastating caricature captures a popular view of the WTO among protesters, but also reveals popular misconceptions about the WTO. Who are these faceless bureaucrats? Are they from the WTO Secretariat in Geneva? None of the international civil servants, including the director general, can make any WTO policy declarations; such statements could only come from a multilateral agreement among all WTO member countries. Are they trade ministers representing their respective countries? The largest WTO members carried pro-environment (European Union) and pro–labor rights (United States) proposals into the Seattle meeting. The cartoon's depiction of spontaneous agreement in the WTO on *anything* is in itself laughable; nothing of significance can change in the WTO without consensus among the entire membership, a process that typically takes many years. The message in the picture also seems to be that the WTO acts as a shadowy world government, eliminating human rights whenever they are inconvenient for world trade. This misperception comes, again, from a misunderstanding of the organization.

In order to construct a more realistic view of the WTO, it will be necessary to understand something of its structure, decision-making processes, and underlying principles. The following discussion will stick to the essential highlights of the way the WTO is structured (no organizational charts, no legal jargon) and its most important activities. We begin with some history and a summary of trade relations up to the founding of the WTO in 1995. There follows a description of the WTO as an international organization and its functions and role in international economic affairs. The chapter then examines the important role of the WTO dispute settlement system and prospects for its reform. Finally, as a preview of coming chapters, we turn to the difficult problem of extending the WTO into nontrade areas, in light of the fundamental value proposition of the WTO to its members.

| *History Matters*

In the previous two chapters, the main point was that trade is good; economic theory suggests that all countries would maximize their economic well-being by unilaterally opening up their borders to free trade. When an economist brings up this point in front of government officials, she is likely to be hooted out of the room as being unrealistic, politically naïve, and impractical. Domestic political considerations, they would remind the economist, prevent the government from unilaterally lowering import barriers. And yet governments have in the end tended to negotiate agreements that move significantly in the direction of freer trade, despite political opposition. Have economists had the last laugh on this issue?

The history of trade relations since World War II suggests that the economics of free trade has indeed won major victories in forging a more open trading system. The means by which this happened, however, actually contradicted the policy advice of economic theory, which is to open markets unilaterally. Trade agreements in the postwar period have managed to overcome the resistance to unilateral free trade by applying the concept of reciprocal trade concessions, which are locked in by tariff binding and similar commitments to prevent backsliding. This method is a device inspired by economics but based on the constraints of domestic and international politics. The catalyst was the bitter experience of the disaster during the years 1929–1945.

The world trading system as it existed in the period after World War I ended in 1919 collapsed almost completely during the years of the Great Depression. Most countries during this time had established bilateral trade agreements with their various trading partners. There was no broad multilateral trade agreement, and the lack of an international institution to anchor trade relations was costly. The response of governments to the great economic contraction of the 1930s was to close their borders to imports in hopes of reserving domestic markets for their own workers and thereby shifting their unemployment problems to other countries (this practice became known as the "beggar thy neighbor" trade strategy, named after a card game that follows a similar pattern). In the absence of any systemic framework for trade negotiations, this policy spread from country to country.

At the same time, international political tensions increased as war clouds loomed in Europe and Asia, and the suspicions among countries threatening military buildups and aggression poisoned trade relations as well. The joint deterioration of national economies and of global economic relations created a vicious circle of suspicion, reduced global trade and finance, and worsening depression. It is difficult to disentangle causes and effects between economics and politics during this troubled time, but it is fair to say that protectionist trade policies were part of a general deterioration in international relations that culminated in world war.

Near the end of World War II, in 1944, representatives of the Allied powers met in Bretton Woods, New Hampshire, to discuss the future of world economic relations. The hope was to develop international economic institutions that would promote prosperity and peace in alignment with the foreign policy goals of the victorious Allies. As a part of that plan, the Bretton Woods meeting led eventually to the establishment of the International Bank for Reconstruction and Development (World Bank), the International Monetary Fund (IMF), and the General Agreement on Tariffs and Trade (GATT).

The GATT was founded in 1947 as a truncated, "provisional" arrangement of the International Trade Organization (ITO). The ITO had been designed as the third leg of the Bretton Woods system but was never ratified. Political opposition in the United States, in particular, was its downfall. The ITO had included an ambitious agenda of economic and trade-related topics, including international agreements on employment and economic policy, economic development and postwar reconstruction, restrictive business practices, intergovernmental commodity agreements, and commercial policies. However, the negotiating countries could conclude a final agreement on only the last of these topics, which resulted in the GATT. Even then, the issue of national sovereignty played a large role in international trade relations. It will be useful to keep this point in mind in the subsequent discussion, since the content of the GATT showed specifically just how far the United States and other countries were willing to go in 1947 to reach a consensus on international trade policies.[1] It was never intended to serve as a permanent international institution, and its lack of a treaty framework meant that it had no members, only "contracting parties." The institutional limitations of the GATT eventually led to the creation of its more formal, treaty-based trade institution, the WTO.

Despite its inauspicious beginnings, the GATT evolved into a highly successful mechanism for trade liberalization. Its success was the result of an evolutionary process of negotiating methods that adapted to an expanding membership and changing agenda over several years. Table 4.1 summarizes the multilateral trade negotiations under the GATT. Because of its limited scope, the GATT covered mainly trade in manufactured products, but trade negotiations in the GATT system succeeded in lowering tariffs in these sectors from a depression-era average of 45 percent to post-Uruguay levels averaging about 5 percent. GATT-sponsored negotiations also resulted in the reduced use of nontariff barriers (NTBs), especially quantitative restrictions on trade, which tend in general to distort trade more than tariffs do.

The first GATT trade talks in 1947–1948 included only the twenty-three founding countries, and led to some 45,000 trade concessions, slashing all participating countries' industrial tariff levels by nearly 20 percent. This early postwar success in trade liberalization was the result of a legacy of extremely high tariffs from the Great Depression and World War II, which were ripe for the cutting, and U.S. willingness to lead the way on most-favored nation (MFN) tariff reductions as part of a new postwar economic order. The next four rounds of trade negotiations, in contrast, were much less successful. The first Geneva Round had harvested the low-hanging fruit of heavy protectionism, and after these tariffs were lowered, political difficulties stood in the way of further cuts. Negotiators attempted to continue with the line-by-line approach used in 1947, but a growing GATT membership was making this approach more difficult. In addition, the United States was no longer playing the same leadership role, as its imposition of escape clause measures and peril point tariff rate floors on trade negotiations prevented tariff reductions below levels that would trigger political opposition at home. Tariff cuts during this period of negotiations averaged only about 3 percent.

More extensive trade liberalization was revived with the Kennedy Round (1963–1967), named after President John F. Kennedy, under whose administration the negotiations began. With an ever-expanding membership, the GATT countries realized that a new approach was necessary, and they adopted a system of linear, across-the-board tariff reductions by broad sectors, rather than the old line-by-line approach. In addition, negotiations during this round addressed nontariff barriers for the first time, which resulted in an antidumping code and introduced preferences for developing

Table 4.1
GATT-Sponsored Multilateral Trade Negotiations, 1947–1995

Trade Round	Date/Countries	Prominent Agenda Items	Outcome
Geneva I	1947 23 countries	tariffs, item-by-item	concessions on 45,000 tariff items; U.S. weighted-average tariffs reduced 19%
Annecy	1949 29 countries	tariffs, item-by-item	modest tariff reductions; U.S. tariffs reduced 2%
Torquay	1950–1951 32 countries	tariffs, item-by-item	8,700 tariff concessions; U.S. tariffs reduced 3%
Geneva II	1955–1956 33 countries	tariffs, item-by-item	broad but modest tariff concessions; U.S. tariffs reduced 2.4%
Dillon	1960–1961 39 countries	tariffs, item-by-item; European Common Market	4,400 tariff concessions; U.S. tariffs reduced 4%
Kennedy	1963–1967 74 countries	tariffs, formula and line-by-line; nontariff measures; codes	overall average tariff reduction 35%; 30,000 tariff items bound; codes
Tokyo	1973–1979 99 countries	tariffs (formula); nontariff measures; codes	average tariffs of developed countries reduced 33%; codes; reduced nontariff measures
Uruguay	1986–1994 103 countries in 1986, 128 by WTO ratification in 1994	tariffs; textiles; nontariff measures; intellectual property; services; dispute settlement	tariffs of developed countries reduced 33%; creation of WTO as single undertaking

Sources: Adapted from Hoekman and Kostecki (1995), pp. 16–17; Evans (1971), p. 12; Curzon (1965), pp. 81, 87.

countries. Despite many difficulties—especially in agriculture, which continued to be highly resistant to trade liberalization—the Kennedy Round reduced industrial tariffs by another 35 percent.

The ever-expanding GATT had ninety-nine member countries by the time the Tokyo Round (1973–1979) was completed. Trade negotiations, which in the early postwar years took a matter of months to complete, were by now lasting several years. The Tokyo Round negotiators again used an across-the-board approach to tariff reductions, combined now with an even broader agenda of nontariff issues and new preferences for developing countries. The overall results were again impressive: a further reduction of industrial tariffs by 33 percent, to an average level of 6 percent among GATT countries, and a number of partial agreements on new, nontariff issues.

Yet the Tokyo Round made it clear that the growing membership and expanding negotiating agenda were pushing the limits of the GATT's ability to secure a unified and universally binding global trade agreement. This fragmentation became evident in the necessity of including in the Tokyo Round numerous codes that dealt with subsidies, product standards, government procurement, customs valuation, import licensing, meat and dairy trade, civil aircraft, and a revised agreement on antidumping measures. The codes dealt with sensitive issues for many countries that were unwilling to negotiate on them and were therefore voluntary. As a result, a country could adhere formally to the core GATT and participate à la carte in any of the codes.

After the Tokyo Round, the pressures to push for more multilateral trade liberalization across several fronts, including agriculture, services, investment measures, and intellectual property, led eventually to the launch of the Uruguay Round, whose results were described in chapter 1. By combining nearly all of the negotiations into a unified, single undertaking within the framework of a fully fledged, treaty-based WTO, the trading system finally got a permanent framework for comprehensive trade liberalization. Despite the persistence of protectionist sentiments in all WTO countries over the years and unresolved trade disputes among WTO members, nearly all countries continue to push for more trade liberalization. The fact that these countries have adapted their negotiating methods, put up with increasingly lengthy trade rounds, and persevered in reaching compromises to achieve agreements provides compelling evidence of the gains from trade—and the value of the WTO.

| The GATT/WTO System

The successes of the GATT negotiations over four decades encouraged countries to extend trade liberalization negotiations into other areas, such as services, trade-related investment activities, and intellectual property protection, as well as agriculture and textiles, which had remained largely exempt

At one point during the Tokyo Round negotiations in the 1970s, when numerous new topics outside the traditional trade areas were being discussed, the joke began to circulate that, if a cat has kittens, then the GATT must be having GITTENS. The next major multilateral trade negotiation, the Uruguay Round, spawned still other negotiating groups and topics, which would eventually be unified into a single undertaking by all members of the newly formed WTO. In order to follow all of the areas and activities currently covered by the WTO, it is necessary to become familiar with the main acronyms. Schott and Buurman (1994) provide an overview, and additional information is available at the WTO Web site (www. wto.org). Here is a brief primer:

ACWL (Advisory Center on WTO Law). Sponsored by the WTO and supported by donations from member countries, this facility is designed to provide legal assistance to developing countries in dispute settlement cases.

ATC (Agreement on Textiles and Clothing). Uruguay Round agreement scheduled to bring textile and apparel trade under WTO discipline by the year 2005. This transitional agreement will liberalize trade that had been restricted by an international system of negotiated quotas under the Multifiber Agreement. When these quotas are finally phased out, the ATC is designed to self-destruct, as WTO rules alone will henceforth apply to textiles and apparel.

CTE (Committee on Trade and the Environment). Created in 1994, this WTO body was established to identify the relationship between trade measures and environmental measures, and to make appropriate recommendations on how the multilateral trading system can be made more compatible with environmental goals.

DSB (Dispute Settlement Body). WTO body that rules on dispute settlement cases under the DSU. The DSB consists of all members of the WTO General Council, that is, all WTO members' representatives in Geneva, who oversee the operation of all of the constituent WTO agreements in general. The DSB rules on actions taken under the DSU.

DSU (Dispute Settlement Understanding). One of the most important new features of the WTO. The DSU established a system of review and procedures for when one WTO member complains that the actions or policies of another member have harmed it through a violation of WTO rules. Typically, a complaint would be followed by consultations, possible arbitration, then the formation of a panel of experts, the panel ruling, possible appeal to an Appellate Body, and, based on the outcome of the case, either compliance, compensation to the complaining country, or eventual retaliation. Panel reports and Appellate Body rulings can be overturned only by a unanimous vote of the DSB.

GATS (General Agreement on Trade in Services). A framework of principles and preliminary agreements regarding services trade, concluded in the Uruguay Round, which has formed the basis for further negotiations since then. It includes a set of basic rules on services trade, annexes dealing with applications to specific sectors, and schedules of market-access commitments. The GATS deals with the fastest growing category of global trade, with many barriers remaining to negotiate.

GATT (General Agreement on Tariffs and Trade). The original agreement that regulated trade policy and sponsored trade negotiations among its member contracting parties, founded in 1947. The original agreement dealt mainly with manufactured products and is now incorporated into the broader family of WTO agreements. GATT 1947 refers to the original text, and GATT 1994 refers to the revised version that emerged from the Uruguay Round negotiations as part of the WTO agreement.

GPA (Government Procurement Agreement). A Uruguay Round agreement that sets up rules for open and nondiscriminatory international access to public tenders for government purchases of goods and services. The rules extend to subcentral governments, such as states and provinces within the WTO member countries signing this agreement. The GPA was not part of the WTO single undertaking and applies only to those countries that signed it.

GSP (Generalized System of Preferences). A system of preferential market access, dating from the conclusion of the Toyko Round of trade negotiations in 1979, offered by developed countries to developing countries. The product coverage, beneficiary countries, and terms of the market access are controlled by the individual developed countries.

LDCs (Least Developed Country). A subset of developing countries representing the thirty poorest members of the WTO, including Angola, Bangladesh, Benin, Burkina Faso, Burundi, the Central African Republic, Chad, Congo (Democratic Republic), Djibouti, Gambia, Guinea, Guinea Bissau, Haiti, Lesotho, Madagascar, Malawi, Maldives, Mali, Mauritania, Mozambique, Myanmar, Niger, Rwanda, Senegal, Sierra Leone, Solomon Islands, Tanzania, Togo, Uganda, and Zambia. These countries receive special consideration in trade negotiations, including more flexible timetables for implementation, reduced requirements for negotiated "concessions" (see "S&D"), and also WTO-sponsored technical assistance. As of mid-2003, ten additional LDCs were in the process of accession to the WTO: Bhutan, Cambodia, Cape Verde, Ethiopia, Laos, Nepal, Samoa, Sudan, Vanuatu, and Yemen.

MEA (Multilateral Environmental Agreements). International environmental agreements and conventions that have trade implications. Part of the agenda in the Doha Round is to negotiate the relationship between existing WTO rules and trade obligations contained in some MEAs, to establish information exchange between MEAs and the WTO, and to eliminate trade barriers to environmental goods and services that could contribute to the goals of MEAs.

MFN (Most-Favored Nation) Clause. This is the main principle of the GATT/WTO system: nondiscrimination. All WTO members agree to treat all fellow WTO members in the same ways as their most-favored trading partners.

NTB (Non-Tariff Barrier to Trade). Any government-controlled trade restriction that is not a simple price-based tax or levy on trade and that introduces unequal treatment of foreign, as opposed to domestic, goods and services. In the broadest sense, NTBs include all government measures, other than tariffs, that discriminate against imports. The goal of most WTO negotiations is to reduce or eliminate NTBs and allow only tariff measures, since tariff reductions are easier to negotiate than liberalization of nontariff measures.

S&D (Special and Differential Treatment). A set of WTO provisions that apply to developing country members, designed to give these countries additional flexibility in complying with WTO obligations and more favorable treatment in multilateral trade relations. These provisions include (1) longer time periods for implementing agreements and commitments, (2) measures to increase trading opportunities for these countries, (3) provisions requiring all WTO members to safeguard the trade interests of developing countries, (4) support to help developing countries build the infrastructure for WTO work, handle disputes, and implement technical standards, and (5) additional provisions exclusively for LCD members.

SPS (Sanitary and Phytosanitary) Measures. A Uruguay Round agreement that allows member countries to use trade controls "to protect human, animal or plant life, or health," as long as the policy is based on sound scientific reasoning and does not discriminate among sources of supply.

TPRM (Trade Policy Review Mechanism). The systematic review of the trade policies and practices of WTO members on a periodic basis. The TPRM originated in 1988 and was eventually incorporated into the WTO agreement. It comprises reports by both the respective member governments and by the WTO Secretariat staff. It is intended for informational purposes, not for use in dispute settlement investigations. The TPRM calls for reviews every two years of the largest WTO members (the United States, European Union, Japan, Canada); every four years for the next sixteen largest WTO members; and every six years for most other developing countries.

TRIMs (Trade-Related Investment Measures). A Uruguay Round agreement that restricts member countries from imposing certain conditions on foreign direct investment, such as requiring local content, trade balancing (i.e., forcing exports to equal imports in net trade of the FDI firm), and foreign exchange balancing. The original TRIMs left many unresolved issues on the table for future negotiation.

TRIPs (Trade-Related Intellectual Property Measures). A Uruguay Round agreement that extended WTO disciplines into the protection of patents, trademarks, copyrights, geographical appellations, industrial designs, and trade secrets. Unlike most WTO rules, TRIPs requires both domestic enforcement and border measures as part of a member's compliance to prevent piracy and other violations. Developing countries were given longer transition periods for the phase-in of TRIPs requirements.

from GATT disciplines. In this regard, one of the most serious problems with the GATT was that its increasingly ambitious negotiating agendas were leading to the voluntary à la carte codes, as mentioned earlier.

Progress in these areas required an expanded institutional structure, which was finally realized in the founding of the WTO at the conclusion of the Uruguay Round trade negotiations in 1994. Building on the GATT structure, the WTO incorporated the original GATT rules (as amended in the Uruguay Round negotiations) and created new multilateral agreements: TRIMs (covering trade-related investment measures), TRIPs (trade-related intellectual property protection), and GATS (the General Agreement on Trade in Services). Along with further tariff reductions and some reforms of GATT rules, the WTO also introduced a revised and strengthened GATT Dispute Settlement Understanding (DSU), now applicable to all of the new areas covered by WTO agreements. Most important was the fact that the WTO was a comprehensive agreement, whose entire set of provisions had to be accepted as a "single undertaking" by all members.

The membership of the WTO as of mid-2003 stood at 146 countries and growing. Critics of the WTO who lament countries' alleged loss of sovereignty by subjecting themselves to WTO decisions should ponder the fact that nearly every country in the world is a member or else wants to be. The basic requirements for membership are that the country's economy have something approaching a market-based price system and a trade policy structure that is amenable to negotiation.

The revised set of trade rules has come to be known as the GATT/WTO system, a designation that acknowledges the legacy of the GATT in establishing the basic principles of multilateral trade rules, extended now to cover the broader set of products and activities represented by the WTO.

The WTO's purpose is to establish (1) a system of trade policy rules upon which all of its members agree, (2) a forum for negotiating market-opening and other trade-related issues, and (3) a dispute settlement system that tries to resolve trade disputes among the members peacefully (that is, without resort to an escalating trade war).

At the heart of the GATT/WTO system lie the principles carried over from the GATT. Most important among these is the most-favored nation (MFN) principle, which mandates nondiscriminatory treatment in trade relations among all WTO members. The importance of this principle is revealed in the fact that it cannot be amended without the unanimous agreement of all member countries. Essentially, this rule declares that WTO members are not allowed to play favorites among their trading partners. The term itself stems from the requirement that each member must apply trade policies to other member nations that are no less advantageous than the policies applied to its "most-favored nation." That is, everybody in the WTO gets the same (best) treatment from everybody else in the WTO: no discrimination, no favorites.

There are exceptions to the MFN rule in the GATT/WTO system. One of the most significant is the permission (under specified circumstances) to form customs unions or free trade areas of limited membership. These arrangements, such as the North American Free Trade Agreement (NAFTA), the European Union, and Mercosur (Argentina, Brazil, Paraguay, and Uruguay), violate the MFN rule in principle by giving the free trade partners special favored treatment. An example of negative discrimination is the use of antidumping and countervailing duties to restrict trade against specific targeted suppliers that violate certain defined fair-trade practices. A more systematic departure from MFN is contained in the Generalized System of Preferences (GSP), which allows more favorable tariff treatment toward certain products exported by developing countries. It should be noted that MFN is such a compellingly simple and powerful concept for conducting trade policy that all of the exceptions to it have always been controversial and are typically motivated by the politics of playing favorites among domestic constituents and trading partners.

Another principle enshrined in the GATT/WTO system is reciprocity in trade negotiations. The system of multilateral trade liberalization can only work politically if all countries that come to the negotiating table are ready to deal, that is, to offer concessions in the form of improved market access measures, in return for market-opening offers by other countries. This negotiating principle—"I will lower my tariffs if you lower yours"—is a key part of the political solution to the problem of overcoming resistance to trade liberalization at home. At home, negotiators will inevitably run into opposition from the domestic industries now exposed to more import competition by the lower tariffs. But reciprocity allows them to go home with a victory in the form of increased access to other countries' markets for the home country's exporters. Economic theory predicts, as shown in chapter 2, that

The WTO represents the idea of multilateral trade liberalization, but the benefits of the MFN clause have not discouraged many WTO members from concluding preferential trade agreements (PTAs) with selected partner countries. PTAs can range from simple free-trade areas (limited to duty-free commerce among the partner countries) to customs unions (free trade plus unified trade policy among all members) to common markets (advanced integration and common policies regarding trade, investment, and factor movements) to complete economic integration (integration of essentially all markets and economic activity, including monetary policy). The best-known PTAs include the North American Free Trade Agreement (NAFTA, an enhanced free-trade area) and the European Union (EU, now an advanced arrangement of economic integration). Yet there are more than a hundred such agreements, most of which have been concluded since 1990. How do these trading clubs fit into the world trading system, and how do they affect the WTO?

Trade theory, as described in chapter 2, indicates that the best policy is for every country to enjoy free trade from all sources. It follows that any efforts to limit trade liberalization to just a few partner countries will be an inferior policy. Viner's (1950) classic treatment of the subject established a cost-benefit test in which the economic benefits for a country from such agreements come from trade creation, based on the expansion of more efficiently produced imports and of new markets for exports within the PTA. The economic cost comes from trade diversion, caused by the fact that the preferential trade partner may be less efficient a supplier of imports than other countries outside the PTA. A comparison of the costs and benefits would allow an assessment of the economic desirability of the agreement.

More recently, economic theory has attempted a broader analysis of the impact of PTAs, including dynamic effects that may affect the members' pathways to greater openness and the possible impact of deeper integration on economic and political structures. For example, joining a free-trade area may contribute to a more rational economic policy, including subsequent multilateral trade liberalization. If PTAs lead to a progressive deepening of economic integration, further economic benefits may accrue beyond what multilateral trade liberalization alone could achieve, such as greater factor mobility, investment, and legal harmonization among the partner countries (although the countries could combine these added benefits with multilateral trade liberalization and be even better off). It is also possible that progress on important trade issues, such as services and dispute settlement, can make progress on the smaller scale of PTAs and eventually pave the way for multilateral treatment in these areas. The downside is that PTAs are by definition discriminatory and work to the disadvantage of those outside the club and also, from an economic point of view, of those inside the club. This is the feature that conflicts with the fundamental MFN principle of the WTO.

Yet the popularity of PTAs is undeniable, for many (mostly non-economic) reasons. In trade policy, countries like to play favorites, and they like to minimize the political costs and uncertainties of negotiations. First, it is easier for smaller numbers of countries to negotiate agreements on trade than it is for the nearly universal WTO membership to conclude a full-blown round of global trade agreements (Fratianni and Pattison 2001). In addition, countries have an easier time negotiating with like-minded or neighboring countries that have similar economic structures. These agreements are easier to sell politically at home, since they typically involve less painful economic adjustment costs and often serve broader strategic goals. In this sense, countries negotiating PTAs have, in contrast to WTO trade talks, greater control over the negotiating agenda and can customize the agreements to fit political goals and constraints. Interestingly, many countries also appear to use PTAs as a device to increase their bargaining power in multilateral trade negotiations, since any increase in the trade preferences within the PTA club tends to increase the incentives for other countries to bargain their way to equivalent market access.

The GATT/WTO rules on PTAs are ambiguous but have been tolerant in practice. Since PTAs would otherwise violate the MFN clause, the original GATT rules had to make an explicit exception for them—contained in article 24—mainly to accommodate existing British Commonwealth trade preferences. The thrust of the rule is that PTAs, such as free-trade areas and customs unions, are acceptable as long as they cover "substantially all trade" among the members and do not increase trade barriers against nonmember countries. These provisions were designed to prevent the use of PTAs as narrow, sectoral trade pacts subject to protectionist abuse. Technically, all PTAs among WTO members require review and approval in order to validate their consistency with GATT/WTO rules.

From the beginning, the GATT/WTO system had a difficult time reconciling article 24 with PTAs in practice. The European Coal and Steel Community (founded in 1951) was in apparent violation of the "substantially all trade" requirement, and the European Common Market (founded in 1957) was also questionable. However, these arrangements were tolerated as a part of U.S. cold war policy at the time. Greater economic integration in Europe, according to this strategy, would serve the purpose of unifying and strengthening Western Europe politically and economically against the communist threat.

The GATT's accommodation of European integration established a dubious precedent that has led to a muddled recognition of numerous other PTAs with controversial features. As a result of the official reviews of the compatibility of such arrangements with GATT/WTO obligations, only a handful have passed the test. The rest have resided in a sort of limbo with neither official acceptance nor condemnation. For trade policy analysts and economists, the main issue of PTAs is whether they are "building blocs" or "stumbling blocs" for multilateral trade liberalization. The general view now is that PTAs are a useful tool for partial trade liberalization and should be used by policymakers as an intermediate step toward broader economic integration and trade opening within the WTO.

The politics of trade, however, imply the continued use of PTAs for both economic and political purposes. The European Union, for example, has now nearly completed its internal economic integration with the introduction of a common currency and monetary policy, which may be a prelude to future political union. In addition, the European Union has many PTAs with other countries, mainly former European colonies. The United States plans to expand the NAFTA to a hemispheric Free Trade Area of the Americas (FTAA) and has concluded PTAs with Israel, Jordan, Chile, and Singapore, and as of mid-2003 had begun negotiations on a proposed Central American Free Trade Agreement (Costa Rica, El Salvador, Guatemala, Honduras, and Nicaragua, along with the United States) and on similar trade pacts with Australia, Morocco, and the South African Customs Union (South Africa, Namibia, Lesotho, Swaziland, and Botswana) (USTR press release, "United States and Chile Sign Historic Free Trade Agreement," June 6, 2003). U.S. special trade representative Robert Zoellick (2002) has explicitly stated that the United States intends to use such agreements as part of a strategy to spur progress on multilateral trade agreements, in addition to political goals.*

In summary, PTAs are beneficial economically if they lead to more and broader integration, especially multilateral trade liberalization. They become a problem when they replace or substitute for open trade policies. For example, any weakening of the WTO would be likely to lead to a proliferation of PTAs as countries would attempt to shore up their major trading markets, at the cost of reduced global trade, efficiency, and welfare.

*For a critical view of Zoellick's trade policy doctrine, see Gordon (2003).

both countries will benefit, on balance, from the exchange of concessions, even though they are not really concessions at all. Each country should lower trade barriers unilaterally to get the gains from trade, but reciprocal market opening makes good economic behavior politically possible. The third crucial principle is the orderly resolution of trade disputes. In any international agreement, there is always the possibility that a member might cheat on the negotiated agreements or otherwise impose new or disguised trade restrictions that negate the benefits of negotiated agreements. The WTO, as noted earlier, has no army and no jail, so there must be a credible process of resolving disputes that protects the integrity of the agreements and of the system in general. Otherwise, the negotiated agreements would lack credibility, and their economic benefits would be more uncertain and therefore less valuable. The WTO dispute settlement process strengthened this part of the trading system by eliminating the ability of a "guilty" party, especially a large and influential country, to veto an adverse ruling. At the same time, the process regards trade retaliation or punishment as a last resort and encourages the parties to negotiate a peaceful resolution of the dispute.

The three basic principles of the WTO—MFN treatment, reciprocity, and dispute settlement—create a simple but powerful framework for ordering trade relations among independent, sovereign countries. The signal accomplishment of the GATT was to harness these ideas into an integrated, self-reinforcing system, which could legitimately claim that if all signatories followed the rules, everyone would benefit. This consensual and collaborative approach is important, since the WTO has no direct enforcement mechanisms and no centralized authority. It cannot punish those who violate the rules, but only allow other members, under certain circumstances and within limits, to retaliate against the violator. The WTO maintains a historical continuity with this tradition by carrying over these principles to the broader areas of trade, investment, and intellectual property.

| *What the WTO Does and How Various Interests Are Represented*

The WTO is an umbrella organization that incorporates previous GATT accords and includes new agreements on trade in services and trade-related intellectual property rights. Unlike the GATT, which bound its contracting parties to a smaller scope of rules, mainly regarding trade in manufactured products, the WTO is an organization whose members commit to adhere to the entire set of agreements in a single undertaking.

The WTO goals, as described in article III of the 1994 Marrakesh agreement, include (1) administering multilateral trade agreements, (2) acting as a forum for multilateral trade negotiations, (3) administering a dispute settlement process, (4) reviewing national trade policies, and (5) cooperating with the World Bank and the IMF to achieve greater coherence in global economic policymaking. Of these goals, the second is the most important, since the goals and activities of the other four items flow from the agreements reached in the negotiations.

The nature of such multilateral negotiations suggests the complicated process that is typically involved in reaching an agreement. In order to focus the discussion as efficiently as possible and to limit the number of negotiating units, the WTO gives legal standing only to nations, as represented by their governments. This provision is mandated by the accepted practice of public international law. Companies, individuals, and other groups or organizations can find representation in WTO negotiations and activities only to the extent that governments incorporate their interests into their negotiating positions.

Recent protests against the WTO have railed against its "undemocratic" nature, so the issue of representation demands some further discussion. Whatever the protest groups have to say about faceless bureaucrats in Geneva, it is their own countries' delegations that have agreed on what the bureaucrats are supposed to do. The question of democracy, in this sense, must go back to the process of forming a negotiating position for each individual country. In most democratic societies, the channels for achieving influence on trade negotiations work through elected representatives and through executive branch agencies. Elected legislators will typically be called upon to vote for or against the final trade agreement, and their influence on the negotiations is potentially significant, since trade negotiators know that their negotiating position must address politically sensitive concerns. This is probably the most direct route for grassroots lobbying to have an impact. In addition, organized lobbies, industry organizations, and other interest groups can exert influence on legislators as well as on government agencies and other officials who have access to the trade policymaking process. In the United States, for example, the U.S. trade representative (USTR) conducts trade policy discussions with interagency task forces composed of representatives from various executive branch departments. These discussions allow a wide range of conflicting views to be thrashed out in advance of higher level discussions on negotiating positions. The USTR also holds discussions with representatives of business and various industries, and some interest groups lobby the USTR directly.

Negotiating trade policy issues in democratic societies therefore involves, in basic terms, a two-stage process (see Putnam 1988): (1) at the national level, identifying the trade-offs and compromises in trade policy that recognize domestic political constraints, and (2) in international negotiations, identifying the trade-offs and compromises necessary to get an agreement among countries that will simultaneously satisfy each country's political objectives at home. Having identified the structure of political influence, it is also clear that actually achieving influence cannot be guaranteed for any specific point of view. Certain environmental, labor, and human rights groups complain, for example, that they do not have their fair share of access or influence on the trade negotiation process. Yet this complaint points to the role of domestic political structures and current administration attitudes, not the WTO as such, as the source of their problem. At the same time, it would be difficult to argue that these concerns have been ignored in trade negotiations, since the United States and the European Union, among others, have pushed for discussion of environmental and labor standards in WTO meetings.

Yet for those groups that are currently frustrated in their attempts to influence trade policy rules through the WTO, this study will offer some alternatives to what must be considered the pipe dream of creating a "green" WTO. Aside from some reforms that may be possible in submissions to dispute settlement panels, the main channel of effective influence will probably be through treaties and conventions that directly address the environmental or social issue. The fact remains, however, that international institutions such as the WTO will continue to operate on well-established rules and traditions that apply to all treaties and official international bodies: it is the governments that make the decisions and define the agendas. Chapter 9 will address the issue of nongovernmental organizations' participation in the WTO in more detail.

| *The Ongoing Activities of the WTO*

Multilateral trade negotiations are momentous events, usually taking many years to complete, but their successful conclusion leaves a number of tasks to be carried out on a day-to-day basis. The WTO has set up mechanisms for both the big picture activities—ongoing trade negotiations and agendas for new negotiations—and continuing operations requiring full-time staff.

The WTO is officially headed by the Ministerial Conference, a sort of committee of the whole of the WTO membership. Each government's delegation to the Ministerial Conference is usually headed by a trade minister or equivalent, and the group meets about every two years, as it has done in Singapore (1996), Geneva (1998), Seattle (1999), and Doha, Qatar (2001). These are major events that usually involve high-level decisions on upcoming negotiating agendas, interim agreements, or other business commensurate with the senior level of representation. The Ministerial Conference appoints a director general (DG), who is in charge of the WTO Secretariat in Geneva. The DG is usually a senior trade diplomat or government official whose primary job is to provide moral leadership for global trade liberalization; to encourage, cajole, or scold governments at critical points in multilateral negotiations; and otherwise to present the WTO case for increased trade to the outside world.

The DG is also officially in charge of the Secretariat's operations, which includes activities ranging from translation services to technical and legal research and trade policy reviews. The WTO has a small staff of fewer than

600, an extremely small number compared with other international organizations, such as the World Bank (6,800 employees), the Food and Agriculture Organization of the United Nations (5,100), and even the International Telecommunication Union (730). Secretariat activities are strictly circumscribed by the WTO agreement and enforced with a correspondingly small budget of about $108 million in 2003.[2] Funding for WTO operations is therefore a small fraction of what other international organizations receive; as the World Bank and the UN Development Program, for example, each have $1.5 billion budgets.

The WTO staff are therefore not in a position to act as a world government, as alleged by some critics, much less to take over the world. One reason is that they simply do not have enough money. Another reason is that the WTO members have made sure that the Secretariat has no rule- or policymaking authority. All power emanates from the collective and consensual agreement of the WTO members.

| Dispute Settlement

One of the most important ongoing WTO activities, and certainly the most visible, is dispute settlement among its members. The WTO rules allow a member country to file a case against another member country to challenge a specific policy or practice, usually on the basis of its alleged incompatibility with the WTO system. If preliminary consultations do not resolve the dispute, the case is reviewed by a dispute settlement panel, which is charged with rendering a judgment as to whether the accused country's policy or practice is in violation with WTO rules.[3] If the panel rules against a specific policy or practice, the "guilty" country is technically required to change its practice or legislation in order to achieve WTO compliance. Either country can appeal the panel's finding on the basis of fact or law to a standing WTO Appellate Body, which can sustain or overturn the original panel's decision. If, after further consultation and possible arbitration, the loser refuses to comply with the panel's ruling, the country that filed the case is allowed to impose retaliatory measures within certain constraints.

The dispute settlement process is perhaps the single most controversial component of the WTO system, specifically where protests over alleged violations of sovereignty, antidemocratic practices, and antienvironmental biases converge. For some WTO critics, it is a question of legitimacy: the panels do not reflect any direct democratic representation, and they seem not to be accountable to any checks and balances. For others, it is an issue of transparency, openness, and access: the panel reviews are not public, and only governments involved in the dispute are allowed to submit testimony. For yet others, the issue is ideological: the panel rulings have in some cases declared environmentally based trade provisions to be inconsistent with WTO obligations.

The director general (DG) of the WTO has an important but somewhat obscure role in the conduct of global trade relations. Some of the more extreme antiglobalists regard the DG as a sort of CEO (chief executive officer) of world trade, imposing free-market trade policy rules on unwilling countries or acting as the lapdog of multinational corporations. Many caricatures of WTO officials as balding, middle-aged plutocrats that appeared in editorial cartoons during the Seattle protests bear a resemblance to Mike Moore, DG at the time, and to his predecessor, Renato Ruggiero. Yet the actual role of the DG is more modest in terms of actual power. Because of the political sensitivity of trade policy, members of the GATT and later the WTO delegated little formal authority to the DG and have kept the Secretariat's staff and budget small. In contrast, the managing director of the IMF and the president of the World Bank have large budgets and staff, with considerable authority over the disposition of loans. The DG's role cannot be one of decision maker, because all decision-making rights are reserved to the WTO members and the bodies to which they explicitly delegate such responsibilities, such as the dispute settlement panels. Instead, the DG has the public role of acting as a sort of cheerleader for trade liberalization, and he actually exercises greatest influence behind the scenes, working quietly to broker compromises, facilitate discussions, scold delegations for their foot dragging and obstructionism, or otherwise move negotiations forward toward a conclusion.

Supachai Panitchpakdi became the seventh director general of the WTO in September 2002. He became the first citizen of a developing country to hold the post, and he is the first to come to the position with a Ph.D. in economics. He succeeded Mike Moore of New Zealand as part of a prior arrangement involving the split of a

six-year term between the two of them; Moore served from 1999 to 2002. The political controversy that surrounded this arrangement is indicative of the way in which the external role of the director general has changed over the years.

Originally, the chief administrative position of the GATT was that of the executive secretary, and the entire GATT Secretariat had but a handful of staff in the beginning. The GATT represented only a part of the proposed International Trade Organization, which never came into being, and little attention was paid to staffing the operations of a supposedly temporary, stop-gap agreement. However, the importance of the GATT and the need for an effective chief administrator became apparent as the number of GATT participants (contracting parties) grew and trade negotiations became more extensive and complicated. By 1965, the GATT had grown in importance to the point that the new position of director general was created.

Sir Eric Wyndham-White was executive secretary and, later, the first DG of the GATT, holding these positions from 1948 to 1968. He distinguished himself as a skillful diplomat, shepherding several rounds of GATT negotiations to their conclusion (see Dam 1970, 339–40). White also established a tradition of long terms and a European identity for the DG position. While the GATT system itself relied on consensus and equal representation among all participants, the fact that the United States and the European countries represented the bulk of world trade had led to a tacit understanding that the DG would be European, with an American diplomat as one of the top GATT deputies. Similar arrangements prevailed at the other Bretton Woods institutions, with the World Bank presidency reserved for the United States and the IMF directorship for a European appointee. At the same time, the long terms for the DG made sense insofar as the role called for an ability to work well with the various national trade delegations, a task made easier by personal contacts and longevity in the position. White's successors were Olivier Long (1968–1980) and Arthur Dunkel (1980–

1993), Swiss diplomats with extensive trade negotiating experience who enjoyed the confidence of the major trading powers.

Stability in the DG position worked well at the time, as the three DGs in the first forty-five years of the GATT oversaw eight rounds of multilateral trade negotiations. Yet the terms of choosing the DG were increasingly questioned by the developing countries, which were joining the organization in large numbers and complaining that the United States and European governments dominated the DG selection process. By the beginning of the Uruguay Round in 1986, the GATT had 103 members, including 80 developing countries, and a more open selection process was put into place. Dunkel's retirement in 1993 triggered an acrimonious debate over the selection of his successor. The United States and the European countries had agreed upon Peter Sutherland of Ireland, but some developing countries were backing candidates from Uruguay and Colombia. In the end, Sutherland was chosen, largely because he was a strong candidate in his own right but also because developing countries were wary of creating a confrontation with the rich countries as the Uruguay Round was nearing completion. However, the signal had been sent: no more automatic DG appointments from the rich countries.

Sutherland served just two years as DG, thereby ending the tradition of long terms. He was given credit for bringing the Uruguay Round to a successful conclusion but stepped down as the GATT gave way to the newly created WTO, which he knew would be eager to start afresh with a new DG. Ironically, the position then went to yet another European, Renato Ruggiero (1995–1999), an Italian diplomat and government official, when the major candidate from a developing country, Mexico's Carlos Salinas (backed for a while by the United States), had to withdraw because of alleged political and criminal scandals. But now a new tradition was emerging: the expectation of a three-year term for the DG, with strong representation among the developing countries in the selection process.

The tension between developing and rich countries reached a peak from 1998 to 1999, as the United States and most European countries backed Mike Moore of New Zealand, and many developing countries (plus Japan, Australia, and the United Kingdom) supported Supachai Panitchpakdi of Thailand. After a long, drawn-out, and sometimes bitter process, a compromise was finally reached in which the DG position would go to Moore and then to Panitchpakdi, each for a three-year term. Moore therefore took over the DG position under difficult circumstances, as many developing country members of the WTO had resented what they considered to be strong-arm U.S. tactics that led to his appointment. All of this occurred as the members were preparing for the Seattle ministerial meeting that would presumably set the agenda for a new trade round. The cloud that followed the controversial DG appointment probably contributed to the tense atmosphere among national delegations in Seattle. The green-room tactics during the meeting (described in chapter 1), which attempted to force a consensus by limiting the participation of many developing countries, only amplified this rift, and the Seattle ministerial meeting ended as a major failure in trade diplomacy.

The WTO's failure in Seattle to begin a new trade round cannot be attributed to the DG, since the responsibility of setting the agenda and negotiating the important compromises lay with the major trading countries, and they blundered badly in this task. Success in the job of DG depends on effectiveness both publicly as an advocate of trade liberalization and also behind the scenes as a quiet diplomat who can bridge the gap between trade delegates on contentious issues. In this sense, the DG's job has become more difficult in recent years, as the term is now limited, the diversity of WTO membership is greater, and the issues are increasingly wide-ranging and intractable. Public criticism of the WTO by antiglobalization groups has put greater pressure on the DG to improve the WTO's image. In addition, the consensus-based governance within the WTO has become extremely difficult to manage well, as many developing countries seek systematically stronger voices. The role of the DG as broker and mediator has become all the more formidable.

After the Seattle meeting, Mike Moore worked hard to address these issues, improving the transparency of WTO information regarding deliberations and documents, spearheading initiatives to improve developing countries' ability to take part in negotiations and dispute panel proceedings, and opening up WTO meetings to outside observers from NGOs of all types. At the Doha ministerial meeting in November 2002, the WTO members finally completed the unfinished business of Seattle by agreeing upon an agenda for the new development round of multilateral trade negotiations. With the launch of the Doha Round, Moore finished his tumultuous term as DG on a positive note.

As Supachai Panitchpakdi assumed the position of DG in September 2002, his position was hardly enviable. The WTO faced many challenges, including contentious negotiating issues, continued antiglobalization sentiment, and a large bloc of developing countries wanting better outcomes and processes in the governance of trade policy. The solutions to these problems will depend in large part on the political will and creative thinking of the WTO member governments and their delegations. Yet history suggests that the DG's diplomatic skills will be required as well in order to move trade liberalization forward.

It is ironic that what was considered one of the most important diplomatic achievements of the Uruguay Round should now inspire such fury. Under the previous GATT system, the dispute settlement regime was much weaker, particularly since a country found "guilty" by a panel could veto the decision in the GATT Council, thus negating any official finding of wrongdoing. Many countries, led by the United States, argued specifically for a strengthened system that would prevent countries from escaping the consequences of an adverse ruling. Developing countries also supported the new Dispute Settlement Understanding (DSU), since it increased their chances of a favorable outcome in disputes with larger and more politically powerful countries.

In responding to these concerns, a few general points are worth noting here, which will be amplified in the coming chapters. First, the member countries of the WTO specifically empowered the Dispute Settlement Body (DSB) to pass judgment on the WTO-compatibility of national trade policies. This function was approved through the free acceptance of the international treaty obligations negotiated in the Uruguay Round and ratified by all of the participating national governments. No secret protocols were annexed to the treaty text; no surprises were sprung on countries after they signed on. To the extent that countries thereby sacrificed sovereignty over their trade policies, this was done consciously as part of a package agreement they chose to accept.

In addition, there are factors that mitigate the impact of apparently lost sovereignty when a WTO member country is found to be in violation of the rules. As the subsequent discussion on specific cases will show, a panel decision typically indicates that governments need to amend their statutes or practices in order to achieve WTO compliance. This requirement often implies that alternative measures are available that can accomplish the goal of, for example, protecting the environment, without violating the MFN principle in the treatment of imports. Of particular interest is the possibility that treaties or other international agreements could be concluded to accomplish the goals of the disputed national law or policy.

The WTO dispute settlement system in practice also allows the dispute to be circumscribed, which prevents an escalation of the problem into an unfettered trade war. In addition, the panel decision cannot force a country to change its laws; as an alternative, a WTO member can provide compensation to the complaining country by rebalancing its concessions (market access measures) in order to offset the economic loss to that country resulting from the disputed practice. Any WTO-sanctioned retaliatory measures that would be triggered by a defiance of the panel ruling must be proportionate and follow certain rules of nonescalation. In the meantime, parties to the dispute often continue negotiations over the issue, which allows other aspects of trade relations to proceed without general disruption. The DSU thus allows potentially inflammatory trade issues to be isolated diplomatically, so that the trading system can continue to function.

Finally, the WTO system preserves national sovereignty through member countries' right to unilateral withdrawal. Any country can withdraw from the WTO on six months' notice, for any reason. In view of the gains from trade enjoyed by WTO members, it is understandable that a country would be very reluctant to withdraw, even when a WTO dispute panel decision goes against it.

The Record of Dispute Settlement under the WTO

The WTO's dispute settlement system has been very active since its inception in 1995: 276 complaints, representing 180 disputed practices, were filed through December 2002. The United States and the European Union appeared most often as both complainants and respondents. However, a significant development under the new DSU is that developing countries are participating much more under it than under its GATT predecessor. Some developing countries have even complained against and won cases against the United States and the European Union.[4] The likely reason for increased developing country participation—and for increased overall requests for dispute settlement consultations—is that the panel decisions cannot be vetoed by the respondent country, as was the common practice under the previous GATT system.

Vermulst and Graafsma (2001) have studied the dispute settlement cases involving antidumping, countervailing duties, and safeguard measures from 1995 to mid-2000. They note that nearly all of the cases that went to panel investigations ultimately resulted in "convictions" on at least some of the allegations. Clearly, a country will not usually go forward with a panel investigation unless there is a very strong case in its favor and the country believes the outcome will benefit itself overall.[5] As noted earlier, the majority of complaints are settled "out of court" through consultations. Of the first 276 complaints, 71 had resulted in panel reports by December 2002, of which the Appellate Body reviewed 48, while 16 more were under active panel review. Thirty-five complaints were settled by "mutually agreed solutions" without panel investigations, and 23 were otherwise settled or inactive. The remainder of the complaints were still at the stage of consultations.

By most accounts, the WTO dispute settlement system has worked well, despite the political difficulties of a small number of cases, to be discussed below. The large number of requests for initial consultations gives testimony to the WTO members' satisfaction with it. The vast majority of cases are settled through consultations or an acceptance of a panel decision and the remedies it requires—usually a change in trade legislation to align national laws and policies with WTO obligations—and do not attract much media attention or opposition from NGOs. In fact the success of the DSU has caused a problem of funding; the case load has stretched available resources in the WTO Secretariat to the limit.

But then there are the special cases. Some trade disputes simply do not lend themselves easily to a third-party, legalistic resolution, as represented by a final panel report or Appellate Body decision. Some of the more controversial cases, for example, have involved high-profile disputes between the largest players, the United States and the European Union. For example, three prominent cases have gone through several rounds of dispute settlement under both the GATT and WTO: EU banana trade policy (WTO dispute panel decision supported the United States), EU trade restrictions based on U.S. beef hormones (decision supported the United States), and export tax credits for U.S. foreign sales corporations (decision supported the European Union).[6]

These disputes raged on for years and, in some cases, even after presumably final panel decisions, the two sides continued to argue over the adequacy of WTO-mandated policy reforms to resolve the issue, and secondary disputes arose regarding the appropriateness and scale of retaliatory measures under the rules. Yet, despite all stubborn resistance to being found "at fault" and conceding defeat in an official WTO decision, there are signs that the disputants may finally be putting at least some of these cases behind them.[7] In other words, there seems to be evidence that definitive dispute panel findings have raised the stakes of opposing the WTO system, even when the most politically powerful players are involved.

Other dispute settlement cases have sparked strong opposition from environmental NGOs, setting up showdowns between national trade law legislation designed to achieve a nontrade goal and that country's WTO obligations. In these cases, WTO critics have argued that the arrangement usurps a country's sovereignty by giving WTO rules primacy over national legislation. A counterargument is that WTO members knew full well what the DSU would be doing when they concluded the Uruguay Round agreement and that the DSU actually protects national interests against the erosion of trade benefits through unwarranted policies and practices by other countries. Chapter 5 will follow up on the sovereignty debate, and chapter 6 will discuss some of these cases in more detail.

A balanced assessment of the DSU recognizes its accomplishments and its problems. Some observers, such as Jackson (2000), have proposed mainly "fine tuning" to improve the performance of the system. There are a number of details of the dispute settlement process that have been the subject of debate, including the use of monetary compensation, professional representation in counsel and panels, and various procedural issues (Hoekman and Mavroidis 2001). One pervasive issue is transparency of the panel proceedings, which in itself has many dimensions. While the information flow under the DSU has improved greatly due to the posting of documents on the WTO Website, other information remains restricted. In addition, participation in and access to the panel proceedings is still limited to governments, a policy heavily criticized by many NGOs. This topic will be considered in chapter 9.

Barfield (2001) has more fundamental objections to the DSU, arguing that the binding legal force of panel decisions is disproportionate to the very limited legislative abilities of the WTO itself. He sees a danger in the DSU's establishment of absolute legal victory in formal disputes, in contrast to the GATT's legally ineffectual veto system, which had the advantage of forcing the disputants to work toward political, negotiated settlements. Barfield proposes a systematic return to nonlegal solutions in difficult dispute cases— mediation, conciliation, arbitration, even perhaps a delay until the next WTO trade negotiations—perhaps through intervention by the director general, who would have to be empowered to take such steps. In addition, he proposes a modified veto provision in which one-third of the WTO Dispute Settlement Body can block a panel report. In the absence of these additional checks and safety valves, Barfield argues, a recalcitrant party may not abide by unacceptable panel decisions and thereby undermine the entire WTO system.

In calling for a "softening" of the DSU, Barfield appears to have in mind the prolonged disputes between the United States and the European Union described earlier, which could theoretically escalate into larger trade wars whenever one side suffers a formal WTO "conviction."[8] Based on the record so far, his judgment of the DSU's faults may be premature; panel decisions in even the most contentious disputes have not led to a breakdown in the system. In any case, the definitive nature of panel decisions, as noted above, seems to have had a salutary effect on general confidence in the dispute resolution process.

Yet the point is that flexibility in dealing with politically charged disputes will certainly be necessary in order to avoid the systemic problems that might accompany a panel decision that places the government of a respondent country in a devastating political situation at home, for example. What is not clear is whether institutional change in the DSU—always a difficult proposition—will be necessary in order to achieve this result. As long as the United States and the European Union exhibit the political will to keep the system intact, confidence in the system will be sustainable. And while no one can necessarily count on this political will, it would take at least as much political will to alter the institutional structure of the DSU, as Barfield proposes, to achieve long-term systemic stability.

In addition, until adequate international institutions in nontrade areas emerge, crossover issues with trade components will be difficult to settle in any systematic way. That said, common sense suggests that WTO panels in the course of their investigations should seek—and also encourage the opposing parties to seek—any and all mutually acceptable alternative solutions in order to avoid trade conflict and to resolve the dispute. Such an approach may be especially promising in cases where the disputes involve a lack of resources and could be settled with foreign aid.[9] Disputes need not be resolved in every case with punitive measures.

The most serious problem with the DSU and its litigiousness is that it still makes the participation of developing countries, especially the poorest countries, difficult. Hoekman and Mavroidis (2001) identify the problems faced by small, poor countries with few resources available to assemble a legal team and prosecute a dispute settlement case. They recommend a number of reforms to improve the access of developing countries to the process, including the naming of a special prosecutor to bring cases for poorer countries, the establishment of independent sources of trade information to identify WTO violations harmful to these countries, and the use of monetary compensation for damages to settle cases.

These proposals have merit but would require institutional changes and cooperative efforts that may not materialize. At the 1999 Seattle ministerial meeting, WTO members took a more straightforward approach by establishing the Advisory Center on WTO Law (ACWL), which makes funds, training, and legal expertise available to developing country trade officials and lawyers for dispute settlement cases. The main problem with the ACWL is that it is dependent on contributions by the wealthier WTO members that have joined the center voluntarily, that is, those likely to be the subject of developing country complaints. However, general funding from wealthier WTO members for developing country technical assistance and capacity building has increased since the Doha ministerial meeting in November 2001 and may offer the most promising way to bridge the DSU resources gap.[10]

The Fundamental Constraint on WTO Reform

The WTO is an organization designed to serve the collective interests of its members by establishing rules and procedures that promote reciprocal market access, nondiscrimination, and dispute settlement. The overwhelming consensus is that the WTO has gone a long way toward its goal of achieving the gains from trade for its members. Its very success has created challenges, however. The following chapters will address the most prominent criticisms of the WTO regarding sovereignty, the environment, human rights and labor standards, the interests of developing countries, and the role of NGOs in the world trading system. In anticipation of these issues, this discussion of the basic structure of the WTO provides an opportunity to outline the principal constraints on altering its structure.

One set of proposed WTO reforms focuses on extending the reach of the system into new, nontrade areas. Achieving these goals would involve the use of trade sanctions as punishment for a country's noncompliance with specific standards, rather than for traditional protectionist purposes of supporting a domestic import-competing industry. The sanctions would therefore be designed essentially to increase the prospects for success in achieving the nontrade goal. For example, many WTO critics disavow any protectionist motivation in calling for a new set of trade rules that would enforce environmental, labor, and human rights standards on the global trading community. A common complaint among many anti-WTO activists is, for example, that they are unfairly accused of closet protectionism. Their position, they declare, is not that trade is bad, but that the WTO rules are wrong. They advocate a trading order "with a human face," to be realized with a new set of rules.

The general outline of such a system of standards would presumably include specific requirements or regulations on such items as pollution control, environmental practices, minimum working ages, working conditions, minimum wages, rights to unionize, and freedom from torture, genocide, and political incarceration. It would also require some sort of certification process, including inspections. The "teeth" to enforce such a global regime of standards within the WTO system would then come from a set of mandated trade sanctions against countries that fail the test or refuse to comply. Another variant of WTO reform to achieve these ends would allow individual countries to establish standards of their own regarding the behavior of foreign countries, enforced independently by unilateral trade sanctions.

Unfortunately, the purity of the motives cannot overcome the fundamental problem of subjecting the WTO system to a punitive overlay of social regulations. Recall that the very existence of the WTO rests on a simple but compelling consensus on the benefits of trade. In particular, WTO rules allow each member country's exporters and importers to make investments in trade activities without having to fear arbitrary market closures and corresponding losses in their investments. The entire thrust of the WTO is to generate certainty in the conduct of commercial policy; without this certainty, the value of the WTO to its members diminishes precipitously.

Consider for a moment the logical conclusion to this proposition. If market access can be held hostage to outside certification of pollution controls, working conditions, and so on, then the benefits of WTO membership go down the drain. The problem does not lie simply in complying with "reasonable" standards; it lies much more in the uncertainty of the costs of compliance with the standards and in the uncertainty of the certification process itself. No matter how much the advocates of such standards renounce any protectionist intent, compliance will often impose upon the country under investigation an additional financial burden or reduced competitive position on world markets, especially in cases dealing with pollution control and working regulations and conditions in poor countries. More important, some external entity must certify a country's clean bill of health, and with valuable and often hotly contested market access at stake, how can such a system ever escape the suspicion that certification decisions will be made politically? International certification commissions and safeguards against conflicts of interest would not dispel these fears, which, by the way, would eventually arise on both sides of the issue. In the end, certification will rely at least in part on the subjective nature of human observations, perceptions, data interpretations, and judgments.

Now step back to ponder the necessary intermediate step. How will such a regime be negotiated? A change in WTO rules would require in principle negotiations leading to a new multilateral consensus. In view of the problems stated above, how do the proponents of such changes imagine the new consensus emerging? Appeals to international brotherhood? Developing countries would say: let the poor brothers get rich before imposing the rich brother's standards. Appeals to natural law and human decency? The developing country response: we resent the requirement of being certified decent by others; besides, what happened to your arguments on sovereignty? Finally, if all else fails: agree to the new rules or the rich countries will simply limit their market access to you unilaterally. After centuries of colonization and the domination of the world economy by the more advanced countries, less developed countries will recognize this approach immediately. But can a world trading order be sustained through the intimidation of one group of countries by another?

The depths of resentment by developing countries against many aspects of the green and social agendas have become clearer in the recent WTO debate. Despite some efforts to portray international solidarity with poor countries on the issues among environmental, labor, and human rights activists, political support for socially based trade sanctions emanates almost exclusively from the United States and Europe. It is not difficult to understand the political economy of this issue from developing countries' point of view. Even for labor activists in poor countries, who are pushing for improved working conditions, for example, what does their cause have to gain under standards-based trade sanctions? Being a necessarily blunt instrument, trade embargoes or even targeted sanctions against specific export sectors could hurt large groups of workers in developing countries as much or more than the recalcitrant government. Progressive labor organizations would furthermore often find it uncomfortable to ally themselves with an external sanctions regime that would typically come across as a bullying force of the rich countries.

Perhaps the most important objection to the sanctions approach is that it is diametrically opposed to the spirit of the WTO and its basic value proposition. Despite the trade sanctions contingency contained in the DSU, the authorization for such measures has been limited to a handful of cases out of nearly 300 filed from 1995 to 2002. The WTO is an organization devoted to trade liberalization, not trade sanctions, and it would be a gross perversion of its principles to introduce new rules with the intention of forcing compliance on unwilling members by using trade as a weapon. It is undoubtedly extremely tempting for those advocating global social and environmental agendas to take advantage of the ready-made WTO framework of trade policy rules and potential penalties and use it as an irresistible enforcement mechanism. But such a move would be internally inconsistent, and the WTO membership would not tolerate a hijacking of its core agreement.

5

The WTO
and National
Sovereignty

International trade policy has always been linked in some way with a country's control over its domestic economic environment, and it is not surprising that the World Trade Organization is seen in some quarters as a threat to the national sovereignty of its members. The WTO, by its very nature, commits the signatories to loosen their control over market access by foreign firms and investors, and it is therefore indisputable that it requires the sacrifice of some measure of national sovereignty. As soon as foreign business is allowed to penetrate a country's borders, either through import competition or export opportunities, the government's control over the economy diminishes.

Many critics of globalization claim that open trade and investment policies deprive countries of control over their domestic economic environments. Openness to global competition, they argue, should not force countries to compromise on their own environmental, health, safety, human rights, and labor standards. Market forces are seen as a damaging influence, imposing severe competitive pressures on industries, which in turn put pressure on governments to weaken domestic standards. It is feared that the resulting ratcheting down of regulations, driven by competition from countries with the weakest controls, leads to a race to the bottom by all countries in order that their firms remain competitive on open global markets. The loss of domestic control is, by this reasoning, a *cost* of freer trade, and imports from weak-regulation countries are a manifestation of "social dumping."

An editorial cartoon entitled "Deregulation" expresses the fears of many WTO critics regarding globalization's impact on sovereignty. A faceless WTO bureaucrat sits as a global judge, gavel at the ready, ruling over all countries' national laws and regulations. He holds a pair of scissors, snipping out portions of a targeted country's documents before him: "Sovereignty," "Democratic Institutions," "Constitution," and "Local Control." A thick marking pen lies at his side, with which he has been making his own WTO amendments and insertions into national laws. The WTO, especially its dispute settlement system, is thus portrayed as an outrageous intruder into national sovereignty, destroying social programs and imposing new laws on hapless countries, the victims of an unaccountable world government. This chapter responds to these fears and perceptions by making three points on the issue of trade and national sovereignty. First, increasing global economic integration is a fact of life that has been embraced by most of the world's countries in their jointly developed WTO trading system, and policies that seek to insulate a country from world markets carry a heavy economic cost in themselves. Sovereignty in an interdependent world must, in other words, recognize the value of reciprocal economic relationships among states. Second, while a country's social regulations may sometimes come under pressure from international trade and competition, as a practical matter a country maintains autonomy over its own regulatory environment through the bargaining process. WTO agreements do not unilaterally or arbitrarily strip away domestic control over a country's internal laws and regulations. Third, a comprehensive solution to the problems of conflicting national social and environmental standards will be possible only by constructing new international institutions—not by grafting new rules onto existing trade agreements and institutions such as the WTO.

| *Sovereignty as an Economic Issue*

Bernard Crick, writing in the *Encyclopedia of the Social Sciences*, defines *sovereignty* as part of a theory of politics that requires every government to have within it a source of absolute power of final decisions and the ability to enforce the decisions. He goes on to observe:

> Political theory has perpetually oscillated between stressing one or the other of the two primal functions of government—survival and betterment. Sovereignty sees the world in the light of survival alone and is most appropriate as a theory when the world of settled expectations seems urgently threatened. (v. 15, p. 77)

It is not surprising, then, that the issue of sovereignty arises as economic interdependence is progressing rapidly, apparently threatening established economic policy. At the same time, the issue also reveals the difficulty that governments have in simultaneously pursuing differing goals of "betterment." Should the country focus on economic efficiency through open trade, and thereby increase its welfare by the traditional measurement of the standard of living? Or should the government seek, through regulation, to generate public goods, such as a cleaner environment, and to guarantee social benefits and standards for its citizens? It is important to recognize that countries can pursue both goals and that one may in fact reinforce the other; richer trading countries also typically enjoy higher environmental quality and more social programs. Yet the economic adjustment and restructuring often required in an open trading environment, which is in itself the vehicle for economic betterment, can nonetheless upset "the world of settled expectations." The central question is whether sovereignty over social policies is really sacrificed in the process.

Sovereignty is a differentiated concept. We must first ask: sovereignty over what? Traditional legal and political sovereignty generally refers to the government's ability to enforce its own laws and to maintain existing political structures within its own borders without foreign interference. This definition corresponds to the traditional understanding of "Westphalian sovereignty," which provided the foundation for the structure of the modern state after the Treaty of Westphalia in 1648.[1] Any voluntary sacrifice of this type of sovereignty would typically require explicit transfers of power to a supranational authority as, for example, members of the European Union have transferred certain policy and legal authority to centralized institutions in recent years.

Another dimension of sovereignty, however, is *interdependence*, or a government's regulation of the flows of goods, services, capital, labor, and information between the home country and the outside world. Krasner (1999) maintains that open interdependence is consistent with Westphalian sovereignty; a country can maintain internal control of its territory, laws, and policies while allowing trade, investment, immigration, and information flows. It is wrong, furthermore, according to Krasner, to claim that globalization has compromised traditional Westphalian sovereignty, which historically has never represented absolute control over external economic relations.[2] Trade agreements and membership in the WTO do not involve a significant sacrifice of legal or political sovereignty, since such an international institution has no control or enforcement power over national legislatures. Member countries do yield some trade policy autonomy by participating in international trade agreements, but there is otherwise no sacrifice of national lawmaking or enforcement powers.[3] In general, trade policy and other external economic policies represent a balance that the state strikes in maintaining internal political control while garnering the benefits of international economic relationships. In the United States, legislators examined this question carefully before the ratification vote on the WTO. While the ability of the WTO to find national laws and policies to be inconsistent with its rules has remained a contentious issue ever since, there was general agreement that the WTO did not compromise the *legal* sovereignty of the United States or any other country. A challenge to sovereignty in this sense refers, for example, to the possibility of the WTO adopting new rules, either by consensus or by majority vote, and then attempting to make them binding on the United States against its objections. In order to avoid this conflict, the WTO charter specifically states that any member that refuses to accept an amendment altering its rights and obligations will not be bound by it.[4]

Increasing trade and economic interdependence have, however, raised different sorts of sovereignty issues. As governments have come to take a more active role in the regulation of domestic economic activity, international trade potentially threatens to interfere with the ability of governments to implement regulations or to protect certain types of economic activity. There is some irony in this development, since it does not really involve a threat to sovereignty in the traditional sense of one government interfering directly with another's domestic jurisdiction or political control. Rather, it entails a possible conflict between the sovereignty of domestic consumers in their consumption choices and the sovereignty of governments in regulating those choices. Imports are a "threat" to domestic regulations to the extent that consumer preferences for imported goods may undermine a governmental policy goal. This type of sovereignty problem can therefore be viewed at least in part as a conflict between the government and its own citizens.

In this regard, *economic* sovereignty is a fluid concept and is measured in degrees, not as an absolute state of being. Consider the extremes. Absolute national economic sovereignty in a market-oriented economy implies *autarky*, that is, complete self-sufficiency and no contact with outside markets.[5] Such an isolated economy would limit the availability of goods and services to national production possibilities. Prices, outputs, and incomes would be determined by internal supply and demand forces, and government fiscal, monetary, and regulatory policies would operate without the influences of exchange rates, trade flows, and international investment. At the other extreme, a completely open economy would be exposed to global market forces, which could significantly affect prices, the rewards earned by labor, capital, and other factors of production, and the incentive structure for production, as described in chapters 2 and 3. Under this scenario, the government's sovereignty over the domestic economy diminishes, not because domestic economic policies are no longer valid, but rather because global competition enters the picture to change the incentives for economic activity.

The spectrum of economic sovereignty suggests that there is a certain trade-off between internal economic control and economic efficiency. This is where the gains from trade enter the picture. Most governments recognize the benefits of at least some international trade: why else would most of them be either in the WTO or knocking on its door? There is, therefore, a practical reason that countries may willingly give up some economic sovereignty: international trade and investment make them better off. In this sense, it is misleading, or at least one-sided, to view "lost sovereignty" as a cost of free trade. It is equally true, and perhaps more compelling, to view lost national income as a cost of *maintaining* autarkic economic sovereignty. A government and its citizens must therefore consider how much overall economic welfare the country should give up in order to retain sovereignty over economic activity. Put another way, the sacrifice of economic sovereignty due to increased trade and investment is the result of a calculated internal decision on betterment.

And what about domestic regulations and standards? In terms of trade-induced social dumping, environmental degradation, and so on, the issue boils down to empirical and cost-benefit questions regarding domestic economic policy. The empirical issue is whether increased trade in itself has compromised national sovereignty by eroding environmental and social standards. Studies of environmental policies have consistently shown that there is little, if any, impact of environmental standards on international industrial location, in part because they represent a small proportion of manufacturing costs. In fact, multinationals tend to gear their internal environmental standards to those of the most demanding market, since future market conditions are likely to require higher standards. This "California effect" tends to lead to upward environmental standards harmonization in some markets.[6]

Basic social protections in advanced industrial countries, such as laws against child labor, are also unlikely to have a large impact on the pattern of industrial location. The products that would be most affected by such laws would not be produced legally in labor-scarce industrial economies anyway. In general, the claims that trade erodes social and environmental standards have often been exaggerated. Nonetheless, many firms vulnerable to imports complain about competing with products from countries with lower labor and environmental standards and try to justify trade restrictions through such arguments. Yet, for import-competing industries, the economic issue is ultimately one of comparative costs, not social policy: their desire for tariff and quota protection is driven by competitive pressures. Sovereignty is not really at issue for these firms and should not be used as an excuse to protect uncompetitive industries.

But consider those cases where differences in social standards, combined with global competition, may have some impact on the firm's choice of location. For example, the high social charges mandated by Western European countries to be paid by domestic employers have arguably caused some domestic firms to relocate some production to lower-cost countries. Even here, the differential would typically have to be large in order for it to play a significant role in uprooting otherwise efficient local production. Worker productivity in advanced industrial countries, combined with the advantages of domestic market infrastructure, location, and supplier reliability, favor local production in the sort of manufacturing that is typical in these countries. Social and environmental standards are rarely enough to tilt the balance the other way. Ross Perot's "giant sucking sound" was therefore not only an inaccurate description of the effects of the NAFTA and trade in general, but also an insult to American workers, whose jobs depend on their higher skill and productivity, not on a paternalistic government protecting them from fly-by-night investment decisions and lower foreign environmental and safety standards.

Regarding European social charges on labor, there is widespread recognition that many such labor policies are flawed by features that distort market incentives and that trade is not the source of the problem. The main economic effects of such policies are domestic: they often lead to inflexible, unresponsive labor markets, a distortion of production patterns, and high unemployment. Reforms would be called for even in the absence of trade. The real economic issue, in the end, is how the regulations are affecting domestic investment, productivity, and growth, for these are ultimately the sources of increasing standards of living. Usually, trade is at most a symptom of the larger problem: the country's loss comes not from the trade accounts but from its inability to generate more economic value because of flawed domestic economic policies.

Of course, a government could insist that it has the sovereign right to continue the costly policies without the competitive pressure of imports. Yet policies to restrict trade will not eliminate the underlying problem of productivity and growth. In addition, the new tariffs or quotas are very likely to introduce additional economic costs due to market distortions, foreign tariff retaliation, and reduced incentives for efficiency and innovation. Special interest groups will come out of the woodwork to claim the necessity of protecting sovereignty in other areas that may be "threatened" by imports. The threat to sovereignty is for the most part a red herring here, unless one wants to make the case that a government has the sovereign right to put its people out of work, unimpeded by imports.

Still, the decision to impose a protectionist regime is the choice made by a sovereign government. Increased sovereignty in this regard comes at a price. Is the government willing to sacrifice increased economic welfare for more internal economic control? It may elect to abrogate the trade agreement and forgo the gains from trade in order to maintain internal economic control. But it cannot have it both ways—closing market access at home while asserting rights to multilateral market access abroad—unless it is in a position to impose its views unilaterally on the rest of the world. The record shows the revealed preference of governments: the WTO's 146 member countries reflect a widespread willingness to sacrifice some sovereignty for the gains from trade.

| *Whose Sovereignty?*

At their most extreme, proposals to use trade restrictions to protect economic sovereignty contain an element of hypocrisy. They imply a double standard by complaining that import competition compromises the ability of the government to impose its own standards but then proposing that the solution lies in using trade policy to force all other countries to adopt the complaining country's standards. In the end, trade policy based on the assertion of national sovereignty typically proposes that the country act as a trade imperialist, dictating the terms of market access based on forced harmonization to all of its trading partners. The only alternative way to retain absolute control over a domestic regulatory regime would be complete isolation and withdrawal from the world economy, which is not only a recipe for economic disaster but is also unrealistic in democratic societies. And so we come back to a plea for "free and fair" trade, even though a global trading system must rest on a *multilateral*, not a *unilateral*, notion of what is fair, unless one dominant country or group of countries can call the shots and force the others to follow.

Of course, many critics of the current world trading system propose a social agenda with admirable goals that all people of good will would support in principle: protection of human rights, global environmental protection, elimination of world poverty, and prevention of the economic exploitation of children, to name a few. The United Nations and the International Labor Organization (ILO) have enshrined many of these goals into several declarations and conventions, which their many signatories support in principle. However, such documents typically do not include compliance measures. Making import market access contingent upon upward harmonization to these standards is presented as a reasonable requirement to impose on the trading system.

This approach raises serious objections, however. The goals may or may not be universal, but the appeal to moral or natural law as a mandate for global action is rarely clear-cut, on the one hand, and is potentially inexhaustible, on the other. For example, Steve Charnovitz has argued that "[g]eopolitical boundaries should not override the word of God who directed Noah to take two of every living creature into the Ark." Jagdish Bhagwati and T. N. Srinivasan respond by noting that, "as two Hindus among nearly 900 million on this planet, we find this moral argument culture-specific rather than universal in its appeal."[7] Pursuing the Hindu perspective, would it not then be consistent for India to argue on moral grounds for trade restrictions against all countries that allow the slaughter of (sacred) cows? Morally based unilateral trade sanctions represent a slippery slope in trade policy because all countries can find moral flaws in the policies of other countries if they look hard enough. The U.S. laws that allow the death penalty are widely reviled in many countries, for example. What is needed is a way to identify compelling global policy issues on the basis of broad consensus, scientific evidence where applicable, and systematic, coordinated action.

Two additional objections to unilateral action are that such measures will either be ineffective, weakening the credibility and resolve of countries to address the issue systematically, or if they are effective, that they will do more harm than good. The Law of Unintended Consequences would often intervene. Thus, attempts to eliminate poverty by enforcing a worldwide minimum wage with trade restrictions would most likely increase unemployment and poverty. A trade ban on goods made with child labor may very well increase child prostitution. Environmental antidumping regulations that prevent poor countries from exporting certain goods would typically reduce economic growth and possibly lead to greater deforestation as alternative fuels are no longer affordable.

| Dispute Settlement and Sovereignty

In managing the conflict between national policies and multilateral trade agreements, the most the WTO can do is to agree upon rules regarding trade policy, to judge if member countries' laws and policies are consistent with the rules, and finally to allow compensation or retaliation in case a violation is found in a dispute settlement procedure. It cannot impose new trade legislation on its membership from above in the manner of a sovereign state overruling local laws.

One view of this popular stream of WTO criticism appears to be that since the Dispute Settlement Understanding is a third-party procedure using panelists and rules outside of the national laws of the respondent country, it allows unelected WTO jurists to pass judgment on issues of great concern to the public interest. In doing so, the WTO allegedly strikes down national laws and thereby subverts domestic democratic processes, echoing the caricature of the WTO snipping out any national laws that it regards as somehow getting in the way of free trade.

As for striking down national legislation, a WTO panel will inform a government if its legislation is inconsistent with WTO obligations, which, by the way, must have been ratified previously by its own national legislative body. To be sure, misunderstandings may occur among national legislators, the country's trade negotiators, and foreign negotiating partners in the WTO regarding what exactly is meant by compliance with a specific rule or provision. Yet this situation can arise under any international treaty obligation. It is up to the government then (not the WTO) to amend its laws in order to restore WTO compliance or to offer other proposals to resolve the issue. If a member government chooses not to do so, the consequences do not include military attack nor invasion by the nonexistent WTO army or police, but rather a process that may include measured retaliatory trade actions by other countries adversely affected by the WTO-inconsistent law or policy. From the perspective of economic nationalism, WTO dispute settlement will be acceptable as long as the home country never loses any cases. Certainly, many countries welcomed the new dispute settlement rules (discussed in chapter 4) as a means of protecting the rights they had won from WTO negotiations. According to the text of the DSU itself:

> The dispute settlement system of the WTO is a central element in providing security and predictability to the multilateral trading system.
> The Members recognize that it serves to preserve the rights and obligations of Members under the covered agreements, and to clarify the existing provisions of those agreements in accordance with customary rules of interpretation of public international law.[8]

In contrast to the common complaint that the WTO threatens its members' sovereignty, the DSU is in this regard an instrument to *protect* the interests of sovereign states, both large and small, that have concluded international trade agreements under the WTO.

It is therefore disingenuous for a government to play the sovereignty card whenever a DSU panel decision goes against it. The WTO system depends on mutual and reciprocal recognition of all of its members' rights and obligations. Obviously, most countries cherish the prospect of having their day in court whenever they allege a WTO violation, and the new DSU establishes a definitive process of identifying WTO violations and correcting them. Yet the deal is that everybody submits to the same process and accepts the results. No system of dispute settlement can possibly operate effectively if one or more members arbitrarily and unilaterally reject the outcome of a process that exists by mutual consent.

Losing a case does not imply losing national sovereignty. The "guilty" country can either accept the decision and comply with it or appeal the decision to the DSU Appellate Body. Typically, countries grievously dissatisfied with a result can also, if its appeals are exhausted, offer partial measures to correct its WTO-inconsistent policies or otherwise attempt to stall for more time. Ultimately, a country can reject the decision and take the consequences (retaliatory action by the complaining country), counterretaliate, or leave the organization, as all members can do for any reason, at any time. This situation may make life difficult for a country found to be in violation of WTO rules, but it is not the same as sacrificing sovereignty.

In addition, the DSU specifically states that the panels cannot make new law: "Recommendations and rulings of the DSB [Dispute Settlement Body] cannot add to or diminish the rights and obligations provided in the covered agreements."[9] In principle, a WTO member, as a sovereign country, makes a commitment to abide only by the specific provisions and rules included in WTO negotiated trade agreements. Knowing this, countries will be very careful in negotiating new trade rules, since their signatures on the final agreement will obligate them to submit to DSU reviews and procedures covering all elements of it. It is no wonder that the Uruguay Round took nearly eight years to negotiate, but in the end, the commitment of sovereign states implies that they are aware of all their rights and obligations. At the same time, Jackson (1999) sees strong indications that the dispute settlement panels favor deference to national government decisions and regulations. DSU panelists themselves recognize a responsibility to exercise judicial restraint and tread very carefully where issues of national sovereignty are concerned.

| A More Sovereign WTO

Some critics of the current global trade regime have suggested that the solution to the problem of diminished sovereignty is to invest the WTO with new social and environmental rules that it would impose on its membership. One proposal attempts to apply to the WTO a sort of enlightened world government model based on the example of U.S. development of sovereign control over internal economic affairs. By asserting federal sovereignty over internal economic affairs and imposing federal regulations and standards, the United States eliminated a potential race to the bottom as an internal competitive issue among the states.[10] The corresponding solution at the global level, it is argued, would be to introduce environmental and social chapters into the WTO.

Such a resolution of conflicting policies and policy goals in the world economy would pose considerable difficulties. The main problem is that the WTO is an international agreement among members. The WTO has no sovereignty over anybody, no ability to enforce decisions, according to the definition given earlier. In fact, the WTO has no power to make laws as such, since it has no legislative powers comparable to those of a national government and, as noted above, its dispute settlement system cannot make new laws. It is also ironic that the same impulse to criticize the WTO for violating a country's sovereignty can be turned on its head to demand that the WTO usurp all member countries' sovereignty in the pursuit of the same goals.

In the current WTO system, sovereignty enters the debate only insofar as WTO rules affect the scope of legitimate trade policy action taken *unilaterally* by member countries. In order to get around the problem of a limited WTO mandate, some WTO critics advocate that the WTO merely incorporate new environmental and social policy rules that would allow member states to take trade policy actions to protect the environment and social regulations, measures that are currently deemed inconsistent with WTO rules. It is important to recognize that the sovereignty issue is quite different if the solution is presented in this way. For the result of such new WTO rules, as noted earlier, would be to allow *one* member country's sovereignty to prevail over others' on these issues. Import market access to the United States, for example, would according to this scenario depend upon the U.S.

Congress's latest environmental or social legislation. Other countries would be forced to harmonize their regulations in order to maintain market access, and the hurdles could arbitrarily be raised on a regular basis by new legislation. "My sovereignty trumps yours" is hardly a fair-minded way to deal with international trade disputes.

A moment's reflection upon this proposal will reveal why the WTO membership, not just the developing countries accused of environmental degradation but many of the advanced countries as well, would reject such reforms out of hand. Allowing one country's legislation to determine unilaterally the terms of market access violates the original intent of the GATT/WTO system, which is to improve the terms of market access through the systematic dismantling of trade restrictions and the regulation of trade policy rules. Without this guarantee, the benefits of membership are vastly diminished, and new rules giving expanded freedom to governments to impose new trade restrictions would severely compromise these measures. It is for this reason that any change in the WTO rules must be approved by a two-thirds majority of all member countries. On any proposal to give new powers to restrict trade on the basis of unilateral environmental or social standards, the overwhelming response among WTO member countries would certainly be "no deal."

Needed: Global Institution Building

A strong indicator of the value of the WTO is the fact that its member countries have voluntarily ceded some control over their trade policies in order to reap the benefits of membership, that is, the gains from trade achieved through reciprocal market access. As an international organization, it is built on the simple proposition that trade is good, and trade policy rules will increase members' wealth as long as everyone abides by them. The WTO is not inimical to other goals of improving welfare in the global commons, but it is rather narrowly focused on what it can do under its members' mandate: seek greater collective gains from trade. At the same time, member countries can leave the WTO, or they can try to gather enough votes to change the rules if they are unhappy with the modest economic sovereignty-for-wealth trade-off that membership implies. Or they can push the rules or violate them and take the consequences, but they should realize that breaching the rules weakens the system and may backfire when others try the same trick. In any case, it is crucial to recognize that the WTO has not stolen sovereignty from anyone; the decision to join or leave ultimately lies with the sovereign state.

The consensus underlying the WTO is therefore tightly focused on the gains from trade, and a comparable global consensus on what should be done to protect the environment or to promote social goals does not, unfortunately, exist. Rather than graft these goals onto the WTO rules, which its members would be unlikely to accept in any case, the proponents of environmental and social agendas need to focus on building their own international institutions to support these goals.

The framework for such institutions already exists in the form of the ILO, various international environmental treaties, the UN Charter on Human Rights, and regional economic associations, such as the European Union and the NAFTA, both of which contain social and environmental provisions. The difficult job will be to generate a consensus among nations on basic principles of global environmental and social standards, with sets of rights and obligations among the members that bind them together. Such institutions will also require credible instruments of collective enforcement, based perhaps on a system of fines, sanctions, or even rewards. A broad-based package of incentives will probably be necessary in order to motivate some countries (especially the poorer ones) to sacrifice some of their sovereignty over these domestic issues to a supranational organization. Yet, in the end, the achievement of global, pooled sovereignty through a world environmental organization or convention on health and safety standards would be worth the effort. For then the organization could proceed on the basis of a collective commitment to action and a legitimate transfer of powers to a multinational authority.

Conclusion

The perceived sacrifices of national sovereignty to WTO membership, as portrayed by the cartoon discussed earlier, are therefore not so clear. The WTO cannot unilaterally force its member countries to change their laws, and furthermore it cannot and should not allow one member to alter unilaterally the rights and obligations of other members nor to impinge on the benefits that members received by taking part in WTO negotiations. The available evidence also argues against the ability of the WTO to nullify social regulations and to create a race-to-the-bottom effect. Countries join the WTO knowing full well that reciprocal market access is part of the deal. Protecting their own WTO-related trade benefits means agreeing to submit, along with everyone else, their trade-related policies to scrutiny. If a policy is inconsistent with the WTO rules that the sovereign country freely accepted and if it compromises the trade benefits of another member, then the country, by prior WTO obligation, agrees to change it. Or it can take all the steps reserved to sovereign states to avoid the obligation, and then take the consequences.

For those who fear the loss of economic sovereignty to international trade and the WTO, there is bad news and good news. The bad news is that global competition is likely to play a large and perhaps increasing role in determining the pattern of economic activity in coming years, diminishing the ability of governments to influence the composition of production, consumption, and employment. The good news is that these same global markets, and the WTO obligations that lock in all member countries' gains from trade, are not as inimical to domestic social and environmental regulations as they may at first appear. The influence of differing standards on the location of production has been small and is usually swamped by other economic forces. These forces have tended to favor the protection of domestic regulatory regimes through the ratcheting up of standards. Attempting to shore up sovereignty by restricting trade would be economically costly and would significantly weaken the WTO. All of this leaves much to be done in terms of pursuing global social and environmental goals. The best approach to achieving these goals lies in building new, dedicated global institutions for them. To be sure, solving the problems will take much hard work and negotiations and probably many years. This is perhaps also part of the bad news. However, if the global issues of the environment and social welfare are worthy of a comprehensive solution, they deserve the same considerable effort that established the lasting postwar economic institutions: the GATT/WTO, IMF, and World Bank. Only through negotiations that establish consensus on these far-reaching (and often costly) goals and the means of achieving them will progress be made. Pooling sovereignty, not clinging to national versions of it in the face of global competition, is the way forward. In the meantime, WTO members—rich and poor, small and large—benefit from a rules-based system that protects the gains from trade, which they have negotiated as sovereign states.

6

Trade Policy and the Environment

There is a comical, if somewhat dated, depiction of the WTO on the cover of *A Citizen's Guide to the WTO*, published by a consortium of anti-WTO activists. It shows a Godzilla-type monster, labeled "GATTzilla," after the WTO's predecessor, ravaging the world's environment, U.S. democratic institutions, and helpless dolphins. Leaking DDT from a canister held in one arm, strangling the dolphin with the other, GATTzilla stomps ruthlessly on the nation's Capitol in Washington, D.C., while holding the globe in its lethal jaws. Nothing, it seems, will stop it from destroying the planet, not to mention the American way of life, unless citizens unite to put an end to the onslaught of free trade.[1]

Much of the emotional opposition to the WTO in recent years has been fueled by the view that it is essentially an antienvironmental organization. The focal point of anti-WTO protests in this regard has been a series of decisions by the Dispute Settlement Body (DSB) that have declared certain national environmental and phytosanitary laws of WTO members to be in violation of WTO rules. The conflict between national laws and WTO obligations has also added the sovereignty dimension to the debate. Increasing competition from manufactured imports has created the fear of a race to the bottom, in which many developing countries with weaker environmental standards supposedly threaten to displace jobs in countries with high standards. The connection of environmental concerns with sovereignty and traditional protectionist arguments makes it a pivotal issue in the current debate over trade policy. All is not as it appears to be, however. Aside from the wildly exaggerated perception of the WTO as an unelected world government, imposing the will of multinational corporate polluters on the world's population, there is widespread misunderstanding about the relationship between trade and the environment. This chapter will show how trade does not typically harm the environment, how the WTO does not prevent countries from following strong environmental policies, and how using the WTO to try to enforce environmental standards is the wrong approach to the problem.

A "Green" WTO

Many environmental critics of the WTO might be surprised to see the green language that accompanied the founding of the WTO in 1995:

> [T]here should not be, nor need be, any policy contradiction between upholding and safeguarding an open, non-discriminatory and equitable multilateral trading system on the one hand, and acting for the protection of the environment and the promotion of sustainable development on the other. (World Trade Organization 1994)

The WTO statement on the environment followed the 1992 Rio Declaration on the Environment and Development, which emphasized the need for a cooperative approach and indicated the problematic nature of using unilateral trade policy measures in addressing environmental issues:

> States should cooperate to promote a supportive and open international economic system that would lead to economic growth and sustainable development in all countries, to better address the problems of environmental degradation. Trade policy measures for environmental purposes should not constitute a means of arbitrary or unjustifiable discrimination or a disguised restriction on international trade. Unilateral actions to deal with environmental challenges outside the jurisdiction of the importing country should be avoided. Environmental measures addressing transboundary or global environmental problems should, as far as possible, be based on an international consensus. (UNCED 1992, principle 12)

What these statements tell us is, first of all, that the WTO as an organization has stated from the outset its intention to avoid conflict with national environmental policies and, in addition, that international consensus is the proper method of establishing global environmental rules. What is glaringly absent from most environmentally based opposition to the WTO is an appreciation of the role of global institutions and consensus in moving forward with global environmental goals.

Yet the problem of achieving international consensus points to the main difficulty inherent in the WTO statement cited above. Since these declarations, little progress has been made in negotiating direct links between environmental and trade policies, despite strong political pressures in some member countries for introducing environmental rules into the WTO (see Shaffer 2001). The Committee on Trade and the Environment (CTE), for its part, has provided a valuable forum for discussions on reconciling environmental and WTO treaty obligations and other crossover issues. However, it has not produced concrete proposals for trade policy reform to enforce or promote environmental goals because it has no institutional mandate to do so. As noted in chapter 2, the WTO's fundamental value proposition for its members is to promote trade liberalization, not to create global environmental policy. Introducing environmental conditions on market access tends to work against that proposition. In the absence of a clear global mandate on how trade restrictions might be effectively used to achieve environmental goals, why should WTO members in general agree to limit the market access that produces the organization's main benefits?

| *Taming GATTzilla*

Because the WTO system focuses on trade policy, its rules do not directly address most environmental issues as they pertain to trade relations today. This apparent gap in specific WTO coverage has prompted some critics to call for a WTO environmental code, in particular one that would allow countries more freedom in imposing trade restrictions in response to a failure of the exporter to comply with environmental rules. However, the general approach by the WTO to trade disputes arising over environmental issues rests on two of its basic principles, nondiscrimination (the most-favored nation clause) and the ban on quantitative import restrictions, combined with a general prohibition on extraterritorial application of production process standards in the treatment of imports.[2] In addition, the GATT/WTO dispute settlement system has rarely authorized trade sanctions (see Hudec 1996, 114), and even under the new system, the rules favor negotiation and leave trade retaliation as a last resort.

Organized environmental protests against the trading system began during the Uruguay Round negotiations. The environmentalist group GATT-astrophe protested Uruguay Round efforts that could allegedly weaken sanitary/phytosanitary and technical standards, harm biological resources through intellectual property protection, and prevent conservation measures through market access commitments (Preeg 1995, 147–48). Another flashpoint arose as a result of the first GATT panel decision on the tuna/dolphin case (see below). One environmental group suggested that GATT really stands for "Guaranteeing a Toxic Tomorrow" (see Charnovitz 1992, 336). Environmental policy and trade policy appeared to be on a collision course.

The environmentalists' concerns were not lost on governments in the industrialized countries, particularly in the United States and Europe, which gave rise in 1995 to the CTE in the newly founded WTO. Yet it was immediately clear that whatever reports came out of the committee would not be able to endorse any substantive WTO reforms, since trade-and-environment policy issues go beyond the limits of an identifiable WTO consensus. Shaw and Schwartz (2002, 129) argue that "the relationship between trade and environment in the WTO is, in effect, being created through disputes." Aside from lofty and hopeful expectations and anodyne generalities that state the merits of both trade and environmental goals, what concrete environmental guidelines acceptable to all WTO members are possible? The following discussion will show that trying to insert environmental content into the WTO itself will be very difficult and that the establishment of processes and institutions to resolve conflicts between trade and environmental goals is the best approach.

WTO Dispute Settlement: The Bane of Environmentalists

The GATT and, later, the WTO got in hot water with environmental groups largely because of a series of dispute settlement decisions that declared national laws to be in contravention of WTO obligations. Some of the more prominent cases are known in shorthand fashion as (1) tuna/dolphin, (2) shrimp/turtle, (3) reformulated gasoline, and (4) beef hormones.

The tuna/dolphin case dates from 1991 and pitted provisions of the U.S. Marine Mammal Protection Act (MMPA) against GATT rules on process-oriented import standards.[3] As described in chapter 2, GATT/WTO rules generally prohibit countries from restricting imports of goods based on the way in which they are produced, unless the content of the product is affected in a manner that justifies regulation. So, for example, countries can legitimately require sanitary conditions of food processing for imports, as long as the same standards apply to domestic products. They cannot, however, restrict imports simply on the basis of how the product was made; this would open the door to all sorts of trade barriers based on moral and political objections to foreign business and government practices and policies.

The MMPA allowed the United States to impose trade restrictions on tuna imports from Mexico that had been caught using purse seine nets, which were shown to have resulted in "excessive" dolphin kills. In addition, the MMPA also authorized a secondary embargo against imports of processed Mexican tuna from other countries, including Europe. The GATT panel decision found the trade provisions of the MMPA to be in violation of GATT rules, which unleashed the ire of U.S. environmental groups and U.S. congressional supporters of the bill.

Like many other cases involving environmental regulations, the Dispute Settlement Body's ruling in the tuna/dolphin case did not condemn the national law itself as a barrier to trade. Instead, it pointed out that the goal of protecting dolphins internationally could be pursued without violating trade agreements. The secondary embargo policy, which banned imports from any country processing Mexican tuna, was also found to be in violation of GATT rules and resulted in opposition from European countries as well.

For all the hoopla surrounding the tuna/dolphin case, the panel report was never adopted, and the ruling itself became a "dead letter" legally (the older GATT system of dispute settlement was still in effect, and panel reports were not routinely adopted). Mexico, which was in the middle of the NAFTA negotiations with the United States, chose not to complicate matters by pressing for adoption of the report. Subsequently, the issue became one of certifying canned tuna as "dolphin-safe," based on the fishing methods used. In 1997, the United States ended its outright embargo on tuna caught using unacceptable fishing methods and focused instead on eco-labeling as part of an international dolphin-protection treaty signed with Mexico and other countries. The certification-and-labeling approach to protecting dolphins has proven to be acceptable under WTO trade rules as of 2003, although the standards used in defining "dolphin-safe" predictably became the subject of controversy.[4]

The shrimp/turtle case involved similar issues and became another cause célèbre among environmentalists. The United States had imposed a ban on imports of shrimp from countries using shrimp-harvesting methods that could harm sea turtles. Countries could avoid the ban if they adopted a certification program based on U.S. practice, which required the use of turtle excluder nets. These measures were designed as incentives for countries to negotiate an international agreement to protect turtles. Malaysia, Thailand, India, and Pakistan challenged this practice in a WTO dispute procedure. The dispute panel ruled in 1998 that the unilateral nature of the U.S. policy was in violation of WTO rules. In particular, the policy's implementation was found to be discriminatory because it required other countries to follow standards and procedures dictated by the United States in order to receive certification.

However, the reasoning of the WTO Appellate Body, which reviewed the panel's results, focused on the discriminatory aspects of the U.S. policy as the problem, rather than the use of trade restrictions based on production methods (the requirement to employ turtle excluder nets), which also theoretically violate WTO principles. Thus, the Appellate Body decision accepted in principle the legitimacy of such trade sanctions under WTO rules, as long as they were designed in a nondiscriminatory manner.[5] The United States, in the meantime, changed its procedures to make a conservation agreement easier to achieve, thereby bringing its policy into compliance with WTO obligations. A new WTO dispute settlement panel turned away a subsequent protest by Malaysia against the revised U.S. procedures, indicating that the protection of sea turtles was consistent with the stated WTO aim of supporting "sustainable development" (Weinstein and Charnovitz 2001). While the environmentalists may have lost the initial case, they won not only the argument, but also the practical victory of an effective policy to pursue their goal (Shaw and Schwartz 2002).

Despite the ambiguous details of the interpretation of the earlier panel decision, the sea turtle became a symbol of alleged WTO victimization, particularly at the Seattle meeting. A political cartoon, "Net Profits," captures the anti-WTO sentiment by showing a turtle swimming helplessly below a "net" made up of grid lines that form a corporate profits chart. A thick and impenetrable solid line marked "WTO" shows the upward movement of "net profits," which traps the apparently doomed turtle below, just as the shrimp nets had drowned turtles because they lacked the proper devices to allow them to escape.

Clever as this picture is in showing how "net profits" kill turtles, it falsely links the WTO to the business interests of Asian shrimp fishers, most of whom work independently or for small companies. Even those convinced that the WTO is in bed with multinational corporations might consider it a stretch to suggest that the WTO was acting simply on behalf of the corporate greed of shrimpers. The eventual outcome of the case illustrated the most obvious alternative solution to the problem, which was the negotiation of an international agreement protecting the animal, with provisions requiring the use of devices to protect them from shrimp nets. Bhagwati and Lehman (1999, 42) suggested an even simpler solution: give the shrimpers the required protective devices as a matter of foreign aid. In this particular case, it seems that relatively modest outlays could have settled a contentious trade issue without compromising WTO rules. In general, political confrontation over the WTO can often be avoided by identifying commonsense alternative measures to defuse or resolve the underlying conflict.

Another WTO ruling focused on the trade impact of U.S. domestic environmental legislation. In the reformulated gasoline case, the United States established pollution standards for both domestic and imported gasoline according to the Clean Air Act. Yet a complicated system of content standards had the practical effect of setting more stringent requirements for some imported types of gasoline, especially from Venezuela and Brazil, than for domestic producers. Whatever the reason for the differing standards, the end result was protectionist; the law gave domestic gasoline producers an advantage over some of their foreign rivals. The United States ultimately had to revise the standards in order to comply with WTO rules. This case shows, however, that environmental sovereignty was not at stake, since alternative guidelines could be found to remove the discriminatory effect. Yet this case is often cited as yet another WTO blow against the environment.

These examples show that the dispute settlement panel and Appellate Body decisions have been attempting to draw a fine line between legitimate domestic policy practices of WTO members and those that violate their WTO obligations. It is important to remember that members of the WTO also have rights under the rules regarding market access, so the controversy over these decisions is not simply one of the WTO trampling on a country's sovereign right to impose trade restrictions. Rather, the DSB decisions also involve the sovereign rights of WTO members to the benefits of the trade agreements they have negotiated. Whose sovereignty is trumping whose? These cases also show that the WTO is not designed to override environmental policies, but rather to make sure that they are implemented and administered in a way that is consistent with the country's trade obligations. The fine line such decisions are drawing cannot, in themselves, force new environmental rules on the global economy, because the WTO consensus does not allow it. Any significant progress in this area will therefore have to occur outside the WTO, in the form of new international environmental agreements that define the obligations of their participants. Dispute settlement rulings under these new circumstances would then proceed to sort out which obligations take precedence. In recent decisions, however, the WTO dispute settlement system has shown considerable deference to domestic environmental policy goals.

| *Frankenfood and the Precautionary Principle*

A final example illustrates yet another type of dispute: how to handle trade in food that is allegedly, but not scientifically proven to be, "unsafe." What is now known as the "Frankenfood" issue began with the dispute between the United States and the European Union over U.S. exports of beef from cattle that had been treated with growth hormones. The European Union had banned the import of U.S. hormone-treated beef, and the United States had argued that such hormones were safe and left no damaging effect. Scientific tests tended to support the United States. The European Union, however, had argued for the validity of a "precautionary rule" that would allow discretion in regulating agricultural goods that may be suspected of being unsafe even if proof would not be available until years later, when additional research would presumably have been completed.

The United States finally prevailed on this legal issue, and the panel declared the EU policy to be in violation of WTO rules. As of early 2003, the European Union had refused to comply with the WTO panel ruling, and this is a relatively rare case in which the United States has proceeded, under the new WTO rules, to impose retaliatory tariffs. There is an important principle at stake in the decision: in the absence of scientific evidence, should countries be allowed to use a precautionary principle to exclude imports at their discretion? The clear danger is that much mischief could result if WTO rules were rewritten to allow countries unilaterally to restrict imports based on the perception that something is amiss in the way the imports were produced. Instead of unilaterally invoking a precautionary principle, assembling an international panel of experts to judge the merits of such cases would be far more credible. This may not be easy if the issue has become politicized. However, the point is that unilateral declarations of scientific judgment without supporting evidence will never be a viable principle in any rules-based system.

It seems that suspicions regarding hormone-treated beef have some popular support in Europe, encouraged in no small part by European beef producers. Yet if this is the main reason for the government's import ban, then an equally effective policy would be to allow the imports but to require a label on the beef in question stating the use of hormones in the cattle.[6] In this manner, the consumer would ultimately be able to decide, at least until such time that any strong scientific evidence provides the basis for stricter regulation.

The controversies over WTO panel rulings indicate that the WTO system is under political pressure to rewrite trade policy rules to allow environmentally motivated trade restrictions. Some commentators assert that the existing political consensus for liberal trade is so tenuous that an accommodation of environmental interests will be necessary to maintain the existing trade order (Esty 1996, 2002; Destler and Balint 1999). This proposition will surely be tested in the coming years. However, to force environmental rules into the WTO would be the institutional equivalent of ramming square pegs into round holes.

Consider now the implications of the GATT tuna decision, described earlier, for the WTO membership "contract." If the WTO were to validate the ability of one member country to impose conditions of compliance with manufacturing criteria ("all tuna sold in the United States must be certified as 'dolphin safe'"), then the conditions of U.S. market access for imports would have fundamentally changed. Henceforth, access to the U.S. market would in this case depend on harmonization with standards of processing determined by the U.S. Congress. Whatever the merits of such rules applied domestically, the worry of other countries is that all of their production processes and even workplace conditions may in the future be subject to U.S. inspection as a condition for U.S. market access, depending on what the U.S. Congress considers environmentally sound. The fundamental value of the WTO's market access guarantees would decline drastically, since the terms of market access could be changed unilaterally by an importing country.

No More Room for New Exceptions

The debate over WTO reforms has often reflected a certain frustration with the apparent inflexibility of the agreement. The proposals for new environmental measures, for example, appear to be no less reasonable than existing exceptions for prison labor (contained in GATT article XXe). They could also be regarded as merely international extensions of existing measures regarding conservation of (domestic) natural resources (article XXg) and protection of human, animal, or plant life or health (article XXb). However, these rules are the legacy of an earlier negotiating environment. Historically, the exceptions, exclusions, grandfathering, and all other GATT provisions that qualify the core GATT principles are largely the result of compromises negotiated in the first major postwar multilateral trade talks that founded the GATT in 1947.[7] They were necessary at that particular time to accommodate domestic political interests (especially in the United States) and yet not so burdensome as to negate the core market-access benefits.

From the date that agreement began, the slate on new amendments was wiped clean; any new measures must now meet the institutional cost-benefit test by the existing membership. In the history of the GATT/WTO system, most institutional changes have been packaged in the form of multilateral trade agreements encompassing a broad range of issues. The only major amendment to the GATT before the conclusion of the Uruguay Round was the agreement on trade and development (part IV) adopted in 1964. It is noteworthy that this amendment was motivated by a desire among the early GATT contracting parties to make GATT membership more attractive to developing countries (see Dam 1970, 23642). It would be difficult to make this same argument with regard to an environmental chapter of the WTO.

| *"Market Failure" as a Basis for Trade Intervention*

A viable global environmental agreement that includes trade provisions must make economic sense, not only for reasons of efficiency, but also for reasons of institutional integrity. In many cases, there is no economic conflict between environmental and trade rules, since the WTO does not impinge upon a country's right to regulate trade according to its own environmental rules, as long as such domestic policies follow basic WTO principles. State intervention in trade for environmental reasons, however, requires a careful examination of economic and systemic costs and benefits.

An economic view of trade policy states generally that government intervention in trade is justified only in those cases of market failure, in which the price mechanism does not fully reflect the costs and benefits experienced by consumers and producers. Most environmental issues involve a case of *domestic* market failure, in which the best policy would be a tax that discourages "bad" behavior or a subsidy that encourages "good" behavior. By this standard, restrictions on imports for environmental reasons would be justified economically only if imports themselves were causing pollution, in which case a nondiscriminatory tariff would be the best policy.

When the foreign activity creates transborder pollution, a different economic problem arises: who pays for the damage when an internationally shared public good (clean air or water) is depleted? The Organization for Economic Cooperation and Development (1976) has established the "polluter pays" principle as the means of resolving such issues, but this approach leaves open difficult issues of measurement, responsibility, and burden sharing. If the pollution is limited geographically, a resolution is usually possible through bilateral or regional negotiations. If the scope of the problem extends to the global commons, the issues of responsibility, burden sharing, economic impacts on countries, and enforcement compliance in the face of free riding become much more difficult. *Free riding* in this context refers to countries that contribute to the global pollution problem but refuse to carry any of the burden of fixing it voluntarily. Trade restrictions usually enter the picture as a means of enforcement rather than as a way of correcting the market failure itself.

Yet even when the elimination of the environmental problem would be economically beneficial to the global economy, coordination and implementation of an optimal solution to the free rider problem (which may involve incentives such as payments to the free rider rather than punishments) are difficult for individual countries to achieve. These issues call for an international environmental agreement that establishes for all member countries rules, responsibilities, rights, and procedures for resolving such conflicts.

| *Harmonization: Is There a Race to the Bottom?*

In contrast to the market-failure approach, a number of proposals for an environmentally sensitive trade regime would require countries to harmonize their environmental regulations. In particular, environmental regulations that affect manufacturing costs would converge to the high level of countries with stricter standards. Proposals for environmental antidumping duties, based on the calculated differences in unit production costs due to "lax" environmental protection, would, it is argued, prevent countries from gaining unfair competitive advantage. In this manner, a global environmental regime would avoid a race to the bottom by countries seeking to outdo each other in exporting pollution-intensive products.[8]

Economic considerations suggest that harmonization is a bad idea, however, for several reasons. First, the imposition of an environmental tariff would merely tend to encourage pollution-intensive production at home, while not necessarily reducing pollution in the foreign country (see Ferrantino 1997, 57). In addition, the economic costs of pollution abatement differ from country to country, and national preferences for environmental quality are a matter for domestic policy and not international coercion. The argument for harmonization comes close in this sense to the discredited reasoning of the "scientific tariff" applied in U.S. trade policy in the past. The argument behind the scientific tariff was that it was unfair for a country to have lower labor costs, therefore an offsetting tariff to equalize costs was justified. The harmonization proposal suggests that it is equally unfair for countries to have lower environmental costs, and countervailing duties should close the resulting cost gap.[9]

The lack of sound economic justification points to serious problems in setting up a regime of global harmonization. The harmonization toward the higher standards would impose additional costs on countries with weaker environmental standards, including not only the direct financial cost of compliance but also the economic cost of misallocated resources. Unless the high-standard country or group of countries can collectively bully the weaker countries into adopting their standards, the weak-standard countries will demand compensation. Alternatively, the rich countries would have to offer the poor countries financial aid and technological assistance to upgrade their pollution abatement measures. Given the diverse economic structures among countries, an acceptable package of concessions would be quite difficult to negotiate globally. For this reason, environmental harmonization efforts have been attempted primarily within regional trade agreements, such as the NAFTA and the European Union.[10]

From a political point of view, the harmonization issue would be more compelling if there were strong evidence of a race to the bottom. Most of the fear of "pollution havens" and their detrimental trade effects stems from anecdotes proffered by politicians, rather than from any systematic empirical research, which tends not to support these claims.[11] The minimal impact of domestic environmental measures is due in part to their small share of manufacturing costs: the U.S. Environmental Protection Agency (1997) estimates that environmental compliance costs borne by U.S. firms have amounted to an average of $22 billion per year, less than 0.5 percent of GDP in 1990. More recent studies indicate that the cost of compliance has typically been much less than was feared by firms and that in many cases there are offsetting benefits of increased efficiency and competitiveness, as predicted by Porter and van der Linde (1995).[12] There is growing evidence, for example, that environmental compliance often works hand in glove with technological advancement. Requirements to reduce pollution tend to encourage the development of more efficient and cleaner production methods. There is also evidence that pollution-intensive firms globally tend to build and invest in equipment for future environmental compliance, rather than planning to retrofit later (Levinson 1996, 452). To the extent that it becomes a problem, a series of national environmental practice codes would provide a possible alternative. Such codes could require the multinational corporations of the headquarters country to apply the same environmental standards to all installations outside that country's borders (see Bhagwati and Srinirasan 1996, pp. 178–79).

A broad perspective shows that environmental and liberal trade policy goals are not necessarily in conflict. Reductions in agricultural subsidies and trade restrictions in foodstuffs would, for example, in many cases improve both environmental quality and economic welfare (Esty 1996). In many less developed countries, trade liberalization in pollution-intensive industries would shift production toward areas where cleaner technologies prevail, improving global environmental quality (Ferrantino 1997). Recent studies indicate that trade that aids development also tends to increase preferences for environmental quality (Antle and Heidebrink 1995).[13] Furthermore, increasing income in less developed countries would tend to increase the alternatives for household fuel and thereby decrease an important cause of deforestation (Ferrantino 1997). Trade liberalization and environmental protection are therefore not at odds in all cases and arguably have an overlapping agenda of mutually beneficial goals.

However, the perceived connection between environmental and competitiveness issues sets up the possibility of political coalitions between environmentalists and traditional protectionist groups. To the extent that environmental rules could be used to restrict imports in politically sensitive products, they tend to serve protectionist purposes.[14] Evidence of this connection appears to be present in proposals for environmentally based antidumping laws, for example.[15] In addition, some groups that base their anti-WTO protests on environmental arguments have received support from labor unions, which do not come to the trade policy table with a purely environmental agenda.

Anti-WTO protest groups correctly recognize that many businesses increase their profits through trade. Many of them place perhaps too much emphasis on the profits of multinational corporations, ignoring the benefits of trade to small businesses and consumers. But should it be surprising to them that the restrictive trade regime they propose would increase the profits of other companies? As the discussion of the adjustment and income effects of trade revealed in chapter 3, the biggest winners from protectionism are often the owners of capital in the protected industries. In this light, the pro-environment, anticorporatist arguments against trade appear to be too simplistic. Limiting imports in the name of environmental protection typically shifts corporate profits from one set of companies to another, with a net loss in total economic welfare. The benefits to workers themselves are often dubious.

Nonetheless, many environmentalists protest that their proposals and goals are free of protectionist intentions.[16] The problem lies in some inescapable facts of life in the political economy of trade. Exporting interests and the governments that represent them typically win market access through multilateral trade negotiations, which fight against the entrenched resistance of import-competing interests in foreign countries. These negotiating battles often involve bitter wrangling and compromise, with much political capital expended by governments in order to achieve the deal. Any introduction of a new basis for trade restrictions will automatically raise suspicions among exporters and their governments that foreign import-competing interests are trying to restrike the balance in their favor, diminishing the value of the original negotiations.

It does not matter in this regard whether or not the defenders of dolphin protection in the United States joined forces with the domestic tuna-fishing lobby in seeking a ban on tuna imports from Mexico, for example. Consider the impact of such a ban on the domestic price and availability of tuna in the United States and its affect on domestic producer interests.[17] Environmental motives may indeed be pure, but the possibility of trade intervention inevitably creates motives to restrict competition and raise prices, which are the very reasons for WTO rules against such measures in general.

It is very telling, furthermore, that the United States found virtually no sympathy among any other GATT member countries in its attempt to apply its domestic environmental law to imports in this case. Opposition came not only from the expected quarters—developing countries with relatively weak environmental regimes—but also from the EU countries, which were drawn into the fray by a secondary U.S. embargo against processed Mexican tuna from Europe.[18] Within the WTO institutional framework, it seems that few countries are willing to tolerate the precedent of unilaterally imposed environmental restrictions on trade, at least when other countries are doing it.

| *Alternatives*

The earlier discussion of conflict between trade and the environment suggested a number of possible ways to resolve the issues without resorting to trade restrictions or a general assault on the world trading system. Depending on the situation, countries can often avoid trade conflicts by revising their environmental legislation to eliminate discriminatory trade effects, by providing foreign aid or technical expertise to countries where the environmental problem exists, by negotiating a system of labeling for the products, or by setting up environmental codes of conduct for multinational corporations.

While countries can often implement such measures directly, it may be necessary to consider a global structure for dealing with environmental problems. An independent international organization dedicated to the protection of the global environment, concluded by treaty among a universal community of countries, would provide the most comprehensive framework for dealing with this issue. Measures to protect the global commons, regulate polluting activities, and set standards would then proceed on the basis of a broad consensus among its global membership. Conflicts between trade policy and environmental protection would still pose problems, but there would at least be a systematic framework for resolving them on the basis of consensus and negotiations among the involved parties and the further development of public international law.

| *Basic Elements of a Global Environmental Organization*

A full description of the ideal international environmental organization goes beyond the scope of this discussion.[19] However, such an organization must at the very least proceed from a basis of consensus, which will bind its necessarily large membership to its goals. In the context of environmental protection, elements of this organization would include:

1. a sound scientific basis for evaluating existing environmental conditions, trends, and requirements for the welfare of the global commons;
2. a framework for assessing the costs and benefits of specific policies and actions to various member countries and for devising market-based intervention measures when needed; and
3. a system of consensual decision making, reciprocal rights and obligations, and balanced conflict resolution that can effectively avoid or settle disputes among members over environmental issues.

Carefully formulated scientific evidence, for example, is an essential means of establishing the credibility of environmental protection proposals and creating a consensus on the issues. Blackhurst and Subramanian (1992) identify improved scientific understanding as a key ingredient in any attempt to achieve international cooperation when the costs to participating countries are positive and the benefits are uncertain, as shown by previous efforts to control communicable diseases internationally. Advances in scientific inquiry into the environment will play a significant role in this process, since a general consensus among scientists may be necessary before a broader political consensus for action can exist.

Economic analysis has often played the role of bête noir to many advocates of strong international environmental protection, but the institutional approach shows that it contains a more pragmatic, political feature. It would be folly to expect an international agreement on the environment among sovereign states to be possible in the absence of an acceptable domestic cost-benefit proposition. In other words, one cannot expect countries to join if they perceive the economic costs to be too high or the burden sharing of costs to be unfair. Furthermore, the associated free-rider problem requires an economic assessment of costs and benefits. What, for example, will it take for a particular member to join the environmental agreement? What compensation (in the form of foreign aid or technical assistance on environmental issues) would be possible or necessary? Even if the consensus among the (presumably large) membership of the international environmental organization decides that economic sanctions are necessary, what will their impact be? Will they hurt other countries besides the violator? In short, as long as environmental agreements cannot repeal national sovereignty, they must acknowledge the importance of economic welfare as a driving force in the decisions of governments on the issues.

Effective dispute settlement, along with other protections of member countries' interests, is necessary as a means of overcoming unforeseen conflicts. A strong dispute settlement system in a global environmental organization will also be necessary to shift what are essentially environmental disputes toward that organization, not the WTO. Sovereign countries are wary of joining an international agreement in which future circumstances may damage their interests. In particular, small, politically and economically weak countries will avoid agreements that expose them to bullying by larger or stronger countries or groups of countries. Environmental standards and enforcement in any international environmental organization will therefore not, in general, be dictated by a single country, region, or small group of countries; such measures must proceed by consensus, with the free riders or violators punished only insofar as the general international consensus allows it.

The features just described will surely be frustrating to many advocates of global environmental protection: they represent what may amount to slow, incremental change based on consensus rather than the aggressive, unilateral measures many environmentalists argue are necessary. It is for this reason that the current debate has focused on the legitimacy of using trade sanctions as a means of compelling countries to conform to specific environmental standards or practices, for trade sanctions offer quick, focused, and some would say "satisfying" action in support of specific issues.

One may argue that, in the past, punitive trade sanctions, taken outside the WTO system, have sometimes worked, in the sense that they have forced countries to alter their policies or at least to enter into negotiations on them. When the institutional integrity of the trading system is not at stake, such strategies may at times be effective, depending on the bilateral balance of power in the confrontation.[20] However, the applicability of unilateral trade restrictions in achieving a new global environmental agreement is surely limited and in many ways self-contradictory. As the following discussion will show, trade may play a more positive role in the incentive structure of global environmental institution building.

| Steppingstones to a Comprehensive International Agreement

A number of international environmental agreements exist in fragmentary form already. There are now hundreds of treaties that deal with the environment (Runge 2001; see also General Agreement on Tariffs and Trade 1992), ranging from toxic waste to species preservation, including twenty that contain various trade provisions. In addition, some regional trade agreements contain environmental provisions. The European Union has gone the furthest in coordinating and enforcing a supranational policy on environmental protection, establishing a legal framework for harmonizing standards among its member countries (Sbragia 2000). The NAFTA also has an environmental side agreement that deals in particular with pollution problems in Mexico.

Because of the ability of regional economic agreements to internalize incentives, it is tempting to consider the possibilities of extending this approach to a multilateral negotiation of environmental accords within the WTO framework. In particular, the success of the Uruguay Round in combining agreements on diverse issues, from market access to trade-related investment, raises the possibility of similar negotiations combining trade and environmental issues. Unfortunately, even these contentious issues pale in comparison to the complications of negotiating a comprehensive environmental protection regime. The TRIPs accord, for example, depended ultimately on establishing a legal framework in Uruguay Round signatory countries for asserting property rights and prosecuting patent and trademark piracy, with generous phase-in periods for the least developed countries (see Schott and Buurman 1994). This agreement was not without controversy and has evolved since then, but it was acceptable as a negotiating topic to all parties, even the skeptical developing countries.

An agreement on global environmental protection, in contrast, would require acceptance of standards on pollution and resource use, regulation harmonization, payment of clean-up costs, pollution control, and so on across several industries, not to mention the negotiation of possible trade sanctions to enforce compliance. Agreement on the terms of such provisions, which would affect a large portion of developing countries' manufactured and possibly agricultural exports, is likely to be extremely difficult in many specific cases. It would also require agreement on legitimizing a substantial increase in government intervention and spending, with the heaviest relative burden placed on the poorest countries. The total cost of such an agreement to its adherents would arguably be vastly greater than any other treaty in history. Finally, the large divergence in environmental conditions, capacities, and levels of development among the countries of the world suggests that an acceptable multilateral agreement is likely to be elusive.

These questions point to some of the more general difficulties in concluding a global environmental agreement, as discussed by Esty (1994). For example, what will constitute consensus in terms of a threshold of participation among the world's countries? Who will decide on compliance by and enforcement against nonparties? Should compliance incentives be negative (trade restrictions) or positive (aid)? How would trade restrictions authorized by an environmental treaty be compatible with WTO rules?

There has already been considerable discussion on how to reconcile WTO rules with existing multilateral environmental agreements (MEAs). The CTE, despite the limitations on its ability to propose WTO reform, has produced extremely useful discussions on resolving such potential conflicts. In principle, there are a number of ways to sort out most (if not all) competing provisions in the WTO rules and MEAs in the context of international law. Most issues could be addressed through a system of consultation and cooperation, combined with a mutual understanding of which treaty would apply in a given situation (Shaw and Schwartz 2002; Marceau 2001). The problem is not the feared "inevitable conflict" between trade and the environment, but rather the lack of international agreements on the environment and supporting global institutional structures and understandings to make them compatible with the WTO.

Founding a world environmental organization, or even reaching a comprehensive agreement on global environmental issues, is clearly an ambitious and probably distant goal. It is therefore perhaps too ambitious to be undertaken all at once. Yet the analysis suggests ways of moving forward. The primary catalysts for environmental awareness include (1) the accumulation of scientific evidence leading to consensus and action, (2) a specific crisis that galvanizes public opinion and motivates governments to take action, and (3) economic growth that promotes demand for environmental quality. Increased environmental awareness is important because it indicates a willingness to support environmental goals at some positive cost to society. The primary catalysts for an expanding scope of bargaining issues are increasing trade and investment. As the gains from trade and investment increase, countries are more willing to create, develop, and expand the institutions that facilitate the mutual gains. For the development of environmental institutions, the important upshot of this increased interdependence is that the growing number of bargaining chips may also facilitate further negotiation on environmental issues.

A major implication of this process is that a global environmental agreement will depend on both public awareness and political commitment to the broad issue of environmental quality and a wide range of international economic issues on which to bargain for a package deal. The latter point turns the current debate over trade and environment on its head: instead of using trade primarily as a weapon to force compliance with environmental measures, the institutional approach suggests the value of trade as a positive incentive to induce voluntary compliance with global agreements. Trade liberalization in this regard provides the leverage for overcoming the resistance to costly environmental protection and offers a potential integrating factor in the mutual rights and obligations of a global agreement. In other words, this model suggests that global environmental protection will require further trade liberalization. In this context, the WTO may yet emerge as an important component in the process, not through the imposition of an environmental chapter, but through its ability to harness the gains from trade as a positive bargaining chip for achieving globally acceptable environmental goals.

Many participants in the debate over trade and the environment, particularly with regard to the WTO, have generally been asking the wrong questions. Many environmentalists and anti–WTO activists have maintained that trade is the means and not the end of achieving the goal of global sustainable development. This statement has been used to insist that trade agreements themselves should not be held sacrosanct; trade is only a tool to achieve larger goals. Evidently, the role of trade in achieving sustainable development is typically negative in that trade sanctions and related punishment are effective tools in getting recalcitrant countries to comply with global environmental standards.

Trade is indeed the means and not the end. But countries have reached a consensus on what at least one important end is: economic prosperity and growth. Trade is the means of achieving that end, and the WTO is the organization set up by that consensus to make sure that the means serve that end. Setting up additional goals, or ends, such as sustainable development (which the WTO itself endorses) is possible, but the groundwork must be laid for it. What are the specific goals of sustainable development and how should they be pursued? Before the nations of the world come to a general agreement on these questions, one should proceed with caution in tampering with a system that does enjoy international consensus and would be severely undermined by measures that compromise its core benefits.

Trade creates gains, on balance, for both parties of the transaction; the flip side is that protection hurts both sides. So trade restrictions to protect dolphins, turtles, and clean air create costs for both the exporting and the importing countries. In addition, they create a political lobby for the protection that may not in any way be interested in the dolphins, turtles, or clean air. But one might respond: but the benefits of the trade restriction are greater. Yet if one is so confident about the benefits, it is not too much to ask to compare the alternatives. Is it indeed possible to protect the environment without resorting to the blunt instrument of trade restrictions? The foregoing discussion suggests many alternatives, from eco–labeling and foreign aid to new international economic treaties, conventions, and organizations. Why are many environmentalists so determined to use trade as a punishment, as a means to force compliance with standards or goals asserted unilaterally?

The short answer is that trade sanctions are the quick and easy way to "do something." In large and politically powerful countries, the lobbying group's efforts can be focused on domestic political lobbying, rather than on the more difficult work of international negotiation. If the beneficiaries of trade can furthermore be successfully demonized as soulless multinational corporations, then the cost of the trade sanctions can be palmed off at low political cost. The WTO, of course, throws a monkey wrench into this strategy, holding countries to international commitments on trade. And so, in the minds of some environmentalists, the WTO must also be demonized as the tool of the multinationals and targeted as part of the problem.

Meaningful progress on protecting the global environment, to the extent that there is international support for it, cannot be made without further progress in developing international institutions. The task is complicated in that political, economic, and legal issues must be worked out. The Rio summit (1992), for example, revealed some of the possibilities, but also the limitations, of international cooperation on the environment. In other international agreements, such as the international treaties and environmental chapters of the NAFTA and European Union, some of the pieces of a nascent environmental regime exist already. Yet countries seeking such an agreement need to develop and promote both global environmental awareness and global interdependence as the means of achieving a global consensus. They must also act as global champions of the idea, playing a leadership role in forging international alliances and coalitions, convincing others of the importance of a global agreement, yet recognizing the trade-offs necessary to achieve it. They must negotiate, cajole, threaten perhaps, compromise, rewrite, and persevere—all to render the vision of a new global institution into something that is convincingly practical and necessary.

To extend the reach of regional environmental pacts to new members, "paid" for with further trade liberalization; to join such regional economic agreements into a single economic area under a single environmental code—these are possible steps to a global environmental order. To negotiate a multilateral accord protecting dolphins; to expand the Montreal Protocol to include a new treaty on global warming, with market-based abatement and transfers or other positive incentives—these measures would make progress toward a global environmental regime. Trade issues would surely remain but could then be treated systematically, as a subject of competing trade and environmental principles, each set of principles established independently by international consensus and law.

| Toward Reconciliation

There are many, many ways in which global environmental goals can be pursued without the use of trade sanctions. Aside from pursuing institutional solutions, through international treaties, conventions, and organizations, foreign aid, and technological assistance, countries are free to impose nondiscriminatory environmental regulations, laws, and taxes on products based on their content and on the impact of their consumption. Trade and environmental goals are, furthermore, not only compatible but in many ways complementary. Trade contributes to economic efficiency, welfare, and growth, which together contribute to the resource base necessary for the pursuit of environmental objectives both domestically and globally. Trade also fosters economic cooperation, which can serve as a springboard for agreement on the environment and in other areas.

These linkages certainly will not eliminate all conflicts between environmental and trade interests. To the extent that treaty obligations conflict, for example, public international law will have to sort out the issues, but this is as it should be in a global system of sovereign states. There will also be issues around which debates will rage over the proper use of trade incentives to achieve nontrade objectives. Perhaps the most important point in this regard is that a cooperative approach is likely to produce more progress than confrontation, threats, and punishment.

Even within the present WTO system, improvements are possible, particularly with regard to dispute settlement, which typically limits the discussion and resolution of conflict to legal considerations of treaty obligations. Either formally or informally, discussions of alternative measures, compensation, transfers, and other forms of bargaining should accompany any WTO dispute, so as to encourage to the greatest extent possible a political, negotiated, out-of-court solution. In some cases, it may also be possible to expand the scope of expertise that is brought to bear in the cases, on the bases of objectivity, balance, and equal access to resources for both sides. This type of expert testimony would require the approval of both sides, but it could provide the basis for alternative solutions or negotiations to resolve the problem.

Institutional and cooperative solutions take time and great effort, which may appear to be too slow and marginalist compared with the decisiveness of directives backed up with the irresistible force of WTO-authorized trade restrictions. Yet it is illusory to expect that a global environmental order can be established cheaply, through the unilateral measures of a few countries, enforced with newly legitimate trade sanctions. In this regard, institutions such as the WTO are both inadequate and inappropriate as means of pursuing the global environmental agenda. It is best in this regard to let the WTO *be* the WTO; maintaining a liberal trade order is its full-time job. Managing a global environmental agreement will be an equally daunting task, no less deserving of a carefully planned and solidly constructed institutional and cooperative framework.

7

Human Rights, Labor Rights, and Trade Policy

Riots and Protests Force Cancellation of WTO Opening Ceremonies

The impulse among men and women of good will to make life better for others is undeniably noble and inescapably problematical when converted to international policy. It is simple enough for individuals to posit the existence of basic "human rights," for example; this has been the subject of thoughtful inquiry by philosophers, religious thinkers, and legal scholars for centuries. Yet the implementation of consistent and workable international policies to promote and defend human rights worldwide poses difficult questions. Can or should trade policy play a role in securing human rights for all people in all countries?

One particularly negative view of the WTO, illustrated in the cartoon "Riots and Protests Force Cancellation of WTO Opening Ceremonies," attempts to make the connection among trade, human rights, and labor rights. It shows a group of dark-suited, cigar-puffing, porcine capitalists, presumably in charge of the WTO, addressing a larger group of Third World workers. The workers, including children, are notably taking part in the anti-WTO protests, sporting signs declaring, "No to WTO" and "WTO Unfair Trade." For the capitalist bosses, however, there is only one issue: "Forget the opening ceremonies. . . . Who wants to work the cheapest?"

While it is true that some anti-WTO criticism comes from developing countries, it is misleading at best to imply that the developing world believes that the WTO works against the interest of workers there. Developing country interests will be discussed in more detail in chapter 8. A more subtle implication of the caricature is that the WTO is insensitive to issues such as child labor, workers' rights, and human rights. Locating cheap labor appears to be the only concern of the WTO or of those whose interests it allegedly protects.

This criticism of the WTO is unfair to the extent that the organization was never intended to monitor human rights or labor standards. A more basic philosophical question, however, is whether trade tends to support or harm human and workers' rights, which deserves a thoughtful response. The WTO itself does not recruit cheap Third World labor for Western capitalists, nor does it declare human and labor rights to be illegal barriers to trade. It does set up trade rules that tend to increase exports from and investment in developing countries, as it does for all WTO member countries. Are these rules detrimental to the welfare of workers and citizens in these countries? Should the rules be harnessed to force governments into better behavior?

The issue of human rights has many dimensions, including philosophical and legal aspects beyond the scope of this study and the competence of this author. This chapter sets out to tackle the practical problems of linking trade policy to human rights and labor rights. First, what are "basic human rights" and "basic labor rights" and how might countries agree on them? In addition, what goals should the international community have with regard to these rights, and how might progress toward them be measured? Finally, what institutional framework is necessary in order to enforce them, and how, if at all, can such a framework be created? A careful consideration of these questions sets the stage for a discussion of the possible role of the WTO in the issue.

Many commentators distinguish between human rights and labor rights in the public debate over the linkage of these rights and trade policy. In some cases, this distinction is useful, especially in identifying the possible economic interests involved in the linkage and, in particular, when labor costs affect trade itself. But in principle the lines between the two types of rights are blurred. It may be reasonable, for example, to define freedom from torture, arbitrary imprisonment, and genocide as human rights that are separate from workers' rights to a minimum wage and to organize for purposes of collective bargaining. However, freedom from slavery, freedom from discrimination, the right to a minimum standard of living, and humane working conditions tend to straddle the fence between the two concepts.

The following discussion will encompass both human rights and workers' rights, distinguishing between them when it is appropriate to fit policies and institutions to one or the other. Yet these two broad classes of rights share a common problem: how to achieve a workable international consensus on definitions, monitoring, and enforcement measures.

| What Are Human Rights?

A practical place to begin the search for consensus on the definition of *human rights* is the UN Universal Declaration on Human Rights. This and other related UN documents attempt to establish basic standards of social, political, legal, and economic existence in all human societies.[1] Right away, we confront hard reality. Its thirty articles present a list of the aspirations to the good-and-just life for all citizens of the earth, as seen through the lens of its Western, democratically minded authors.

Aside from basic rights to life and liberty and freedoms from slavery, arbitrary arrest, and discrimination, the declaration asserts political, legal, and economic rights modeled on Western constitutions and cultures. Examples include the right to a public hearing and trial, the right to property and its protection (including intellectual property), freedom of expression, freedom of consensual marriage, the right to a democratically elected government, and the right to equal pay for equal work. All people have the right to both "just and favorable" conditions of work and remuneration and also "rest and leisure." All have a right to an adequate standard of living, medical care, and free public education.

The declaration, which dates from 1948, is clearly a wish list that came out of the heady days of postwar reconstruction. It is a statement of how things should be, rather than an enforceable set of rules backed by hard commitments and credible force. The achievement of such high standards of human rights would presumably be the result of informed governmental social and economic policies in all countries, combined with international cooperation, development, and aid. At the time, there was an optimistic glow that emanated from the promise of benevolent welfare-state economics to solve all problems of human need. The intervening decades of continuing global poverty, as well as the inability of even the rich countries to eliminate their social problems, have shown the limits of, and ultimately the false promises of, government intervention to achieve these lofty goals. Human rights cannot be realized merely by declaration.

We need, then, to go back and reformulate the question. Whatever human rights one may feel are worthy of our aspirations, the relevant question is this: what human rights can and should be defended or enforced internationally? The answer may depend on whether countries intend to enforce those rights unilaterally or through international or global agreements.

If the standard is one of global agreement, the list will be short, simply because the common acceptance of core human rights must span many diverse cultures, societies, economic systems, and levels of development. Legal scholar Patricia Stirling cites international customary law to include in this short list "freedom from torture, collective punishments, prolonged arbitrary detention, genocide, slavery, or threats to commit any of these acts."[2] These are what might be called the core "passive" human rights, the freedom of all people from actions taken against them, based on their existence as human beings.

If enforcement proceeds unilaterally, then the definition of human rights is likely to grow considerably. Since the enforcing country's policies will be subject to domestic influences, it is also very likely that political and economic elements will find their way into the definition. Some countries, particularly the United States, have defined human rights in terms of "democratic" rights and freedoms. In contrast with the core passive human rights described above, these may be termed "active" rights, such as the freedoms of speech, expression, and travel or movement and the right to elect a representative government. Human rights defined in this manner focus on the individual's right to act affirmatively, without interference from the state.

Another set of human rights extends the definition more clearly into the economic dimension. Proposals for a "social clause" to enforce workers' rights are based largely on conventions negotiated within the International Labor Organization (ILO). Examples of core workers' rights include the freedom of association, the right to organize as unions, the right to collective bargaining, the prohibition of forced labor, and child labor protection. Some proposals have also included nondiscrimination and health and safety guarantees at work.[3]

| The Enforcement Issue

As the brief discussion of definitions has shown, any policy measures taken to enforce human rights on a global basis will depend on finding a universally accepted notion of what the basic, nonnegotiable rights of human beings are.[4] Once the definition of human rights takes on political or economic content that may not be recognized universally, then the protection of human rights becomes a matter of regional or unilateral enforcement. The problem of definitions tells us something about the problem of using trade restrictions to enforce human rights.

To the extent that at least a core set of human rights deserves international protection, it would seem logical that a vast majority of the countries of the world would take it upon themselves to conclude treaties to that end. The most notable achievement in international human rights enforcement, viewed historically, is probably the negotiation of several antislavery treaties, beginning in the 1800s. Prohibition of slavery is perhaps the most prominent example of a human right that is recognized as an enforceable, established rule of customary international law.[5] Aside from the universal moral indignation associated with slavery, the fact that its practice usually requires international trafficking has made it easier to suppress. No country wants to be known as a slave trader. What remains of slave trade, allegedly in some African and Asian countries, occurs clandestinely, usually within national borders or through black market operations.

There are many treaties and conventions that address other human rights issues, but their enforcement mechanisms are usually weak. For example, there are treaties that declare genocide, apartheid, and torture to be either crimes against humanity or "acts violative of fundamental freedoms and human rights."[6] In these cases, the human rights violations typically occur within a country's borders, and any enforcement measures would require strong external coercion, if not direct intervention within the target country. The world community has generally been unsuccessful in enforcing human rights in the face of violations in these and other areas. This conclusion probably holds even in the case of South African apartheid. While international condemnation against apartheid dated from its official promulgation in 1948, and a series of UN and other sanctions began in 1962, the government of South Africa successfully circumvented international investment, trade, financial, and military restrictions for decades.[7]

Beginning in 1985, expanded economic sanctions against South Africa included embargoes on coal, oil, arms, gold, and access to capital markets. These and other policies, such as the Sullivan Principles, which established a multinational corporations' code of conduct, appear to have made a positive contribution to change. However, the reforms that finally led to the dismantling of apartheid in the early 1990s were arguably the result primarily of internal pressures.[8] Hufbauer, Schott, and Elliott (2003) conclude, "Overall, economic and political conditions inside South Africa were clearly the most important factors influencing the outcome in this case and economic sanctions can be credited with, at best, a modest contribution" (Case 62–2, p. 17).

Here is the main problem with the enforcement of human rights from the perspective of a trade economist. In the absence of a world government with sovereign powers and policing capabilities in all areas of the globe, there is no easy way to take action against human rights violations within a sovereign state. Verification of the violations is often costly and uncertain; getting international support for action is difficult; and making the action against the target country effective is often as painful for the enforcer as for the target country. In addition, political and strategic considerations often trump humanitarian principles. The sad but enduring truth is that governments rarely rise above their own self-interest or take on the domestic political risks of foreign entanglements in order to defend human rights.

The discussion in chapter 5 concluded that countries will voluntarily sacrifice a measure of their national economic sovereignty if the gains (from trade, for instance) outweigh the costs of lost sovereignty. Governments conduct a similar cost-benefit analysis in their decisions to sign treaties, especially if, as signatories, they may be obligated to take certain actions in the future. The United States, for example, has been very reluctant to sign many human rights treaties and conventions because treaty requirements may impinge on its sovereignty.[9]

The practical consideration is that treaties may restrict the country's options. What if the treaty requires retaliation against countries that have strategic significance to the signatory? What if enforcement leads to an unwelcome change in the internal or regional political balance of power? The treaty's enforcement provisions are generally effective, of course, only to the extent that they lock in a credible threat of concerted action against the violator. Yet it is the inflexibility of this arrangement that deters the country seeking to retain maximum independence in its foreign policy. Building a multilateral front against human rights abuses is extremely difficult in this context.

In addition, the multilateral treaty or convention has the disadvantage of opening up the signatories to standards they may find unacceptable. Human rights violations allegedly occur not only in Third World dictatorships, but also in advanced industrialized democracies. The United States and many other countries, for example, have refused to acknowledge capital punishment as a human rights issue, in contrast to European views on the matter. The United States has also run afoul of the Convention against Torture, which it ratified in 1994, for its use of electroshock devices on prisoners and harsh prison conditions.[10] The United Kingdom has allegedly violated human rights conventions in the detention of prisoners in Northern Ireland.

The United States has opted for the alternative of unilateral actions in attempting to enforce human rights standards on other countries. Unilateralism alleviates the problem of coordination and implementation but sacrifices the broad consensus and coverage that are often needed to prevent circumvention of the enforcement measures. This problem is often compounded by the selective nature of alleged human rights violations announced unilaterally. The United States has often imposed economic sanctions against countries it accused of human rights violations, generally based on antidemocratic practices. As noted earlier, this definition of active human rights has political content that detracts from its universal acceptance. Even fellow democratic countries may not regard this class of rights to be enforceable. European countries, for instance, have declined to join the ongoing or previous U.S. sanctions against Cuba and China, respectively, taking a commercially pragmatic view toward relations with these countries.

| Human Rights, Trade Sanctions, and the WTO

It seems therefore that human rights enforcement suffers from either the insufficient resolve of multilateral treaty provisions or the narrowness and lack of international support of unilateral measures. Could a "human rights chapter" of the WTO solve the problem and create an effective global enforcement mechanism? There are two general approaches to including human rights in the WTO rules, and both of them are bad ideas. One idea would be to make core human rights enforceable through mandatory WTO-sanctioned trade restrictions. The other would be to include some menu of human rights issues among the general exceptions to WTO disciplines (in GATT article XX, for example).

The first and most serious general objection to using WTO-approved trade restrictions to enforce human rights standards is that such measures would be contradictory. Many of the principles and goals of the WTO play a significant role in advancing human rights (see Petersmann 2000). The United Nations' secretary general, Kofi Annan, has explicitly made this link:

> The goals and principles of the WTO Agreements and those of human rights do therefore share much in common. Goals of economic growth, increasing living standards, full employment and the optimal use of the world's resources are conducive to the promotion of human rights, in particular the right to development. Parallels can also be drawn between the principles of fair competition and nondiscrimination under trade law and equality and nondiscrimination under human rights law.[11]

In addition, the origins of the GATT/WTO system, which was created as a response to the devastation of the economic and political turmoil of the 1930s and 1940s, points to a broader role for trade liberalization in the quest for universal human rights. The contribution of the WTO to peaceful trade relations and to the peaceful settlement of trade disputes has reduced a significant cause for political conflict and war, situations in which human rights are most likely to be abused. A multilateral system of trade agreements tends to create stability in international relations and to increase economic welfare for all participants, conditions that play an important role in supporting human rights (see Lim 2001, 282).

Beyond the basic problem of undermining the environment for human rights, using the WTO as an enforcement mechanism is problematical because the organization was never intended to address this issue and has no institutional framework or resources to deal with it. Some observers have tried to identify a WTO link with human rights through a provision that allows member countries to restrict imports made with prison labor.[12] There is no evidence, however, that this provision was anything more than a fair trade measure designed to prevent countries from using unfairly cheap labor to boost export competitiveness.

Proposals for automatic WTO-authorized trade sanctions to punish human rights abuses usually begin with the assumption that all member countries recognize the core human rights to be protected, implying the narrower definition described earlier. In addition, only WTO member countries, which by definition would recognize the enforceability of the specific core human rights, would be subject to punishment. The practical roadblock to such an arrangement is the same one that tends to discourage any international agreement that preempts government decision making. The WTO, a consensus-based agreement, is highly unlikely to achieve consensus on automatic rules regarding human rights abuses. The usual complications of strategic interests would often loom large. Giving up sovereignty on this matter would carry large downside risks for some countries, especially large and politically powerful ones.

A related problem is that the WTO does not have the institutional capacity to investigate human rights violations. The GATT and, later, WTO members have always tightly circumscribed the activities of the Secretariat, most notably by restricting it to a small budget. It was forty-five years after the founding of the GATT that the new WTO members finally saw their way clear to instituting the Dispute Settlement Body to address matters of central concern to the organization. How easy would it be, then, to establish a similar body for matters that have never been part of its mandate? Inevitably, controversies over the composition, procedures, and conclusions of a WTO investigative body on human rights would arise. The high stakes of the economic sanctions would politicize the entire process.

The objections to a WTO role go beyond these cynical observations on statecraft. Trade sanctions, even if effective in inflicting pain on the target country, are not necessarily the most appropriate response to human rights abuses. Trade is a blunt instrument and can often inflict damage on unintended targets. If, for example, a WTO member country, such as the Congo Republic, is accused of conducting official policies of torture and genocide, would a trade embargo really help the matter if it hurts consumers and workers in that country, especially the low-income citizens who are most vulnerable to such measures? This point goes back to the basic contradiction between human rights and WTO-approved trade restrictions discussed earlier. Is the creation of a trade sanctions–induced humanitarian crisis in the target country the best response to the bad behavior of its leadership?[13]

The debate over sanctions against Iraq in the wake of the 1991 Gulf War shows the pitfalls of such actions. To the extent that they were effective in isolating Iraq economically, one might claim that the sanctions were successful in hurting the target: the dictatorship of Saddam Hussein. However, even if that is true, the collateral damage was significant. The politically weak, low-income citizens of a country like Iraq have little power to circumvent the embargo. In contrast, the dictator's virtual monopoly on resources and power allowed him to survive and even tighten his grip on the country, while exploiting the suffering of the country's people for political purposes.[14]

The alternative to embedding core human rights into WTO obligations would be to include the possibility of unilateral human rights–based trade restrictions in the General Exceptions portion of the WTO agreement. This provision would amend WTO rules to allow individual countries to impose discriminatory trade restrictions based on a determination of human rights violations. To be at all workable, such a provision would have to define the specific human rights violations that would justify trade intervention. Otherwise, it would be possible to cook up charges of human rights violations against nearly every country. Examples of crimes and potential violators include discriminatory treatment of minorities, women, and immigrants (inflicted by most countries around the world in one way or the other); the death penalty, any cruel and unusual punishment, and inhumane treatment of prisoners (as alleged against the United States and many other countries); and undemocratic political systems and repression of democratic rights (as in many authoritarian regimes and possibly also in other countries with either right-wing or left-wing governments that are politically unacceptable to other countries).

The underlying problem in allowing an expansive definition of enforceable human rights within the WTO system goes back to the fundamental value proposition of the WTO, discussed in chapter 2. The main purpose of the WTO is to provide predictable rules regarding market access, which reduces a critical element of uncertainty in international trade. An open-ended human rights clause could easily lead to a proliferation of unilateral trade restrictions, which would negate the value of the WTO agreement to its members.

An equally daunting problem with this type of human rights clause in the WTO would arise in the investigation and verification of human rights abuses. As noted above, the WTO does not have the staff or resources to conduct independent investigations of human rights abuses. Presumably, the enforcing country would have gathered information, which would then culminate in a determination of a human rights violation. If that conclusion were challenged in the WTO, then the Dispute Settlement Body would have to judge the merits of the case, as long as such policies were held to WTO disciplines. The WTO would have to add a human rights investigation unit, with a staff of legal experts and judges in this area and a budget to match.

Finally, we come again to the question of the appropriateness and, indeed, the effectiveness of trade restrictions for purposes of combating human rights abuses. A detailed study of the effectiveness of economic sanctions by Gary Hufbauer, Jeffrey Schott, and Kimberly Ann Elliott points out the difficulties in designing sanctions to achieve specific goals.[15] Their analysis covers 103 cases of sanctions imposed by various countries and international organizations in order to alter the military, political, or human rights behavior of specific governments between 1914 and 1999. The general conclusion of the study is that it is difficult to make sanctions work, and it has become even more difficult in recent years. In sanctions cases prior to 1970, 27 out of 61 cases (44 percent) were deemed successful in terms of achieving some demonstrable change in policy or behavior. From 1970 to 1999, however, only 38 of 132 sanctions cases (29 percent) were judged to be successful.

This result may seem paradoxical: with increased interdependence and globalization, one might expect international sanctions to have more, not less, impact today than in the past. Yet the fact is that globalization has dispersed economic influence, which makes it more difficult for even a strong economic power or coalition of countries to isolate, punish, and influence others. There are conditions and rules that will increase the likelihood of success, but the cost may be high and the path difficult.[16]

What we can conclude from the discussion so far is that trade and human rights are not directly connected in most cases, and the gap between the two poses major problems for using trade to enforce human rights. Trade becomes a tool of pure punishment, which may hurt the wrong persons in both the target country and the enforcing country. There is typically no consistent and logical way to link and calibrate trade restrictions with human rights abuses, which makes it difficult to achieve international consensus on a systematic set of sanction rules and guidelines. These factors do not bode well for any incorporation of human rights elements into the WTO.

At the same time, we must recognize the potential power, in absolute terms, of trade as a source of political leverage. In general, trade sanctions may be able to influence a target country's behavior regarding human rights, workers' rights, the environment, or other types of government policies. Trade, in other words, may be effective as part of an enforcement mechanism to achieve nontrade goals. Yet the unilateral use of sanctions, undisciplined by international agreement, is damaging not only in terms of the direct economic cost of restricted trade but also in the systemic cost of undermining accepted WTO trade rules.

Is there a way out of this apparent dilemma? In principle, countries have the ability to impose economic sanctions, including targeted trade restrictions and embargoes, within the WTO system. The WTO rules contain a general nonapplication clause, which allows a WTO member country to deny WTO treatment to another country, but it can be invoked only at the time the new country joins the organization. The United States has made use of this measure occasionally in conjunction with the Jackson-Vanek amendment in trade relations with countries that do not allow free emigration.[17] There is also a wide-ranging but rarely used national security clause, which can allow discriminatory trade restrictions in times of an otherwise unspecified "emergency in international relations" (GATT article XXI). It is also possible to suspend normal MFN treatment between specific WTO members. The United States used this approach to break off trade relations with original GATT members, such as Cuba and Czechoslovakia, after communist takeovers in those countries (Jackson 1989, 205). The WTO rules do not require documentation of human rights abuses or other unacceptable behavior; the country simply asserts its sovereign right to single out another country for exclusion from normal WTO relations. Clearly, this is an extreme measure, but it provides a safety valve for rare cases of complete, across-the-board, unilateral sanctions.

In terms of developing multilateral or even global mechanisms of human rights enforcement, the principle that applies here, as it does everywhere else in this study, is that political will supporting a solution of the underlying problem must be strong enough to support international institutions dedicated to the issue. This development needs to precede the linkage with trade. In this case, an international mandate for protecting human rights is necessary, with international agreement on definitions, standards, procedures, responses, and remedies. A remedy that included trade measures, applied systematically according to clearly defined rules, would at least theoretically be compatible with the WTO system, subject to international law.

What is lacking here and elsewhere is therefore an international institutional framework for protecting human rights with specific actions based on consensus. Political will and international cooperation have unfortunately not proceeded far enough to make such consensus possible. In the meantime, trade sanctions remain an unsatisfactory method of dealing with the problem.

Workers' Rights

What is the difference between human rights and workers' rights? As a conceptual issue, workers' rights are in many ways a subset of human rights, in the sense that work is an essential element of human existence. The terms of employment, remuneration, working conditions, and institutions of worker representation are therefore important aspects of life for most people on the planet. The plight of many—one might say, most—workers in the world ranges from unsatisfactory to deplorable, by the standards of the advanced industrialized countries. And so workers' rights have become a human rights issue.

The earlier discussion about definitions sheds some light on the difference, however, between core human rights and workers' rights. The workplace as an economic entity differs across the spectrum of economic systems and levels of development. Socialist systems typically guarantee employment and basic benefits and impose unified wages; capitalist systems tend to base labor allocation and pay more on a meritocracy of education and training. Poor countries often have systems of low wages and no benefits, with little de facto regulation and labor institutions; rich countries have highly differentiated labor markets, often mandate benefits, and allow varying degrees of collective bargaining. The ILO has indeed identified a set of core labor rights, to be discussed later in this chapter, but there is no corresponding consensus among ILO members on how to enforce those rights. As the UN Declaration on Human Rights showed, we can all dream about the ideal conditions for work and other aspects of life that we would like to see everyone enjoy, but establishing a practical way to reach the goal is another matter.

The heart of the workers' rights issue in trade policy, however, is based on perceptions of fairness. Foreign wages and working conditions have long played a significant role in trade policy, going back at least to the seventeenth century.[18] The argument for protection on this point has traditionally been that lower wages in foreign countries give those countries an unfair advantage in competing with goods produced at home with higher wages. Comparative advantage theory, as discussed in chapter 2, puts this argument to rest at the theoretical (if not the popular) level. Low-wage and high-wage countries typically trade with each other to their mutual advantage—based on efficient exchange and on the proper adjustment in labor and other resources internally (there's the rub, politically). At a practical level, the greater productivity of labor in high-wage countries, where labor's value increases because it has more education and physical capital with which to work, justifies the wage differential without disadvantaging those workers in the global marketplace. Specialization tends to result in an allocation of jobs that use lots of education and advanced machinery to the high-wage countries and those that use more physical or unskilled labor to the low-wage countries.

It is clear that such economic explanations offer little comfort to workers in labor-intensive industries vulnerable to import competition in high-wage environments. In rich countries, workers in the clothing, footwear, and steel industries, as well as those involved in assembly-line manufacturing or the production of commodity goods may face painful adjustment prospects, as described in chapter 3. Protecting their jobs and wages often comes down to an argument that foreign wages are unfairly low. This argument extends to differentials in benefits, working conditions, and institutional rights (to form unions, for example) that may affect the cost of labor.

One element of support for proposals to protect workers' rights therefore comes from a highly motivated constituency of workers in advanced countries. One does not need to be a cynic to recognize that statements by industrial unions in rich countries in support of workers' rights in poor countries are statements of self-interest. Any success in equalizing the labor-cost differential tends to reduce competitive pressure and, with it, the painful adjustment pressure of imports. This observation is merely further evidence of comparative advantage and the political economy of trade. There is trade *because* the labor is relatively cheaper abroad; that is often the basis of the foreign country's comparative advantage. Realizing the gains from trade requires the economy to adjust, and lower-skilled workers in rich countries are often displaced as a result. Is it fair, then, that workers in poor countries receive low wages and endure working conditions that would be unacceptable in rich countries, when the result is that cheaper imports displace rich country workers from traditional manufacturing jobs?

The fairness issue, viewed in this way, is a compelling political force domestically, as shown by the disproportionately high levels of protection received in rich countries by the industries listed above, through tariffs, quotas, and antidumping duties. Beyond the simple political economy question of jobs and wages, however, lies a nagging ethical question. Should working conditions and labor laws be subject to enforceable international standards? Politically, protecting the wages and jobs of a subset of workers in rich countries would not, in itself, be sufficiently compelling to motivate broad-based international support for workers' rights. In this regard, the connection to human rights is quite important and introduces the key political issue. What labor practices go beyond the pale to the extent that international consensus on their ill effects is possible? The ennobling and unifying goal of protecting human rights in this regard lies in the objective of improving the lot of otherwise vulnerable and disadvantaged groups, of safeguarding them from unrestrained cruelty, exploitation, and oppression. Once such practices have been identified, the next question is whether the enforcement of the relevant workers' rights would actually improve the lot of workers in general around the globe.

| Child Labor and Sweatshops

Child labor and sweatshops represent labor practices that are widely condemned. They are widespread in the world economy and are, sadly, a fact of life in many poor countries. There is evidence to suggest that some export goods, particularly from certain developing countries, have been made using child labor or under sweatshop conditions. The question that the world community and governments must face is how to move toward an elimination of these practices. However, using trade policy to correct the situation would probably not be effective and would in addition cause unintended harm.

The ILO (2002) estimates that 246 million children worldwide, approximately one in six between the ages of five and seventeen, are working. In addition, 179 million child workers are exposed to various forms of abuse, ranging from semislavery and debt bondage to long hours and dangerous working conditions, and two-thirds of this group are under fifteen years of age. The largest percentage of child workers lives in the Asia/Pacific region (60 percent of the total), followed by sub-Saharan Africa (23 percent), and the Latin American/Caribbean region (7 percent). Most child laborers, about 70 percent, work in agricultural and related sectors. About 8 percent work in manufacturing, wholesale, and retail trade.[19] A subgroup of this last category, estimated by Save the Children Fund at 5 percent of the total (cited in Lawrence 2002), includes child workers who are involved in the production of export items, primarily in the apparel, footwear, and sporting goods industries.

Sweatshops may be defined as work environments with one or more of the following features: long hours with meager wages, crowded conditions, unsafe or unsanitary facilities, poor lighting and ventilation, and harsh treatment. Sweatshops are most often associated with developing countries, but such facilities have been discovered in New York, San Francisco, and Paris as well. Sweatshop conditions often overlap with instances of child labor, as they are found primarily in labor-intensive, light manufactured goods sectors, such as apparel, footwear, toys, and sporting goods.

While child labor and sweatshop conditions have been linked to the production of these export items, the full extent of such practices is unknown. Studies on the subject disagree on the extent to which manufactured exports from developing countries are "tainted" in this manner.[20] The worst practices appear not to occur in firms owned or managed directly by multinational corporations (MNCs). Typically, most sweatshops are small, independent, locally owned enterprises that sell to regional distributors on a subcontracting basis for mass markets in the United States, Europe, and Japan. Such goods therefore often enter the multinational supply chain through indirect channels.

The ILO has sponsored international conventions to ban certain forms of child labor and to set goals for the eventual elimination of all exploitative forms of it. Yet signing these international agreements only pays lip service to the issue. Governments have found it difficult to move beyond a condemnation of the practice in principle. To be sure, policy measures that can contribute to eliminating sweatshop and child labor practices are difficult to design. Since these practices exist in some—but probably a minority—of factories that produce traded goods, trade restrictions against countries where such facilities have been found would punish all producers of these goods in the country, regardless of their behavior. Other policy measures to suppress trade or to force a divestiture of MNC assets in developing countries would also be ineffective in dealing with the problem. According to one report, sweatshop and child labor conditions are actually worse when locally owned factories are producing for local consumption, with little outside scrutiny. The biggest problems with labor standards in developing countries lie outside the traded goods sector.

In dealing with child labor as a public policy issue, one must first recognize that it is deeply ingrained in the economics and cultures of many poor, underdeveloped societies. It would be fantasy to expect that, if only child labor were effectively banned, all children would show up in school the next day, getting the education that will liberate them from poverty. In many cases, child labor is the result of low family income, which cannot wait for the possible benefits of schooling in the distant future. Schooling is often unavailable anyway. So, in some cases, it may be best to focus on increasing the economic opportunities of adult breadwinners, which in such poor countries will come from both better domestic economic policies and from increased access to export markets and foreign investment. More international aid to support schools in these countries, combined with schooling arrangements on factory grounds (for young workers or for the children of parents who work there), may then establish a framework for building a more advanced structure for the family income and education incentives that are essential for economic development.

The sad truth is that the alternatives to working in an apparel factory may be much, much worse for many children in developing countries: begging, crime, child prostitution, pornography, and jobs in nontraded sectors with more dangerous working conditions. When a documentary aired showing the use of child labor in garment production for Walmart in Bangladesh, there was an immediate outcry in the United States and a congressional threat to ban all imports from Bangladesh linked with child labor. Several Bangladeshi factories then dismissed thousands of young workers (mostly young teenage girls), many of whom ended up in more dangerous lines of work, including prostitution, and few of whom went to school (Denny 2001, 21).

The long-term solution must come from a transformation of a subsistence economy with a large labor surplus to one in which industries can begin, capital can accumulate, educational resources can become available, and upward mobility can become possible. Stable and rising family income will be a key element of this process. The success of many previously poor countries in making this transition has relied largely on access to export markets in light manufactures. These markets must therefore remain open in order to provide the opportunity for development.

Government policies that would actually help these countries improve their labor standards are therefore the same policies that would improve their standard of living. Aside from trade liberalization and greater (not less) foreign investment, the rich countries could provide more foreign aid, including the construction and funding of schools. Yet this is a huge project. In the meantime, the high public profile of many multinational corporations and retailers in the rich countries can play a role.

Real progress on the issue will be possible only if policies aim at the economic roots of it. In addition, MNCs have found that allegations of exploitative labor practices are potentially bad for business and have therefore begun to monitor the hiring policies and work conditions in their foreign factories. Sporting goods manufacturer Reebok and toy maker Mattel responded to reports that sweatshop and child labor were used in the production of their products by taking steps to eliminate subcontracting, institute inspections, and enforce higher workplace standards (Tierney 2000; Slater 2000). Nike, Adidas-Salomon, and Disney have similar programs. Public relations considerations in developed country markets appear to provide a compelling incentive for MNCs to adopt voluntary corporate codes of conduct involving some assurance or certification of "no sweatshops or child labor used."

Globalization has not created the problem of poor labor standards, despite the protests against multinationals and their alleged exploitation of labor in developing countries. Yet, ironically, the best way to improve the situation would be to increase globalization. Already, international scrutiny has raised awareness of the problem, and the corporate response has established the beginnings of industry codes of conduct. Trade and investment can make a crucial contribution to productivity, increased wages, and economic growth. Far from being the cause of the problem, international trade and investment may yet provide the keys to making progress in eliminating sweatshops and child labor.

| Workers' Rights and Trade Negotiations

While economic transformation through better domestic policies, foreign investment, trade, and aid may provide the best long-term foundation for eliminating abusive labor practices, many countries still favor a concerted global approach to influence governments directly. There seems in this regard to be little disagreement in principle about the goals, but finding an effective multilateral way to persuade governments to enforce international labor rights has so far been elusive. It is interesting to note that there has been a long history of attempts to include workers' rights in multilateral trade negotiations, but without success. The United States, for example, has proposed workers' rights and labor standards as a trade issue at least since the 1948 negotiations over the Havana Charter (see Watson, Flynn, and Conwell 1999, 63–76).

It has become clear over the years that the treatment of workers' rights as a competitiveness issue, in which creating a level playing field is the goal, will guarantee failure in any multilateral negotiation that includes developing countries. Efforts to make social dumping the basis for trade sanctions, based on gaps in wages, benefits, and other labor cost elements, has in the past met—and will continue to meet—with a sharply negative reaction from low-wage countries. The labor cost gap is in this sense a major source of comparative advantage, and policies to use that criterion to restrict trade cannot avoid the tinge of protectionism they inevitably carry.

Punitive trade restrictions to enforce labor standards would have other problems as well. Would such sanctions be effective in changing government policies in targeted countries? The record of economic sanctions suggests that their ability to alter behavior is doubtful. Who would get hurt? Trade sanctions would reduce employment opportunities in the target country for many workers that the policies are presumably designed to help. Another serious problem is the lack of connection between trade and the more serious allegations of workers' rights abuses. As noted in the discussion above regarding child labor and sweatshops, many of the worst cases of exploitation occur in plantations, mines, construction firms, and small businesses that serve only domestic markets.[21] Trade sanctions would miss the target, while inflicting damage on export industries that typically offer the best prospects for economic growth and, indirectly, social progress.

The economics of labor markets in developing countries are often harsh but difficult to circumvent. Proposals for an international minimum wage, for example, may appear at first to offer hope of a higher standard of living.

Yet workers are hired in any market on a cost-benefit decision. Hiring will continue only as long as the value of a worker's output per hour exceeds the total cost per hour of hiring the worker. Worker productivity in less developed countries tends to be low, which is the main reason that the prevailing wage in those countries is correspondingly low—and the main reason that high-wage workers in rich countries can compete on world markets as long as their productivity is correspondingly high. Setting the wage above the market level implies that the hiring will stop short of clearing the market, a formula for worsening unemployment. For this reason, no serious current proposal for workers' rights contains a global minimum wage (an idea popular in the 1970s).

The political success of strategies to establish and promote global labor standards must connect to humanitarian constituencies and other associated political forces across a wide range of countries. The best prospects for achieving progress lie in institutions other than the WTO. In this regard, slogans such as "trade with a human face" are not helpful. The underlying issue is not trade, but rather "work with a human face," which must be promoted by domestic labor policy reforms, moral suasion, and economic opportunities and incentives.

| *Why Not the ILO?*

The International Labor Organization is an institution designed specifically with the purpose of promoting and protecting workers' rights and welfare globally. It was founded in 1919 and became a specialized UN agency in 1946. Its membership includes not only governments (with nearly universal representation) but also trade union organizations and employer associations.[22] The charter of the ILO contains many of the elements that were later included in the UN Universal Declaration on Human Rights, described earlier:

> The ILO formulates international labor standards in the form of Conventions and Recommendations setting minimum standards of basic labor rights: freedom of association, the right to organize, collective bargaining, abolition of forced labor, equality of opportunity and treatment, and other standards regulating conditions across the entire spectrum of work related issues. It provides technical assistance primarily in the fields of vocational training and vocational rehabilitation; employment policy; labor administration; labor law and industrial relations; working conditions; management development; cooperatives; social security; labor statistics; and occupational safety and health. It promotes the development of independent employers' and workers' organizations and provides training and advisory services to those organizations. Within the UN system, the ILO has a unique tripartite structure

with workers and employers participating as equal partners with governments in the work of its governing organs.[23]

It would seem that the ILO is set up as the ideal institutional framework for establishing and protecting workers' rights on a global basis. Yet, if this is the case, why is it that many labor advocacy groups and NGOs insist on shifting this burden to the WTO?

The answer lies primarily in the lack of a systematic and effective enforcement mechanism and the apparent unwillingness of ILO members collectively to develop such mechanisms. The essential difference between the ILO and the WTO in this regard lies in the contrasting nature of the goals, incentives, and processes in the two organizations. The WTO's mandate and structure have for the most part successfully internalized both the benefits of membership—the very real gains from trade—and the costs of violating the rules through the principle of reciprocity. WTO rules refer primarily to trade policies and therefore deal with external, state-to-state relations. All members benefit from nondiscriminatory market access, and any government that unilaterally reduces this benefit for the other members is subject to an equal withdrawal of benefits in retaliation.

The ILO, in contrast, has established goals regarding *internal* standards and policies regarding labor, issues beyond the reach of easy international verification and enforcement. There is nothing about ILO membership akin to the gains from trade that provides a direct incentive to comply with these standards or conventions, as each state retains sovereignty over its internal policies. There is, to be sure, a sense of moral obligation attached to participation in ILO conventions and agreements, and this should not be underestimated. In addition, the ILO has established a reporting mechanism (not always faithfully followed by some members) and processes for investigating infringements of the conventions, in some cases even those involving non-signatories.[24] Article 33 of the ILO charter includes the possibility of collective condemnation and even sanctions against countries in flagrant violation of ILO conventions. However, it has been difficult for the ILO membership, although nearly universal, to see its way clear to a comprehensive system of establishing enforceable workers' rights.

Among the numerous nonbinding ILO agreements that have been adopted by large numbers of countries is the Declaration on Fundamental Principles and Rights at Work.[25] This document establishes the goal of setting a global framework for workers' fundamental rights, including freedom of association, the right to collective bargaining, the effective abolition of child labor, and the elimination of discrimination in employment and occupation. It also stresses the need to assist ILO member countries in attaining these goals through technical cooperation, advisory services, and "efforts to create a climate for economic and social development" (paragraph 3). The declaration also notably insists on delinking workers' rights from protectionist policies:

[L]abor standards should not be used for protectionist trade purposes, and . . . nothing in this Declaration and its follow-up shall be invoked or otherwise used for such purposes; in addition, the comparative advantage of any country should in no way be called into question by this Declaration and its follow-up. (paragraph 5)

The declaration is a political document, not a legally binding convention. The question therefore remains as to how the goals of the declaration can be most effectively promoted. All ILO members must report on their progress in achieving its goals, but this provision again provides, at best, only moral suasion.

ILO article 33 allows the governing body, an executive tripartite committee, to recommend measures to secure compliance with legally binding ILO conventions. This article was first invoked in March 2000 against Myanmar (Burma) because of that country's refusal to change its policies regarding forced labor. With only limited means of enforcement through the ILO itself (that is, a suspension of ILO technical assistance), the accompanying recommendations could only suggest that member countries review their relationships with Myanmar and consider measures that might provide incentives for compliance (see Elliott 2000). Prior debates on the use of article 33 against Myanmar showed that several developing countries were clearly uncomfortable with the idea of ILO-mandated sanctions, even though they were indirect and unspecified. Part of the problem lay in the fact that "renegade" trade sanctions against Myanmar had already appeared in some local jurisdictions in the United States (see Moritsugu 2002), and any ILO measures to encourage sanctions could set an unwanted precedent for broad and possibly uncontrollable trade-based retaliatory measures.

Myanmar's violation of ILO workers' rights standards was extreme and indeed exceptional in leading to the very first article 33 action, but it is evident that many countries see a slippery slope in the broad range of labor rights that could be subject to ILO condemnation and sanctions, weak as they are. Until the point where ILO sanctions were first proposed, most countries could safely sign on to the conventions without risking the sort of critical international scrutiny that could lead to punitive enforcement measures. This institutional feature of the ILO points out the basic problem it faces: the willingness of its members to endorse high-sounding principles but not to develop effective mechanisms to enforce them.

The Myanmar case illustrates both the possibilities and the limitations of pursuing the goal of enforceable labor standards through the ILO. While there is a mechanism for identifying shortcomings and abuses, based on ILO conventions, consensus on the issue of enforcement is weak, and the ILO itself provides very little in the way of incentives for compliance. It is therefore easy to recognize the appeal of using the WTO as the mechanism for a universal sanctions system. The proposed formula is easy: violate international labor standards and get hit with trade sanctions. This provision could easily be written into a WTO social chapter, so the argument goes. Yet the fatal flaw of such proposals is that the WTO rules are subject to tight, consensus-based control by its membership over collective rights and obligations. In the absence of universal agreement on labor standards, a social chapter that could compromise the WTO's contractual benefit of market access for all its members would quickly be vetoed.

The best institutional response to issues of global workers' rights would be an ILO empowered with incentive mechanisms to promote compliance with standards established by a consensus of participating countries. Some observers have suggested that, in the absence of a strengthened ILO in these matters, there will be strong political pressure for the WTO to fill the vacuum, if not with a social chapter, then with expanded rules to enforce labor standards, perhaps through a broader interpretation of the prison-labor exception in GATT article 20 to include "forced labor" (see Elliott 2000). Pushing the WTO rules in this direction would be problematic, however, since the ILO definition is probably too broad to accept as a new WTO obligation. The definition itself could become negotiable but probably at a high cost to the developed countries supporting the idea.[26]

Finding a way to generate the political will needed within the ILO to enforce even a small set of universally recognized workers' rights will not be easy. There are two elements to the problem that must be addressed. One is the need for a more ironclad prohibition of protectionist trade sanctions in any ILO article 33 actions, whose vague call to retaliation may be keeping some countries from supporting the system. Alternatively, the ILO members must clearly define (and win support for) cases where trade sanctions are an acceptable enforcement measure.[27] The second element is that specific alternative compliance measures, including not only negative diplomatic sanctions but also positive inducements, should be considered in ILO article 33 recommendations. Foreign aid for education, infrastructure, and capacity building for the domestic enforcement of labor regulations could contribute to better working conditions and the ability to comply with ILO conventions and provide politically more acceptable carrots rather than sticks as incentives. This approach would require greater coherence in international institutional cooperation, since World Bank loans, for example, may need to play a large role in supportive aid projects.

In the meantime, the ILO offers a forum and a platform for another promising approach to labor standards. Beginning in 1972, the ILO sponsored a tripartite conference to establish a labor code of conduct for multinational corporations, which was adopted by the governing body in 1977. The code does not have a supporting enforcement mechanism, and its scope does not include purely domestic firms. However, moral suasion may add power to its impact. A similar code was adopted by the Organization for Economic Cooperation and Development (OECD), which consists largely of industrialized countries.[28] Bhagwati and Srinivasan (1996) have proposed an extension of the OECD code, which would require all multinational corporations to adopt the environmental standards of their respective home countries in all foreign operations, a concept that could apply to worker and social policies as well. As indicated in the discussion of child labor and sweatshops, many multinationals have discovered that voluntary and self-imposed compliance with labor standards makes good business sense.

International codes of conduct that are voluntary will always remain less than satisfactory for those who see hard rules backed up with credible enforcement as the only reliable way to make progress in these matters. Although a hard regime of enforceable rules is likely to remain elusive, it is at the same time well worth remembering that corporations are sensitive to issues of human rights and workers' rights, which are increasingly a matter of good business practice. The Sullivan Principles, which arguably played a positive, if perhaps not decisive, role in expediting the end of apartheid policies in South Africa, may provide a model for promoting global social standards in multinational corporate practices.[29]

| Conclusion

The WTO has neither the design, the capacity, nor the resources to monitor either human rights or workers' rights in its regulation of trade policies. This conclusion does not imply that these rights are impossible to protect effectively across borders. It does indicate that the thorny problem of establishing a viable system for their protection demands a more comprehensive solution, which must be open to both negative and positive compliance incentives, as well as voluntary measures by governments and businesses. Above all, the role of trade liberalization in creating the economic and relational foundation for progress and cooperation in these areas must not be underestimated.

In the end, the greatest barrier to progress is the lack of appropriate global institutions. Countries must find common ground on the underlying principles of human rights, workers' rights, and the measures that are acceptable to promote them and defend them. This agreement, if it is to occur, can only happen independently of trade negotiations and trade policy rules. Otherwise, protectionist motives will always be suspected, tainting the effort. The WTO system is also not set up to allow for human rights exceptions to its disciplines. Countries are allowed under the WTO rules to suspend normal trade relations with other countries under special circumstances. These provisions are rightly designed as exceptional measures, and they generally must apply across the board. The danger with expanding an exceptions approach is that it would institutionalize a unilateral determination of standards and an erosion of the system of trade rules.

We sometimes come to a point in the debate on this issue where the discussion of economic impacts and trade-offs is abandoned. Opponents of trade with country X on grounds of alleged human rights violations or forced labor practices may well argue that no economic argument is applicable. The behavior of country X is despicable and therefore country X should be shunned, in trade and other aspects of international relations. Yet moral decisions on economic policy never occur in an economic vacuum. Economic analysis can inform, without necessarily dictating, the proper policy in such circumstances. An economic assessment can predict, for example, how much a trade embargo will cost the target country and the enforcing country. It can show how the burden of the cost will be shared by workers and factory owners in both countries. Political considerations also suggest the possible value of allowing trade to continue and contribute to economic growth and rising standards of living, which are usually linked to the development of democratic institutions and an improved environment for workers. Ideally, this sort of information should be gathered and debated before the government chooses its policy.

The record indicates that economic sanctions in general are ineffective in achieving their policy goals and should give pause to policymakers whose decisions may be affecting many different groups, both at home and abroad. The admonition against unilateralism also suggests the problematic nature of pursuing policies based on self-proclamations of moral superiority. Unilateral assertions of moral superiority in trade or in any other policy action directed against other countries are typically manifestations of political power and are often in direct conflict with the notion of a global commons or natural law. If the principle being defended is truly and compellingly universal, it should be possible to assemble a large coalition in its favor and to devise ways to encourage and promote compliance with it.

WTO and the Interests of Developing Countries

WTO'S LEVEL PLAYING FIELD

What do developing countries have to gain from membership and participation in the WTO? This question has generated much controversy recently, as anti-WTO protesters claim that the organization facilitates the exploitation of poor countries by multinational corporations, the continuation of low wages and unacceptable working conditions, abuses of human rights, and the despoiling of the environment worldwide—all in the name of corporate profit. In this view, the WTO is alleged to be antidevelopment.

Most economists and trade professionals, in contrast, regard the WTO as the catalyst for economic growth and emergence from poverty. While democratic and social reforms are not necessarily a direct consequence of increased trade, the general view among trade professionals is that economic growth tends at least to support greater democratic participation, increased regard for workers' and human rights, and greater preferences for environmental quality.

Indeed, the subject of economic development is so broad and deep that this chapter cannot possibly do justice to it and all its many multidimensional and interdisciplinary elements. Even the narrower topic of trade and development is large and complicated, and we can only touch on the more important aspects of it. However, it is important to note at the outset of this chapter that economists generally agree that trade is an important and even crucial component of economic development. As a matter of revealed preference, developing countries have been joining the WTO in droves in recent years, and nearly all of them outside the WTO are currently trying to get in. This trend should not be surprising, given the earlier discussion on the gains from trade and the associated benefits of technological transfer, access to new products and product ideas, and exposure to the rigors of best practices and competition on world markets. The agenda of the Doha Round of trade negotiations also highlighted the importance of development issues in an effort to harness trade for growth, especially in the world's poorest countries.

This chapter will focus on the relationship between developing countries and the GATT/WTO system. It should be clear, in view of all the evidence, that trade is important to developing countries and that their continued engagement in the global trading system is essential as a matter of development strategy. However, the theoretical benefits of trade do not necessarily imply that WTO membership has always done an adequate or sufficient job of promoting economic development in poor countries. There are many instances in which the gains from trade liberalization for developing countries have not been all they were cracked up to be. In particular, the least developed countries in the world have not improved their standards of living in recent years (see Michalopoulos 2001, 34; "Is It at Risk?" *Economist*, Feb. 2, 2002, pp. 65–67). Yet the reason for this problem appears to lie more in their limited access to globalization than in their exploitation by it.

One clever editorial cartoon, "WTO's Level Playing Field," presents the view as many developing countries surely see it. There is a level playing field of economic opportunity in the world, but the problem is that there are two of them—one for the developed Northern Hemisphere and one for the developing Southern Hemisphere. The developed countries of the North play on their own field, while the developing countries of the South play, upside down, on the underside of the northern field, and nowhere do the two meet. The fields are set up to be separate, with no contact between them, except for an occasional curious glance between the top of the world and the bottom, perhaps at WTO ministerial meetings.

In view of the widespread disappointment among many developing countries regarding the functioning of the WTO, it is nonetheless telling that their governments are intent upon reforming WTO internal governance and striking better deals in trade negotiations, rather than abandoning the basic principles of the organization. This approach contrasts sharply with some of the external protests against the WTO, which tend to view the organization and its capitalist underpinnings as rotten at the core.

Ironically, much of the current protest accuses the WTO of exploiting developing countries, while at the same time the protests target alleged abuses that occur largely in the developing world. Thus, the environmental and social standards proposed to eliminate exploitation in the WTO system would result in trade sanctions and barriers against these same developing countries. Certainly such measures would tend to have their largest economic impact on the citizens of the developing countries, as noted in chapters 6 and 7. The fact that much of the protest is nominally targeted at multinational corporations or authoritarian dictatorships does not change this assessment.

Beyond the concerns of social and environmental groups, the developing countries themselves have often complained bitterly about the WTO. Their concerns tend to be of a more mundane, but nonetheless important, variety. Market access, timetables for reforms, compliance with WTO procedural requirements, and WTO governance may seem to be obscure and esoteric issues, but they represent major focuses of developing country negotiating efforts in the WTO, with potentially large implications for their gains from trade, especially among the poorest countries in this group.

It is therefore important to maintain a broad perspective when considering the interests of developing countries in the WTO. It is also important to remember that interests among developing countries also diverge on many trade matters. This chapter will take the approach of identifying the core benefits of WTO membership for developing countries and also the elements of WTO membership that relate to economic development. The central focus will be the role that the WTO plays in securing the gains from trade for developing countries.

| The Benefits of Developing Country Membership

Developing countries join the WTO for the same basic reasons that other countries join: to gain from trade liberalization and to become part of a process that makes the gains easier to achieve. The multilateral nature of WTO trade agreements is especially attractive to smaller developing countries that would otherwise have a difficult time negotiating many different bilateral trade arrangements. The WTO system allows countries to plug in to a global trading network with a unified, broad-based negotiation process. When compared with the alternative approach of regional and other preferential trade agreements (as described in chapter 4), the WTO offers the advantage of providing an automatic framework for maximizing the breadth of market access. Many developing countries have tried to increase market access, specialization, and efficiency through preferential trade agreements, without much success.

Developing countries can still reap potentially large gains from trade from further trade liberalization in general: their industrial tariffs average 13 percent, compared with 3 percent for the richer countries. Lower tariffs will cause the economies of developing countries to allocate their resources more efficiently, which will allow the development of more successful export industries. Furthermore, they stand to gain especially by lowering trade barriers with each other, since many natural trade opportunities with other developing countries in close proximity and with similar market characteristics and income levels are still being suppressed by tariffs and other trade restrictions (Bhagwati 2002). A particularly important benefit for developing countries is the WTO's rules-based system, which includes an effective dispute settlement system. All WTO members benefit from this aspect of the WTO, but developing countries (and other small and less politically powerful countries) are able to resolve trade conflicts through the WTO in ways that would not otherwise be possible for them. This is not to say that the United States and Europe can no longer throw their weight around in trade relations, but the DSU gives all countries their day in court, a fair hearing of their case, and a decision by an independent panel of judges. Prior to the strengthening of dispute settlement in the WTO, the United States had often taken unilateral actions under section 301 of its trade laws, which left less powerful trading partners with little leverage to negotiate (see Bhagwati and Patrick 1990).

| ## The Trade and Development Process

The institutional benefits of WTO membership described above provide a general case for how the WTO helps developing countries achieve the gains from trade. It is worthwhile, however, to review briefly how the economic benefits of trade contribute to the broader process of economic development. Development may best be understood as a process of transformation. Harry Johnson describes the process from an economic point of view:

> The development problem of the less developed countries is one of converting a "traditional" society predominantly based on subsistence or near-subsistence agriculture and/or the bulk export of a few primary commodities, in which per capita income grows slowly or may even be declining as a result of population pressure, into a "modern" society in which growth of per capita income is internalized in the social and economic system through automatic mechanisms promoting accumulation of capital, improvement of technology, and growth of skill of the labor force. (Johnson 1967, 44)

The development process takes place in a broader political, social, and legal environment, so many different pieces of the puzzle must be in place. Specific pieces include political stability, monetary and exchange rate stability, and a legitimate system of laws and property rights. Other factors include an adequate natural and human resource base and favorable geographical location. External resources through foreign aid may also play an important role. Supportive policy measures may also be important, such as education to develop human capital, basic health care and disease control, and infrastructure development for transportation and communication. In general, implementing a broad and properly balanced array of economic, political, social, and legal policies to support the various aspects of the development process is also important for promoting development.

Trade is only one of many pieces of the development puzzle, but it is an important piece. In the transformative process of development, trade itself may be regarded as a process rather than merely as a commercial activity. The gains-from-trade discussion in chapter 2 emphasized that countries benefit from trade through specialization and exchange. At the same time, the reallocation of resources implies a process of adjustment, which is supported by an economic and legal system of incentives to facilitate factor mobility and investment. The process extends to the role of trade in exposing firms and potential entrepreneurs to new products, production processes, and technologies and in motivating the search for new market opportunities. The transfer of technologies, technical know-how, and best-practice production and management techniques occurs largely through trade and trade-related foreign investment. In this regard, the full benefits of trade will also require an economic environment conducive to entrepreneurship, import-export trade, and foreign investment, as well as market access for the country's exports abroad. The WTO plays its most direct role in this process by creating an international environment of certainty regarding market access and related economic activities.

Trade therefore enters the development process with a number of possible roles. In the earlier stages of development, where the country may be producing a limited range of commodity goods, foreign markets may create a vent-for-surplus to bring unused resources into production. At this stage, the improved resource allocation and increased output may allow increased savings and capital accumulation.[1]

At more advanced stages of development, trade is associated with progressively more sophisticated manufacturing and product differentiation, based on technology and skills transfers. In many cases, export-led growth contributes to development by increasing factor supplies and productivity, providing the proper price signals and incentive structures (Riedel 1991), and encouraging inward foreign direct investment (Balasubramanyam and Salisu 1991). In essence, export-led growth has been identified with a set of "dynamic efficiencies," that link the exporting country's exposure to the rigors of world markets with competition-driven learning by doing, improved information exchange, and reduced transaction costs (see Krueger 1980; Meier 1995, 483–85). The process role of trade in development is important because the structure and pattern of a country's imports and exports will tend to change as development advances.

The benefits of trade to economic growth in general therefore appear to reside at least as much in the various impacts of openness to international commerce and competition as they do in the more traditional static welfare gains demonstrated by economic theory. In fact, trying to pinpoint the contribution of international trade to economic growth in statistical models has proven to be very difficult (see Frankel and Romer 1999), largely due to the problem of identifying a clear sequence of causality. Nonetheless, the body of evidence linking trade to increased income and economic growth is large and growing.

In this regard, the global trading system embodied in the WTO becomes crucial to the development process. If countries undergoing development—at whatever stage—find that their most beneficial pattern of imports and exports changes, then it is important that world markets remain open to trade. Balassa (1980) has identified the trend in shifting comparative advantage as economies grow and evolve. Moving from commodity production to simple manufactures, such as clothing and footwear, allows the country to enjoy comparative advantage in labor-intensive goods—as long as export markets are open to these politically sensitive goods. Progressive capital accumulation and development implies increasing comparative advantage in producing such goods as consumer electronics, steel, and even automobiles, and later even more advanced products. The gains from trade in this case presuppose a system of open market access that respects an evolving pattern of market-driven comparative advantage over and above discriminatory, politically driven trade regimes. The principle of nondiscriminatory, predictable market access, as noted earlier, is the hallmark of the WTO system.

| ## *Special and Differential Treatment*

The foregoing discussion presented what is generally accepted as the mainstream view of economic development. There are certainly competing models, notably those based on fundamentally different views of the world. Marxist models of development, for example, do not accept many of the basic assumptions of market-based economics. Instead, they typically focus on the goals of removing industry and agriculture from private ownership, redistributing political and economic power to workers and peasants, and designing state-run central plans for economic development. Market-driven free trade will be anathema to such a policy regime. Some of the more extreme opposition to the WTO comes from left-wing anticapitalist groups in developed and developing countries whose models of development simply cannot be reconciled with the GATT/WTO system on ideological grounds.

Political and economic views regarding the role of trade in development have tended to waver between the two basic and conflicting poles of free trade and unimpeded markets, on the one hand, and interventionist planning, on the other. The GATT was founded in 1947 with 23 members, 11 of which could be considered developing countries. Over the years, the number of developing country members of the GATT and its successor, the WTO, has grown in both absolute and relative terms. Of the WTO membership in early 2003 of 146 countries, 120 were either developing countries or countries in transition to a market economy. The issue of the proper role of trade policy in development has therefore always been important in the formulation of GATT and WTO rules. This importance has increased over the years, as the role of developing countries in the organization has grown. In earlier years, the view toward trade in the development process tended to be tentative, skeptical, and decidedly more interventionist in spirit. More recently, many (not all) developing countries have embraced trade-opening measures, sometimes unilaterally. Yet the legacy of the earlier years lives on in the special and differential (S&D) treatment traditionally given within the GATT and, later, the WTO to developing countries.

S&D treatment is based in large part on the view that developing countries may have a more difficult time adjusting to trade liberalization than developed countries. There are both economic and political components to this view. Until recently, the accepted economic wisdom had been that developing countries may not benefit initially from trade-driven resource reallocation as much as developed countries. Many economists have regarded the presence of market failures, including the lack of well-developed capital, resource, and product markets, information gaps, insufficient investment in infrastructure, and factor immobility, as barriers that would prevent the struggling economy from garnering the full benefits of trade. Furthermore, pessimism about the course of commodity prices seemed to suggest that such countries would suffer from declining terms of trade.[2] For many economists and government officials, trade barriers to help infant industries and correct balance-of-payments difficulties represented legitimate policy measures to promote development. The accompanying political element to the S&D argument is that poorly functioning markets, combined with the lack of government capacity to provide safety nets (adjustment assistance, welfare payments, and so on), make it more difficult and painful for poor countries to adjust to trade liberalization. S&D treatment, in the form of reduced requirements for reciprocal tariff concessions, would make it more attractive politically for these countries to take part in trade liberalization.

During the period of massive decolonization and economic reconstruction after World War II, the upshot of this thinking was for the GATT to carve out exceptions to the general goals of liberal trade for developing countries. The UN Conference on Trade and Development (UNCTAD), founded in 1964, reinforced this approach. Under the leadership of its first secretary general, Raul Prebisch, the UNCTAD promoted the concept of import substitution industrialization (ISI) as a policy formula for development (see Meier 1995, 355–60, for an overview). In general, this idea incorporated the use of import tariffs, the identification of local demand, and economic planning to develop domestic industries to replace imports.

The underlying assumption was that the industrialized, developed world represented the core and the developing world the periphery of the world economy. Left to market forces, the periphery would depend on trade in commodities for its path to development, which would in turn be futile because of the perceived trend in falling commodity prices, continued dependence on industrialized imports from the core, and the corresponding inability to break out of poverty. Therefore, according to this view, the periphery could catch up with the core only by closing off their domestic markets from import competition and developing industries on their own.

The GATT was dominated by developed industrialized countries, and while not embracing the Prebisch approach, it did attempt to accommodate the "special needs" of developing countries in terms of trade policy rules. Specific portions of the GATT allowed for exemptions from the normal rules prohibiting import quotas and requiring tariff binding, so that developing countries could protect infant industries and redress balance-of-payments difficulties. The GATT later developed the Generalized System of Preferences (GSP), in which developed countries give preferential tariff treatment to certain developing country exports. In negotiations, the GATT allowed developing countries to participate without the expectation of reciprocity on their part. The developing countries were, in other words, allowed to "free ride" on trade liberalization and get increased market access for their exports without having to give up additional domestic market access to foreign imports.

| Chump Change for Developing Countries?

Special and differential treatment has always been controversial among economists, who have noted that such halfway trade liberalization does not fully remove trade distortions. For example, a country that enjoys preferential market access because it faces lower tariffs than its rivals will shift resources toward production of that good domestically. However, the preferential tariff creates a distortion by tilting market access and production incentives toward countries that may not in the end have comparative advantage in those products. S&D treatment as it pertains to tariff preferences, nonreciprocity, and exemptions from market access rules has been strongly criticized by many trade economists (see Krueger 1999; Finger and Winters 1998; Bhagwati 2002).

The counterargument is that such preferences are unlikely to cause serious economic distortions, given the array of products and suppliers subject to GSP treatment. Furthermore, it seems that the advantages imparted by GSP, nonreciprocity, and other S&D measures are largely political. Such arrangements make it easier for the governments of developing countries to take part in trade negotiations and become more integrated in the world economy, because they reduce the need for domestic concessions, such as tariff reductions.

Ironically, there has never been a very strong economic case for S&D treatment based on correcting market failures. Economic analysis, furthermore, shows that countries benefit by making market access concessions, so the question arises as to whether such measures are true acts of kindness by the developed toward the developing countries. A closer examination casts further doubt on the actual benefits of S&D treatment for the developing countries. It has often been alleged that special treatment gives them only "crumbs from the rich man's table." Many developed countries, for example, exempt textile, clothing, and agricultural products from GSP treatment, which are typically of greatest importance to these countries as export goods. In addition, excusing developing countries from reciprocity has arguably led to their marginalization within the GATT/WTO system (see discussion on internal governance below). Most of the important bargains at trade negotiations are the result of trade-offs among the major players, and without reciprocity there can be no true equal partnership in the negotiations or in the organization as a whole.

As the structure of trade negotiations and trade policy rules has become more complex, the nature of S&D treatment has expanded. Aid programs to help governments of developing countries acquire economic and legal expertise in their delegations and preferential treatment on compliance with TRIPs and other harmonization standards are among the benefits of special treatment. If one begins with the fact that the world trading system has become more legalistic and complicated, it is difficult to oppose the offers of aid and less stringent compliance schedules for developing countries, especially the least developed among them. In the day-to-day grind of ongoing committee work in Geneva, in technically challenging, multisector trade negotiations, or in a complicated dispute settlement case, professional services are extremely valuable, and the poorest countries often lack the resources to support the minimal requirements of a trade delegation. Developing the domestic regulatory institutions required to comply with WTO standards regarding TRIPs, sanitary and phyto-sanitary measures, customs valuation, and industrial standards, is expensive (see Wilson 2002). Financial aid to facilitate the infrastructure for fuller participation in the WTO seems only fair.

And yet, the S&D system remains unsatisfactory in principle, even as the governments of developing countries lobby for its continuation and expansion. The mercantilist aspect of the GATT/WTO system has tended to encourage this sort of thinking (see Wolf 1987). Over the years, it has become institutionalized and is perhaps a difficult legacy to suppress. Yet at this point it would perhaps be best for developing countries to use S&D measures as bargaining chips for more advantageous trade-opening measures elsewhere.

| The Built-In Agenda

In the broader scheme of developing country interests in the world trading system, S&D treatment does not provide a truly compelling case for WTO reform. On the other hand, there are plenty of development issues left over from the Uruguay Round of trade negotiations that require additional attention and follow-up. This situation illustrates the high stakes and the growing role in the world trading system of developing countries, which have much to gain from its continued stability and negotiating framework.

Two areas of trade policy reform in the Uruguay Round were particularly important to the large group of developing countries: agriculture and Multifiber Agreement (MFA) restrictions. The Uruguay Round succeeded in opening up some aspects of agricultural trade, which has long been protected and distorted by a myriad of tariff and nontariff barriers, export and domestic subsidies, and regulations that discriminate against imports. Many developing economies could benefit greatly by further liberalization in this sector. However, many of the market-opening measures are limited, and the policy reform rules are often ambiguous, so that true liberalization cannot be assured.[3]

Perhaps the greatest potential benefit for developing countries from the Uruguay Round was the plan to dismantle the long-standing system of textile and apparel protection provided by the MFA. Trade restrictions implemented under this plan by developed countries have represented the single most damaging barrier to manufacturing expansion and exports by many developing countries, for which these products would typically have served as steppingstones to industrialization and economic growth. Despite the Uruguay Round agreement to terminate the MFA at the end of 2004, the liberalization efforts are heavily backloaded, so that most of the improved market access is not scheduled to occur until near the end of the transition period. In the meantime, there is a clear danger that backsliding can occur or that countries will impose alternative import restrictions, either through safeguard protections built into the agreement or through antidumping (AD) and countervailing duty (CVD) measures.

Such trade law measures represent yet another potentially severe barrier to trade. AD and CVD cases are directed against imports selling at prices that are unfairly low or that are allegedly subsidized. Imports from developing countries are particularly vulnerable to these charges, since trade law measures often target commodity-type price-sensitive imported goods.[4] There was some, but limited, progress in reforming trade law–based contingent protection in the Uruguay Round. Experience in the United States has shown that import-competing companies and industries often initiate trade law investigations when trade liberalization reduces traditional tariff or nontariff protection.

In addition, the developed countries that make extensive use of AD and CVD laws have set a bad example, which a number of developing countries are now unfortunately imitating. Until the 1990s, the vast majority of AD cases, for example, were filed by a small number of developed countries: the United States, members of the European Union, Canada, Australia, and New Zealand. From 1990 to 2000, however, there was a sharp increase in the total number of AD cases filed and in the number of developing countries by which they were filed. During the second half of 2001, developing countries initiated 121 AD investigations, compared with 65 from developed countries, and yet the majority of cases were filed against exports from developing countries (WTO press release 287, Apr. 22, 2002). This is a dangerous trend that harms the entire world economy, since AD laws are often subject to abuse and arbitrary administrative guidelines.[5]

The developed countries have hardly covered themselves with glory in their trade policies regarding agriculture, textiles and apparel, and AD and CVD measures. One can certainly condemn them for such damaging policies, not only toward developing countries, but also toward their own consumers. This situation provides yet another compelling reason for additional trade liberalization for all countries.

| Trade-Related Intellectual Property

One of the most controversial outcomes of the Uruguay Round was the conclusion of an agreement on trade-related intellectual property (TRIPs) rights enforcement. Essentially, this agreement extended to all WTO members the obligation to harmonize their domestic laws to global standards regarding the protection of patents, trademarks, and trade secrets.

There are two basic problems with TRIPs from the perspective of economic welfare for developing countries. First, the agreement appears to favor overwhelmingly those economically advanced countries holding patent and trademark rights, with possibly detrimental effects on poor countries importing intellectual property products. Second, and more subtly, the introduction of this sort of harmonization-of-enforcement measure into the WTO sets a possibly dangerous precedent that may open the door to other proposals that would make trade subject to environmental, labor, and human rights standards. Subjecting trade to these tests is widely regarded as particularly pernicious for the interests of developing countries.

The economics of intellectual property (IP) protection are complex and defy efforts to devise uniform policy guidelines. The reason for this state of affairs is that IP rights impart monopoly power to the holder, which in turn implies at least temporarily a transfer of economic welfare from the consumer to the producer. Looking at the overall economic welfare for society (the global society, in this case), such monopoly rights may be justified if they provide the incentive for entrepreneurs and scientists to develop new inventions and technologies. But then, how much monopoly power in the form of IP protection is enough to guarantee this outcome? The final balance sheet of economic costs and benefits of IP protection cannot, in practical terms, be derived theoretically, because there is no way to identify in advance all of the parameters and conditions that could tilt the balance either way. This assessment can only proceed on the strength of empirical evidence as it emerges.

Nevertheless, IP-related trade has increased significantly in recent years, and international shipments of books, movies, music, chemicals, pharmaceutical products, certain types of machinery, electronics, alcoholic beverages, and cosmetics with IP content now represent some $1 trillion in trade annually (Maskus 2000). It was inevitable that it would become an important trade issue. One can make a strong economic case for TRIPs as a component of the WTO trading system, based on a consideration of developing country interests. First, TRIPs will improve the incentives for foreign direct investment (FDI) and licensing of technologies in countries that previously had weak IP protection. This is because corporations are reluctant to manufacture, sell, or license products in countries where copying and piracy are not prosecuted. A second and related advantage is that TRIPs will improve the incentives for companies to develop technologies—particularly, medicines—of special interest to developing countries. Maskus (1998) and Yang and Maskus (2001) report a significantly positive response of inward FDI and licensing to an increase in patent rights in developing countries.

Against these putative benefits, one must consider the potential costs to developing countries or any countries that are net importers of IP-intensive products. The most direct, measurable, and immediate costs are the increases in prices that are likely to accompany enhanced IP protection. McCalman (1999), reported in Maskus (2000), uses a static model to estimate the theoretical impact of TRIPs on the value of patents in place in 1988, had the agreement been in force during that year. His conclusion is that the value of patents would have increased by $5.7 billion for U.S. firms and $1 billion for German firms (the two big winners). These sums would have been transferred from most of the rest of the world, including the rest of the European Union, Japan, Canada (the biggest single loser), Brazil, India, Mexico, and presumably all or most other developing countries that are net importers of IP-protected goods.[6]

There is, in principle, the possibility that the incentive structure of global IP protection will eventually allow developing countries to cultivate their own intellectual property. Some IP capital presumably exists already in these countries, in the form of indigenous medicines and geographically based products. There is also scope for developing indigenous, IP-protected music, art, and literature, which is the subject of some World Bank project aid. However, net inflows of IP-related profits probably lie in the distant future at best for most developing countries.

A number of economists, including strong free-trade advocates, have condemned the TRIPs agreement and advocate its repeal (see Srinivasan 1999). Aside from the discouraging economic welfare arithmetic for developing countries, there is a clear danger that TRIPs has opened a Pandora's box, which exposes the WTO to demands for rules on the environment, labor, and human rights. To put this issue in perspective, however, one must also consider that, in the absence of TRIPs, the United States would surely have proceeded with unilateral measures under section 301 provisions of its trade law, which allow retaliatory measures against countries that fail to enforce the IP rights of U.S. firms. So one argument in favor of TRIPs is that it has brought an otherwise unilateral practice under WTO discipline. Yet a similar discipline could also theoretically have been enforced under an enhanced World Intellectual Property Organization (WIPO), a UN agency founded in 1974 (its roots go back to the Bern Convention in 1883), which specializes in IP issues.

The counterargument is that the WIPO has always been weak, with no credible enforcement mechanism, and could therefore not extend significant IP protection internationally. The U.S. pharmaceuticals and entertainment industries strongly favored a WTO approach because of the leverage that the issue of trade provided in both the negotiation of the TRIPs agreement and the follow-up enforcement provided by the Dispute Settlement Body, which acquired "teeth" in the Uruguay Round. And with this argument we come back to the Pandora's box problem, since environmental, labor rights, and human rights activists can make exactly the same arguments for including clauses in the WTO to establish international standards in these areas, including trade sanctions for noncompliance. Including TRIPs in the WTO weakens the argument to keep environmental, labor, and human rights clauses out, issues that may further damage developing country interests.

The approach of this book has been that the WTO should be allowed to focus on trade alone and that nontrade issues should be handled by strengthening institutional frameworks, provided either by existing treaties and conventions or by developing new ones. The WTO is overloaded even without the additional burdens of monitoring compliance in nontrade areas (Ostry 2000). It would have been much better, based on this approach, to channel IP negotiations into strengthening WIPO or specific IP treaties and conventions, even though IP products are increasingly traded. The point is that IP protection regimes operate as domestic regulatory bureaucracies and require additional government intervention, which gets the WTO into areas beyond its core issue of market access.

One must acknowledge at the same time that efforts to get the TRIPs genie back into the bottle are likely to be futile, and many trade observers are counseling against suggestions that developing countries try to scale back the agreement (Watal 2000). In the meantime, there are numerous ways in which improvements can be made within the existing TRIPs framework and agreement. The technology and resource gaps, combined with the transfer problem, remain the most troublesome issues. Jeffrey Sachs (1999) has proposed a form of foreign aid to be granted to, for example, pharmaceutical companies that develop new medicines to treat tropical diseases.

Other forms of international aid to developing countries to offset the TRIPs-related price increases, linked to critical health or other development needs, are also worth pursuing.

The TRIPs agreement has evolved to strike a balance between the interests of patent holders and those of product users on this issue. In one of the most significant developments at the WTO ministerial meeting in Doha, it was agreed that compulsory licensing for patent drugs would be required in circumstances of medical emergencies, such as HIV/AIDS, tuberculosis, malaria, and other epidemics, in any country where the patent was not held. This means that drug production would be permitted in such cases without the royalty payments to the patent holder, but the agreement was limited to those countries that had the domestic capacity to produce generic drugs. The more difficult question of allowing countries without any drug production facilities to import the drugs without violating TRIPs was not resolved at Doha. However, the Doha Declaration did extend the deadline for the least developed countries to implement the TRIPs provisions regarding pharmaceutical products until 2016.[7]

The ongoing adjustments to the TRIPs agreement indicate its difficult fit in the WTO system. Future negotiations are likely as countries continue to probe their way through an international agreement whose balance of benefits to producers and consumers of IP goods and services is still unclear. The progress of the WTO revisions shows that, contrary to the perceptions of many critics of the WTO, member countries, including the United States, have been willing to revisit the TRIPs agreement to resolve difficult issues regarding its impact on developing countries. Further goals should include plans for technical assistance and capacity building to facilitate TRIPs compliance for developing country members and assistance to enhance and develop IP products in developing countries themselves. WTO members should also be ready to deal with the political consequences of dispute settlement cases when TRIPs compliance does become an issue. For developing countries, especially the poorest among them, some sort of negotiated package of aid and assistance will often be superior to a legal ruling by a WTO panel.

| *Internal Governance and Green-Room Politics*

One of the major flashpoints of the Seattle conference, as noted in chapter 1, was the issue of decision making and representation. The controversy erupted over claims by several developing countries' delegations that they were systematically excluded from crucial meetings and discussions at the Seattle ministerial meeting.[8] These charges have led to a broader discussion of possible reforms of the internal governance system of the WTO.

It is necessary, first of all, to put the issue in perspective. Charges of "lack of representation" by smaller member countries (not just developing countries) in the WTO are not new; they go back to the GATT system as well. As noted in chapter 4, the WTO is a consensus-based body based on the principle of one member, one vote. Given that unwieldy framework, certain methods of consensus building have evolved over the years. All WTO members recognize the power structure of the organization, with the United States and the European Union at the top. This hierarchy does not mean that the United States and the European Union control the organization, but it does mean that consensus on the major issues must generally begin with them. Typically, small numbers of WTO members concerned with specific issues meet to discuss them and to draft positions on them. As negotiations proceed, larger numbers of WTO members are drawn into the talks. This process often takes place informally and works well as long as all truly interested parties have access to it (see Sampson 2001, 7).

At more advanced stages of negotiations, when positions on major controversial issues must somehow be reconciled, the GATT/WTO system uses what has become known as the green-room meetings, named after the color of the decor of a room in the Centre William Rappard in Geneva, where such talks often took place. In these meetings, groups ranging in size from four to thirty-four member delegates hash out compromises on important issues, which are then typically brought to larger circles of WTO members or, in some cases, to the full membership for review and approval (see Blackhurst 2001). Participating countries typically include some combination of the United States, the European Union (representing its fifteen members collectively), Canada, Japan, and other developed countries and some of the larger developing countries, such as India or Brazil, or countries representing the interests of blocs of smaller countries.[9] Indeed, developing countries, especially India and Brazil, have often played important roles in multilateral trade negotiations since the Tokyo Round.

This system of representation, text drafting, review, and approval developed as an efficient method of conducting negotiations within an otherwise unmanageable framework; including all WTO members in every meeting would clearly be impossible. However, the size of the WTO has grown and the negotiating landscape has changed since the traditional system developed, and there is a strong case for reforming it. In terms of sheer numbers, more than three-quarters of the WTO membership are countries with developing or transitional economies, with thirty more waiting to join. The increasing number and dominance of developing countries in terms of membership strains the traditional governance system.

In addition, times have changed from the early postwar days of the GATT, when the accepted wisdom was that developing country involvement in the trading system should be limited, qualified, and conditional. The implementation of S&D treatment also implied a lesser role for them in trade negotiations, especially because of the suspension of reciprocity for developing countries. Many negotiations up until the Uruguay Round involved multilateral codes that allowed à la carte membership; a country only needed to negotiate if it wanted to join that specific agreement. The Uruguay Round instituted the principle of an all-or-nothing "single undertaking," that is, you adhere to the whole negotiated agreement or not at all. This change increased the importance of broad participation. As noted earlier, many developing countries have also come to recognize the importance of trade in general as a vehicle for economic growth and want to maximize their opportunities for negotiated trade expansion.

The increasing desire of this group, representing the vast majority of WTO members, for a voice and participation in WTO affairs finally clashed openly with the strained institutional structure of decision making at the Seattle ministerial meeting. Director General Mike Moore and U.S. trade representative Charlene Barshefsky, facing the prospect of a total collapse of the talks, pushed for a rapid agreement on a face-saving communiqué in the only way they knew: a green-room summit of an "inner circle" of WTO members. This effort was doomed anyway but was doubly disastrous in that it alienated many developing country delegates, who were left outside the door.

| Green-Room Remedies

Finding a systematic way to improve the representation of developing countries and small countries is a major challenge. The IMF and World Bank use executive boards of twenty-four members for internal governance, but those institutions are structured differently, and such an arrangement would be more difficult to implement in the consensus-based WTO.[10] The GATT experimented with a permanent "consultative group of 18" (CG-18) in the 1970s and 1980s, but it was not successful in overcoming the problems of exclusion and lack of transparency.

WTO director general Supachai Panitchpakdi acknowledged the importance of internal WTO governance reform when he entered the position in 2002 (Panitchpakdi 2002), and despite the difficulties he has indicated his support for some sort of advisory board modeled along these lines (Panitchpakdi and Young 2001). Blackhurst (2001) proposes formalizing a twenty-four-member consultative board or advisory council to replace the informal green-room negotiations. Membership would follow the traditional arrangement of permanent seats for major trading countries, with rotating seats to be shared by groups of other WTO members, based on either regional representation or similarities on trade-related issues. Schott and Watal (2000) propose a less formal steering committee of twenty members, organized along similar lines. As one possibility, they propose a configuration that assigns seats to the European Union, United States, Japan, PRC/Hong Kong, Canada, Republic of Korea, Mexico, Israel, and South Africa as single country or unified voting entities and then regional seats to the Association of Southeast Asian Nations (ASEAN), the European Free Trade Association plus

Turkey, Australia/New Zealand, the Central European Free Trade Agreement (Czech Republic, Hungary, Poland, Slovak Republic, Slovenia, and Romania), North Africa/Middle East, South Asia, Mercosur, the Andean Community, Africa (two seats), and Central America/Caribbean community. Meetings and minutes would be reported to the WTO as a whole with full transparency and would never result in votes to bind the entire membership. A key challenge for this proposal is to devise a system that allows WTO members with common interests on any given issue at stake in the meetings to enjoy the appropriate level of representation.

Flexibility will be a key element of any successful reforms. Former WTO director general Mike Moore has commented that the organization is like "a parliament without parties, whips or standing committees; with no speaker and no rules about tedious repetition" ("Playing Games with Prosperity," *Economist*, July 28, 2001). In this regard, the smaller WTO advisory board will need to offer a deliberative framework for the larger group of member governments, that is, it will need to provide a way of organizing and focusing common interests into representative groupings. The WTO, in other words, needs a sort of party system to represent common interests across the issues. The system should promote the building of coalitions on important issues, but at the same time assure that individual countries' views are adequately and predictably represented in the smaller advisory board's meetings.

Some nascent elements of such a structure exist now. For example, the Cairns Group represents major agriculture export interests with a coordinated negotiating platform, much as a political party would. A fully developed system of political representation of this sort would align like-minded textile and clothing exporters into a representative group, with members identifying with that particular platform. Similar groupings could coalesce for countries on either side of important issues: IP goods importers and exporters, antidumping hardliners and reformers, environmental harmonization advocates and opponents, and so on. Obviously, a single WTO member would belong to many such "parties," according to its particular interests on various trade issues. Two countries could share interests on one issue and oppose each other on the next issue; there is no prospect for a simple two-party system here. The important element is effective representation: the major points of view on specific issues must be at the table to carry the torch for members not present.

Within the framework of a WTO advisory board, with flexible participation based on the issues, it seems eminently possible to devise a comprehensive system of representation along multifarious party lines. Participation would be determined by the issue at hand and the declared adherence of members to specific parties (or perhaps even factions of parties, if such subdivisions emerge). In some cases, the regional groupings would be appropriate. However, the variable political geometry of trade issues suggests that the composition of the board for any given topic should be issue-driven, with grouped seats determined by the agreed-upon proxies of the various interests involved and assigned to a representative country.

The key principle to keep in mind when discussing internal WTO governance is that the important work of the organization, and the benefits it delivers to its members, can proceed while its members debate the merits of reforms to improve the system. None of the members, and especially the developing countries, have an interest in throwing the baby out with the bath water and undermining or destroying the system.

| *Capacity Building*

The issue of governance is tied to another critical circumstance for the least developed countries among the WTO membership: being able to afford a mission to the WTO at all. From a cost-benefit perspective, a poor country would weigh the costs of funding a WTO delegation against the estimated value to the country of the gains from having that representation. These gains would come from increased benefits in terms of market access and other trade liberalization due to its representation in key negotiations or in ongoing committee work in Geneva, the value of bringing cases under the DSU, and so on. It might be tempting to leave this decision to the governments of the countries involved, difficult as the choices are for countries with few resources.

Yet garnering the gains from WTO membership is not such a simple matter of this cost-benefit choice for poor countries. Rich countries determine many of the terms of membership, which raises the issue of fairness. Aside from the expensive nature of maintaining a standing delegation in Geneva, compliance with WTO rules has become increasingly burdensome, as noted earlier regarding the TRIPs and customs valuation requirements. In addition, reforms in dispute settlement have increased the reliance of litigants on expensive legal services. Perhaps more important, there is a network effect associated with this problem. Global society gains from the widest possible participation of countries, through their governments, in its institutions, to the extent that it allows for maximum representation in achieving agreement or consensus on critical transnational issues. When the cost of participation excludes poor countries or downgrades their ability to take part in negotiations, then the resulting agreements are less than representative of global society, and in political and ethical terms less than legitimate. In addition, an exclusive decision-making process runs the risk of perpetuating the poverty that lies at the root of the problem.

Among developing countries in the WTO, 70 percent have missions that are in some way handicapped by underfunding, according to Michalopoulos (2001, 159). Some of the problem is simply a lack of staff; some of it comes from overdue arrears to the WTO. While developing countries, especially the larger ones with more resources, do enjoy the chairmanship of many WTO committees, the overall developing country representation in standing committees is less than proportionate to their membership in the organization (Michalopoulos 2001, 160–64).

The WTO rules and negotiated agreements have made provisions for the least developed countries' circumstances in many cases, as noted in the S&D discussion earlier in this chapter. There is also an effort under way by richer members to fund WTO capacity building for the least developed countries through training programs. The Advisory Center on WTO Law, discussed in chapter 4, is designed to help poor countries bring and prosecute dispute settlement cases and is also very helpful in bridging the gap. However, a long-term and systematic commitment by richer WTO member countries to improve the participation of the poorest countries across all of these dimensions is needed. The Doha Declaration has acknowledged this problem as part of the agenda for the development round of trade negotiations, and WTO-sponsored funding of capacity building, based on voluntary contributions by member countries, has begun.

| What the Developing Countries Need from the WTO

Antiglobalization protesters appear to be afraid of the WTO for the damage it allegedly inflicts upon developing countries. This view is unfortunate and counterproductive to the extent that it has a negative impact on trade liberalization. Indeed, the true and tragic damage would occur if trade liberalization stopped, cutting off a crucial avenue of growth for poverty-stricken countries.

What the developing countries need is more trade and foreign direct investment, not less. They need a system of obligations that will discipline their trade policies and keep markets open for their exports. They need, even more, a system of rules that gives them, as the smaller, weaker, and more vulnerable players in world trade, the best possible chance of pursuing their trade interests among the larger and more politically powerful developed countries.[11] The overwhelming evidence is that policies encouraging more open trade enhance and promote economic growth. The fact that there are other complementary policies that may be necessary does not detract from this major conclusion. Economic growth cannot be systematically sustained by policies that restrict a country's abilities to specialize its production on the basis of comparative advantage, to absorb foreign technology, to learn from global competition, and to exchange its goods and services internationally.

The sad truth is that the least developed countries are falling further behind in the world economy and have not, in general, benefited greatly from trade liberalization. This is not because the trading system itself has failed, but rather because these countries have not been able to take advantage of it. Perhaps the most important role of the WTO in the world economy of the twenty-first century will be to cultivate a trade environment that is conducive to economic growth in the world's poorest countries. Nearly all developing countries recognize the potential from trade and that is why they have joined the WTO.

There are many contentious issues within existing WTO agreements on which developing country members have a strong case for revision, amendment, follow-through, and reform. The Uruguay Round agreements, for example, included provisions for an end to the MFA, which now may be threatened by backsliding, high tariffs, and AD cases. In general, there is still an unacceptable disparity between the playing fields of economic opportunity of the developed and developing countries, as implied by the cartoon discussed earlier. The WTO can do its part to improve the situation by focusing trade negotiations on development issues, as it has committed to do in the Doha Round, and by making WTO governance more inclusive. The WTO's internal governance system is not perfect, and developing countries have made their disappointment with it clear in recent years. Yet the response of the developing country delegations has not been to abandon the WTO, nor to condemn its existence, but to demand institutional reforms, which are capable of proceeding without endangering the onward march of trade liberalization.

To get the process moving forward, the world—especially the developing world—needs to keep multilateral trade liberalization on track. Many observers, WTO critics and advocates alike, from both developed and developing countries, have pointed out the shortcomings of the Uruguay Round and of the WTO in general. This chapter has duly noted many of these criticisms. Yet further progress on redressing these problems, improving the functioning and operation of the world trading system, and providing the global environment for economic growth in poor countries can proceed only within the context of a strong multilateral system. In particular, past experience has shown that forward momentum is essential for consolidating and building on existing trade liberalization agreements. All of the old and new issues need to be put on the table in a new, comprehensive multilateral trade round. This is the best development and growth agenda.

9

NGOs, Multinationals, and Global Trade Governance

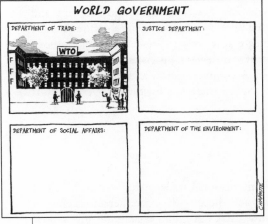

WORLD GOVERNMENT

DEPARTMENT OF TRADE:

WTO

JUSTICE DEPARTMENT:

DEPARTMENT OF SOCIAL AFFAIRS:

DEPARTMENT OF THE ENVIRONMENT:

CHAPPATTE

The increased visibility of nongovernmental organizations (NGOs) as participants in the trade policy debate has raised serious questions regarding the legitimacy of the traditional system of representation in the WTO and in the global economy in general. Is the WTO a closed club ruled exclusively by trade interests, especially the commercial interests of multinational corporations (MNCs), to the detriment of all other interests? Do governments unjustly exclude nontraditional interest groups from any role in trade policy? What possible role might NGOs play in the WTO and other global institutions, and how should they be represented?

A political cartoon on the state of global governance highlights the view of many WTO critics among the NGOs. It shows four panels, which represent various branches of "world government." The first is a "Department of Trade," represented by a fortified and shadowy WTO building, with armed guards protecting it from a band of protesters outside its walls. The other panels are labeled "Justice Department," "Department of Social Affairs," and "Department of the Environment." All of these panels, of course, are blank: trade is the only issue represented in "world government." This cartoon perceptively illustrates the inchoate nature of the current global governance architecture, even as it casts a skeptical eye on the WTO, one of the few organizations that can be regarded as both global and effective in carrying out its mission. But why is trade the only panel with a well-developed institutional structure?

It is also telling that the cartoon regards the WTO as a world government, as though the WTO exercised autonomous, independent authority and dictated laws to its global subjects. Chapters 4 and 5 addressed this issue at length. Yet the envious suspicion by NGOs of an allegedly powerful WTO under the insidious influence of MNCs explains their strong interest in gaining access to its decision-making structures. Why, some NGOs ask, cannot other social and environmental issues receive equal representation with trade in global governance? Is it not reasonable to include representatives of these interests in the WTO?

This chapter examines governance in the global trading system with regard to NGOs and MNCs. The major actors in the governance issue are workers, consumers, businesses, especially those engaged in importing, exporting, or competing with traded goods, and national governments, which must play a pivotal role in bridging the gap between institutions and the demand for transnational representation. The challenge for governments and for advocates of trade and nontrade issues lies in developing a comprehensive system of international governance that is open, representative, and responsive. The WTO is but one part of this developing system of global governance, but it will need to establish communication and policy links with representatives of nontrade issues when there is a legitimate overlap of interests.

| *The Variety of NGOs*

There are many stakeholders in international trade policy. As described in chapters 2 and 3, workers, firms, and those with a commercial interest in the production process have a direct stake in trade, since trade affects their wages and returns on investment. Consumers are also important stakeholders in trade, since they benefit from the lower prices and greater variety that typically come with trade liberalization, and industrial consumers benefit from access to competitively priced imported inputs for their production. In addition to these traditional actors in trade policy, there are also a number of new participants in trade policy discussions, such as environmentalists and advocates for labor standards, human rights, and other issues. These groups perceive a link between their respective issues and trade, either through trade's direct impact on the issue or possibly through the use of trade sanctions as a mechanism to promote their goals. Finally, governments themselves have strategic, political, and economic interests in trade as matters of domestic and foreign policy. Under the current WTO system, governments are also the main representatives of their populations in negotiating trade agreements and reflect the overall best interests of their constituents as a whole—or do they?

Traditional participants in the trade policy debate are represented through industrial or company lobbies (especially large firms and MNCs), unions, exporter or importer associations, and consumer advocacy organizations. Elected representatives with strong constituencies linked with one of these interest groups may also play a role in trade policy formulation. The voices of each group do not always carry equal weight among policymakers, but they do have a visible stake in the outcome, and a government's negotiating position typically recognizes their interests. The new trade stakeholders, in contrast, in many cases do not have access to the channels of trade policy influence, largely because the WTO system itself has resisted entering these nontrade areas in its multilateral negotiations. As a result, these groups have attempted to influence the WTO through NGOs, often organized on a transnational basis, which have organized protests against the WTO in Seattle and elsewhere. They claim to have global constituencies based on environmental and social issues. They therefore also claim to have a legitimate stake in WTO issues, insofar as trade policy affects these goals.Much of the opposition to the WTO has come from NGOs that claim to represent "global civil society" and that demand a voice in the WTO and other global organizations. Such groups represent a wide variety of interests, such as environmental protection, labor and workers' rights, human rights, and the special concerns of poor countries. Less well known are NGOs that represent business interests and advocate free trade. More than 700 such groups officially registered as nongovernmental participants in the WTO meeting in Seattle, and it is estimated that there are many thousands organized worldwide—29,000, according to one estimate quoted in the London *Economist*.[1]

And just what is *global civil society*? Civil society traditionally refers to any and all groups and organizations that exist separately from the state and the market (Carothers, Barndt, and al-Sayyid 1999), including political parties, interest groups, ethnic associations, and religious, cultural, and community organizations. The term is very broad in that it encompasses all groups of citizens that are organized in some way for a specific purpose or activity. *Global* civil society implies a set of groups connected internationally by a common interest, such as environmental quality, working conditions, human rights, or (less visibly) economic benefits tied to expanding trade, whether or not they are organized internationally or as a political interest group. The question then becomes how the interests of global civil society achieve recognition and representation either domestically or internationally.

In this context, NGOs play a significant role in representing civil society, providing organized channels of political influence, civic participation, and education. The UN Department of Public Information defines an NGO as "any nonprofit, voluntary citizens' group which is organized on a local, national or international level."[2] By this definition, everything from the local chess club to national political parties would (or could) qualify as an NGO. It seems that the critical distinction between an NGO and any other non-profit group or organization lies in its purpose and aspirations. As a practical matter, an NGO appears to be any such group that goes to the trouble of being recognized in this manner, usually in the hope of being represented in larger organizations, conferences, or policymaking bodies. Achieving recognition as an NGO typically involves a formal process of certification or credentialing, and the standards may vary. Yet NGOs also include groups that represent business interests, workers, or consumers who benefit from trade, which are not commonly associated with civil society. The broad UN definition cited above therefore also includes many private, but nonprofit, interest groups representing industries, national exporters, and trade associations. This component of the NGO population complicates the representation issue, as will be shown later on.

In considering the wide range of private interest groups participating in the trade policy debate, it is revealing to examine the list of NGOs that attended the WTO ministerial conference in Doha, Qatar. Among the nearly 600 NGOs were familiar names such as Oxfam, Friends of the Earth, Greenpeace, Third World Trade Network, and Public Citizen's Trade Watch, as well as Act-Up and ATTAC, which have played notoriously disruptive roles in antiglobalization protests. Trade unions, religious organizations, and humanitarian and human rights groups also attended. These NGOs are typically linked with the views of what has become known as global civil society. However, also in attendance were many business-oriented groups, such as chambers of commerce from various countries and industry and trade associations representing manufacturing, agriculture, and service sectors. These are groups traditionally associated with the commercial interests of trade agreements. They generally represent the business—as opposed to civil—part of global society, but their NGOs are constituted formally in the same manner, and it would be virtually impossible to separate them from groups with social, environmental, or humanitarian orientations.

Furthermore, there is generally an underlying political strategy associated with all NGOs, which is to establish a presence in all forums that deal with issues they wish to influence or monitor. Clearly, registering as an NGO for purposes of attending the Doha ministerial meeting is for many such groups a parallel form of their domestic lobbying activities. Failure to gain access to the decision-making process or to achieve influence domestically increases the importance of seeking international channels of influence. Yet even if a domestic lobby enjoys domestic influence, it will still be motivated to duplicate its presence in other forums if influence there is—or later becomes—a matter of competition among the various NGOs.

In analyzing the role of NGOs in global governance, it is useful to distinguish between the "advocacy" and "technical" functions of NGOs (see Ostry 2001). Pure *advocacy NGOs* are designed to lobby on behalf of an issue, mobilize public opinion in favor of it, and achieve political influence.

Technical NGOs primarily provide expertise or other specialized knowledge of an issue. Some NGOs combine both functions. For example, Friends of the Earth lobbies for particular environmental causes and at the same time has a scientific and legal staff that could contribute amicus curiae briefs to a legal proceeding or advise a drafting committee on the technical aspects of an environmental treaty, law, or policy. Some NGOs, on the other hand, have specialized in the advocacy role to the point of being primarily *mobilization* NGOs, which act as focused information centers for specific issues and rally broad support from other NGOs for a particular cause or event, such as protesting the WTO at Seattle or opposing the Multilateral Agreement on Investment (MAI). Public Citizen's Global Trade Watch, founded by Ralph Nader, is a prime example of a mobilization NGO.

| *Multinational Corporations*

Multinational corporations are the business-sector counterparts to NGOs in the global governance debate. These are companies that have extended the scope of their operations beyond the confines of a home market to foreign direct investments (FDI)—that is, building or purchasing production facilities and related physical capital—in other countries. The total stock of global FDI in 1998 was $4.1 trillion (Graham 2000, 4). MNCs play a significant role in generating the gains from trade for both their home and their host countries, since they reallocate resources internationally to maximize efficiency and profits, a process that typically requires trade in both inputs and final products. They have added an international dimension to the firm's "value chain" (Julius 1994), in many cases making each stage of production and distribution an issue of global management and resource allocation. It is not surprising that MNCs have a large stake in the world trading system, for their business strategies depend on open markets for the movement of goods, services, and capital.

The impact of MNCs collectively on global trade is enormous, since FDI and trade are often tightly interrelated. It is now estimated that more than half of global trade is linked to FDI through imports of inputs and intermediate goods (often from a firm's own subsidiaries) and exports of final products. As opposed to the common view that FDI uproots entire firms and deindustrializes the home country, what generally happens is that this sort of corporate strategy promotes an international division of labor, with the home and foreign countries each specializing in certain parts of the production and research and development (R&D) processes. Building a manufacturing facility in the host country introduces additional capital into the country's economy, which raises labor productivity and local wages. In addition, the MNC often brings new technologies, know-how, and best management and operational practices to the host country. In the home country, the outsourcing of certain parts of the production process increases efficiency and allows greater specialization. As in the case of trade adjustment described in chapter 3, FDI may lead to the dislocation and reduced wages of some workers, which suggests the political advantages of worker adjustment policies. However, the advanced developed countries typically identified as host countries also have inbound FDI from other countries, which increases further the economic benefits and adjustment opportunities of global foreign investment for all participating countries.

Many of the largest MNCs are huge, with output levels greater in value than many countries in the world. Yet, in addition to these behemoths, there are many more MNCs, an estimated total of some 40,000, with ownership links to 200,000 affiliates. Most MNCs, some two-thirds of them, operate within and between the developed countries, although there is a small but growing number in the developing world. MNCs based in the United States, for example have about 80 percent of their FDI installations in other developed countries, with about one-third focused in manufacturing; one-third in finance, insurance, and real estate; 10 percent in petroleum; and the rest in wholesale trade, services, and other industries (U.S. Bureau of Economic Analysis, cited in Burtless et al. 1998).

Many critics of the WTO regard MNCs as the great villains of the world economy: secretive, manipulative, and ruthless in the pursuit of global profits. One of the key developments in the antiglobalization movement was the campaign coordinated by several NGOs against the Multilateral Agreement on Investment, which the Organization for Economic Cooperation and Development (OECD) had attempted to negotiate in the mid-1990s. The MAI negotiations attempted to establish common rules on national treatment and investor protection for multinational investment among the twenty-nine OECD members, which include the United States, European Union, other Western European countries, some Eastern European transition economies, and Turkey. Despite the modest slate of investment liberalization reforms and a policy impact limited to the OECD countries, many antiglobalization activists seized upon the MAI as a clandestine plot to allow MNCs free rein in the global economy, eliminating jobs in developed countries, exploiting labor in developing countries, and creating pollution worldwide.[3] In 1998, the protests against the MAI became politically embarrassing to some OECD governments, and the negotiations collapsed (Graham 2000, chaps. 1–3).

The MAI debacle was significant for a number of reasons. Buoyed by their victory in defeating the MAI in 1998, antiglobalization NGOs turned their sights on the 1999 WTO meeting in Seattle. The WTO, for its part, was considered complicit in supporting MNCs, since the Uruguay Round had concluded agreements on TRIMs and TRIPs after much MNC lobbying and was the next likely forum for investment negotiations. The MAI was therefore a lightning rod for NGO protest activity, which spread quickly to the WTO. In addition, MNCs became the poster children for antiglobalization, embodying the supposed evils of big business, aided and abetted by supposedly secretive organizations like the OECD and the WTO. Finally, the failure of the MAI negotiations pointed out the high profile and the political hazards of the MNC interface with governments.

Because of their transnational nature and also because of the size of the largest among them, MNCs deal prominently and visibly with governments, often at high levels. They benefit greatly from more openness in international markets and freedom from local regulation in host countries. In order to make progress in their agenda, they invest heavily in lobbying at home and abroad for international trade and investment policy liberalization. The stakes of maintaining and liberalizing global markets provide strong incentives for MNCs to try to influence global trade and investment rules.

As a matter of public policy, governments must decide whether or not more open markets are better for their respective economies. The trend in recent years has been for governments to support open markets and FDI, with the expectation, based on economic theory, that increased FDI and trade are good for the host countries as well as the MNCs. Empirical research has also tended to support this conclusion. Yet the highly visible role of MNCs has also raised fears that they have too much power. In many cases, environmental, humanitarian, and anticapitalist NGOs have been formed in order to oppose MNCs as agents of globalization.

Given their size and capacity for political influence, there is certainly the possibility of manipulation and abuse, especially when large MNCs deal with corruptible host governments. Their focus on profits is not the problem, however. On the contrary, their positive contributions to economic activity and the spreading of technology occur as the very result of profit opportunities. Most MNCs are also accountable to their stockholders and are subject to domestic regulation in their home countries. These are potentially powerful channels of influence and scrutiny. It is noteworthy that the financing and activities of most NGOs are not usually subject to the same scrutiny, oversight, or transparency measures.[4]

In other words, the activities of MNCs are subject to both legislative and public pressure, even when it comes to their activities beyond the borders of their home countries. For example, many MNCs have signed on to the UN Global Compact, established in 1999 and based on the Sullivan Principles of corporate responsibility.[5] Signatories agree to follow a code of conduct that supports social justice and human rights in all areas where they do business. While such agreements have no direct enforcement provisions, they suggest that moral suasion may be a more powerful force in international business than is commonly recognized. As noted in chapter 7 in the discussion of child labor and sweatshops, MNCs have found voluntary standards and self-monitoring to be sound business practices. In the end, bad global citizenship in the form of exploitative corporate behavior may invite a backlash from increasingly well-informed consumers. The abilities of a firm to hire the best and most qualified employees, to raise capital, and to manage its public and political affairs at home increasingly require sensitivity to global social issues.

For their most severe critics, such measures will hardly be enough.[6] Yet domestic political channels in the MNC's home country are still the best way to raise the issues and exert influence. In contrast, trying to attack MNCs by attacking the WTO misses the target. For one thing, MNC influence on the WTO has often been exaggerated. The largest of the MNCs certainly wield a great deal of political influence, but mainly through domestic channels. The first is through lobbying efforts in their home countries, where they play a large role in setting national agendas for trade negotiations and also have access to unilateral trade protection through antidumping and countervailing duty laws.[7] The second channel lies in their relationships with the governments of the countries hosting MNC foreign operations. It is important to keep in mind that many countries, and indeed localities even within the developed countries, have been courting FDI for the economic benefits it brings. Most governments have come to view FDI as an overwhelmingly positive contribution to the recipient country's economic development and growth. This view is based on the underlying economics of international capital mobility and related activities.

Such bilateral relationships always carry the danger of abuse, as special deals may be struck to bypass taxes or regulations, for example. In addition, many governments, especially in developing countries, want to retain as much control as possible over the terms of FDI, which is why they also have a strong interest in TRIMs. Yet this issue is being sorted out in the WTO as a matter of negotiation among sovereign states, not as the result of MNCs dictating the rules to helpless governments.

Within the WTO, the MNCs can indeed exert strong influence, but it is typically tempered through the mediating factor of governmental representation. In the years before the conclusion of the Uruguay Round, U.S. multinationals (and other U.S. firms), for example, could—and did—lobby their home government directly for unilateral action under various forms of section 301 of U.S. trade law. Together, these provisions allowed unilateral actions by the United States to "pry" open foreign markets and to retaliate against any foreign trade practices deemed "unreasonable."[8] By bringing investment and intellectual property issues into the WTO through the TRIMs and TRIPs agreements, and by strengthening the dispute settlement system, trade policy issues of concern to MNCs were channeled into a multilateral forum. Under the WTO system, only governments have standing, and a government must therefore decide whether to bring a case before the Dispute Settlement Body, based on national interests and an associated assessment of trade-offs in commercial diplomacy. This does not eliminate the influence of MNCs on the trading system; active lobbying; aggressive, unfair trade-law enforcement; and accommodating domestic trade officials still give them considerable clout. Yet the elimination of unilateral measures tends to moderate the influence of the MNCs and of domestic business in general on trade policy.

One sign of the restraint on political influence is that many MNCs advocate WTO reform that would allow them to file dispute cases directly, without governmental intermediaries (see Julius 1994). Such proposals cast serious doubt on claims that MNCs somehow control the WTO or dictate trade rules or dispute settlement decisions. In addition, MNC activities are subject to increased public scrutiny, providing another channel of influence for NGOs. In general, stakeholders in trade issues, whether they are NGOs, MNCs, or other interest groups, have their most direct influence on trade policy through their national political institutions. For those concerned abut MNC political power, the best institutional arrangement is one in which governments can negotiate agreements and represent the broader interests of their domestic constituents in the WTO, keeping all interest groups involved at the domestic level of the policy debate. Other channels of influence for nontrade issues can also be developed in new international institutions.

| *Governments as the Dominant Players*

The WTO is set up as an intergovernmental organization, in which national governments alone have standing. This system of representation raises the question of how democratic the WTO is, since the delegates involved in the negotiations seem to be far removed from grassroots political constituencies in their home countries. Many critics of the WTO have accused it of being antidemocratic, elitist, and focused exclusively on business interests, especially those of MNCs. The criticism has two basic elements. The first is the complaint that the machinery of trade policy, staffed with "neoliberal technocrats," is biased against any inclusion of nontrade issues in trade policy. The second is that the WTO itself is off limits to any representation on nontrade issues through NGOs. In order to evaluate these criticisms, it will be necessary to examine the political process of establishing trade negotiating positions in the WTO. It is extremely important to gain an understanding of the underlying politics of the WTO, because one's perspective on the process of decision making significantly affects one's attitude toward the issues of institutions and global governance in general.

The critical, "democratic deficit" view of the WTO tends to employ a conceptual framework of decision making that emphasizes the role of a technocratic elite in trade negotiations and WTO dispute settlement. According to this view, trade officials hold a neoliberal view of the world economy, characterized by a strong preference for market processes and competition over government intervention at the national level. Trade diplomats from the member countries work together with officials from the WTO Secretariat to frame trade liberalization agreements, with limited accountability to the citizens in their home countries. This trade elite is ideologically oriented toward free markets and will resist any infiltration of environmental, labor, human rights, gender, or any other nontrade issues into trade agreements, rules, or dispute settlement decisions, no matter what grassroots support may exist for these measures at home. Based on this view of how the WTO works, it follows that the WTO can only regain democratic legitimacy if it systematically incorporates environmental and other social stakeholders into the negotiations and implementation of trade rules, for example through NGO representation (Esty 2002).

It is certainly true that trade diplomats are focused on trade, and they can also be described in many cases as technocrats, since trade issues tend to be complicated and require specialized (especially legal) knowledge. Regarding the economic ideology of trade officials, WTO civil servants tend to be neoliberal in their outlook, which is not surprising, given the WTO's role in trade liberalization, but it is important to remember that this group has no independent power, as noted in the account of the WTO Secretariat's strictly circumscribed functions in chapter 4. It is, however, highly inaccurate to regard all WTO delegates, even those from the rich countries, as neoliberal in their outlook. It would be more accurate to describe them as mercantilist, which is consistent with the negotiating framework of the WTO.

Furthermore, the extreme characterizations of the WTO as an elitist club of unaccountable free-trade bureaucrats receive little support from the facts. Shaffer (2001), for example, has taken up this question and documented the activities of the Committee on Trade and the Environment (CTE) within the WTO in an effort to determine the extent to which representatives reflected the views of their national environmental constituencies and whether there was a systematic bias toward trade—as opposed to environmental—perspectives. His conclusion is that negotiating positions did not reflect a uniform, technocratic, neoliberal bias but rather revealed both the internal conflicts and the dominant, mercantilist positions of the various countries. Elements of environmental protection did tend to appear when there was an associated trade advantage for the country, but the ultimate negotiating goal remained consistent with the WTO bargaining framework, which was to seek market access for the country's exports and keep or enhance import protection for domestic industries as a bargaining chip.

These and other accounts of trade policy formulation tend to support a different conceptual framework for understanding WTO negotiations, one that is based on a two-tiered process of bargaining (see Putnam 1988). In this view, international trade talks first require that a country establish a *domestic* consensus on its negotiating position; this job is not left to an independent elite acting on its own in Geneva. In richer countries with extensive government bureaucracies, this process typically takes the form of interagency negotiations, in which competing constituencies are represented in various ministries or departments (foreign affairs, labor, environment, commerce, and so on). Otherwise, internal governmental processes establish negotiating terms and goals based on overall national interests. In many countries, there is an important check on negotiated agreements that comes from the ratification process through national parliaments or legislatures.

An important element of most WTO members' approach to trade negotiations, however, is that their ultimate goal is to maximize national gains from trade as part of the WTO value proposition, as noted in chapter 2. A national position in trade negotiations that has the goal of achieving gains from trade presumes a national political consensus on the gains from trade, which typically involve an accommodation of opposing constituencies. Internal political bargaining is typically necessary in order to secure the necessary legislative support for the trade agreement. Specifically, compromises with opponents of increased trade have always been part of the process of trade liberalization and have given rise to antidumping and countervailing duty laws, trade adjustment assistance, subsidies to politically influential industries, the GATT escape clause, the Multifiber Agreement, and other sectoral protectionist policies. In addition, domestic lobbying, especially in the United States and the European Union, continues to shape national bargaining positions on politically sensitive trade issues. The history of domestic trade debates and international trade negotiations since the Second World War and the origins of specific GATT and WTO trading rules themselves reveal the high degree of political compromise that has been necessary to move trade liberalization forward. While this progress has indeed been impressive over the years, it has not proceeded without hard bargaining and compromise *within* countries, as well as between countries. It is therefore inaccurate to characterize trade policy as the exclusive province of a neoliberal technocratic elite. Too much is at stake domestically for that to be the case.

A variant of the democratic deficit view is that critical social interests do not receive adequate representation in domestic policy. Advocates of environmental, labor, human rights, and other nontrade agendas aver that they are shut out of domestic trade policy decision making, and many of them are calling for increased participation by advocacy NGOs in both national policy formulation and the WTO itself (Esty 1998, 2002). These critics maintain that governments have a responsibility to give equal time, or at least sufficient policy access and influence, to nontrade stakeholders in trade policy decision making. Most governments do in fact concentrate trade policy matters in executive agencies (as opposed to elected legislatures), which tends to streamline the negotiating process and remove a bias toward protectionism.[9] It is also clear that the WTO's value proposition tends to focus governments' attention directly on trade and the traditional domestic trade-offs associated with it. Governments implicitly understand that opening WTO negotiations to nontrade issues will complicate the negotiations, although both the United States and the European Union have introduced such issues into trade discussions as a result of domestic political pressures.

In order to make progress on resolving trade policy with nontrade issues, it may be useful to reformulate the problem. Access to influence on trade and environmental, labor, and human rights policies is politically contestable and subject to the available policy channels for deliberation. The final international negotiating positions of governments on trade and other issues depend on their judgments of the national interest and the available venues for pursuing their goals. In the absence of an international bargaining framework on the environment, for example, environmentalists must compete with trade interests (and any other lobbyists with trade axes to grind) in order to attain influence on trade policy, which they see as instrumental in achieving their goals. From their perspective, such a policy process may appear to be unfair, given the government's participation in the WTO consensus and the importance of the gains from trade. But the most promising alternative may be to develop new or strengthened international bargaining channels on the environment, where their views and positions will encounter a more efficient negotiating framework. In other words, the alleged democratic deficit may be more easily rectified through the creation of dedicated global institutions or other negotiating opportunities to deal with these issues. Instead of seeking to close the gap by adding social chapters to the WTO or by altering WTO rules to allow more trade restrictions—which would erode the WTO consensus by undermining its fundamental value proposition—advocates of nontrade goals could push hard for new regional and international agreements, conventions, and organizations that would give them a direct voice in these matters.

Governments formulate trade policies and negotiating positions according to the political calculus they face. One would normally expect a compelling national interest with implications for trade policy to come to the fore in a representative government's trade policy or trade negotiating position. But what if the political system is less than democratic? What if a compelling (even popular) domestic interest does not have the requisite political backing to achieve representation in that country's policy formulation? What if the issue or interest is transnational in nature, such that individual governments cannot—or will not—give adequate consideration to it in their policies and positions? In light of these questions, it is not difficult to imagine that the traditional system of representation in a global, intergovernmental organization may fall short of fully representing global civil society.

The Representation Debate

Antiglobalization protesters often complain that their domestic trade policy institutions are closed to them and also that the transnational nature of their constituencies makes domestic political channels inappropriate anyway. They claim that the WTO and other global economic institutions are unbalanced because of the presumed influence of MNCs and free-trade ideology on them, and they demand a more democratic system of representation in them.

Yet the establishment of democratic representation by NGOs in WTO decision making would be extremely difficult and would certainly not receive the necessary political support of WTO members in the foreseeable future. Governments of the largest and most influential countries that belong to the WTO, for the most part, are democratically elected, and the larger NGOs are active in these democratic countries. One might therefore question the legitimacy of their demand that they be afforded a second bite at the policy apple when they have failed to persuade their home governments of their case, notwithstanding their claim to a transnational constituency. The work of the WTO, furthermore, is to negotiate agreements that can only be implemented by governments, which must consider the relevant trade-offs for their economies and populations as a whole.[10] Direct participation by NGOs in this process would be disruptive and unproductive. There are many other ways for NGOs to play a significant role in the WTO, but direct representation in the negotiations or decision-making process is not one of them.

An associated problem is the issue of confidentiality in negotiations, especially in some aspects of (especially bilateral) trade talks and also in certain stages of dispute settlement cases. Governments prefer, for various reasons, to deal with their negotiating counterparts away from public scrutiny. At stake is the effectiveness of the negotiation or dispute settlement process. Full public awareness of the issues and bargaining positions of the parties involved would in many cases prevent the parties from reaching an agreement, which may then result in an outcome detrimental to all parties.[11] Some may object in principle to any such nontransparent aspects of traditional statecraft. Yet the principle of confidentiality in negotiations enjoys not only long-standing acceptance and legitimacy in international relations but also theoretical support as a facilitator of compromise. Many observers agree that any WTO negotiations that involve "horse trading" should be conducted in executive session, which still leaves room for possible NGO participation in the WTO in most of its discussions, which are generally unrestricted.

Establishing the democratic legitimacy of NGOs is another problem. In the absence of global elections, there is no legitimate democratic process of determining NGO representation in international institutions. Various NGOs claiming to represent a common constituency often do not agree on important policy questions. Thus, even a general recognition of environmental interests in the world population does not solve the problem of which environmental NGOs will speak definitively for the global environmental constituency, for example.

A related and important problem arises in allocating representation among all the competing types of NGOs. The discussion of NGOs in trade policy and anti-WTO protests has usually focused on NGOs that have mobilized large numbers of participants in events on behalf of environmental and social causes. Their high public profile has often given rise to an implicit assumption that NGO agendas automatically provide a complementary balance to the business interests that presumably dominate the WTO. Yet there are many pro-business, pro-trade NGOs as well, and the presence of anti-WTO groups on the streets does not justify their representation at the policy bargaining table. The application of one environmental advocacy group for a seat at the WTO decision-making table would spawn a similar application from (or creation of) its opposite number. There is no practical and legitimate way to include some NGOs based on their political orientation or ideology while excluding others, in an effort to create a more balanced representation of global civil society in the organization.

Many NGOs that advocate nontrade agendas have argued that the pro-business lobbies already have representation through their domestic influence on national trade policies and do not deserve "double representation" as NGOs at the WTO. This assertion is not self-evident, however. Many environmental and social NGOs have extensive lobbying activities in the United States and in European countries, and those countries' trade delegations have raised nontrade issues in WTO deliberations. In the United States, there is now a systematic environmental review of trade policy and other public notice provisions for trade negotiations (see Loy 2001). Trying to engineer a balanced, level playing field of disparate and opposing interests through selective NGO representation at the WTO would therefore be an arbitrary and dubious enterprise. Furthermore, if the NGOs that represent populist issues assume that participation in the WTO will assure them more democratic, equalizing access to global institutions, they had better be prepared for a strong push by well-funded opposing interests for participation and access as well.

Expanding Public and NGO Access to the WTO

In a broader sense, public participation in the WTO involves issues of communication, information, and dialogue, and the WTO Secretariat has taken several steps to improve these aspects of its external relations. The Marrakesh agreement, which established the WTO, provided for "consultation and cooperation" with NGOs, and additional steps have been taken more recently to increase this function. The WTO Website has been expanded since 1999 to become both an instrument of public relations and a research tool. Thousands of unrestricted documents are available online, including texts of dispute settlement decisions, the WTO budget, and background information on current negotiating topics. The WTO has also initiated a series of symposia on trade and nontrade issues linked to the WTO, which includes the participation of many speakers and groups highly critical of the WTO.

More open dialogue and communications are administrative issues that can generally be managed by the WTO Secretariat without much controversy. To allow deeper participation in WTO meetings may require more formal approval by the collective WTO membership. Most proposals envisage a limited role for NGOs as observers and in some cases contributors to more routine WTO deliberations, but also perhaps in dispute settlement hearings. The issue of NGO participation has unleashed a lively debate among WTO observers. At one end of the spectrum of opinion is the belief that more formal and deeper NGO participation can only improve the flow of information, degree of openness, and democratic nature of the WTO (Esty 1998). NGOs, according to this view, possess specialized knowledge and expertise that can help make more informed decisions in DSU cases and contribute to a better understanding of the environmental, human rights, and labor rights implications of trade negotiations.

On the other side of the issue are those who fear the intrusion of anti-WTO forces in NGO clothing. Since the avowed purpose of most NGOs is to influence (that is, to change) WTO policies, often in a fundamental way, many observers regard their goals with suspicion. Robertson (2000) notes that many (not all) NGOs exhibit an antithesis to the principles of free trade and the functioning of markets, which form the basis for the WTO's system of trade rules. The concern is that, by admitting NGO input into WTO activities, such as dispute settlement, or by granting them a formal presence in WTO meetings, the outcome would therefore be to undermine the organization as a whole.

In this regard, there is an underlying tension that lurks behind proposals for more WTO openness. Commercial diplomacy has until recently been conducted away from public view by specialists in the arcane arts of trade law and economic statecraft. They are no strangers to controversy, opposition, and political conflict but have typically conducted their work, even the more routine meetings, in Geneva without extensive scrutiny from public interest NGOs. Howse (2002) has noted that many younger staff members in trade delegations are attuned to nontrade issues and amenable to discussions with NGOs. Even so, revising the traditional practice of closed doors and confidentiality may be difficult, especially if many NGO observers are basically opposed to the organization. The operation and functioning of the WTO rest on a professional staff of trade experts and national delegations of trade diplomats, who are unlikely to welcome with open arms groups that vow to "fix it or nix it" or to make the WTO "sink or shrink."

A systematic approach to this question will, first of all, require some sort of NGO credentialing. Open access to the WTO by any and all of the many thousands of NGOs would only create chaos. The United Nations, as noted earlier in this chapter, certifies NGOs for participation in UN-sponsored organizations, and a similar procedure would be necessary for expanded NGO access to WTO activities, given the large and growing number of

NGOs that have registered for attendance at WTO ministerial meetings.[12] At the same time, the terms of NGO participation are likely to be subject to the same sort of bargaining that takes place in trade negotiations, since the WTO membership must in principle approve it by consensus. This will be especially true for any NGO role in activities that affect negotiations or DSU outcomes. Ullrich (2000) suggests various ways that the WTO could approve NGO participation, such as simply changing a few words in its preamble, but it would be naïve to expect the process to be that easy.

It is noteworthy that, among WTO members, developing countries have shown strong opposition to the participation of NGOs in most cases, particularly with regard to environmental and labor issues and the submission of amicus curiae briefs in dispute settlement cases.[13] Most NGOs are based in developed countries, and although there are increasing numbers from developing countries as well, the northern NGOs dominate in terms of membership, political clout, and funding. The main concern of developing countries is that a modification of WTO rules to set environmental and labor standards, enforceable with trade sanctions, would work to their detriment. In addition, some NGOs have legal expertise and resources that may be greater than those of many developing countries, which could be used in dispute settlement cases, for example, against the interests of the poorer countries. Such a large bloc of opposition in the consensus-based WTO implies that any eventual NGO participation would be highly circumscribed, unless large and influential developed country WTO members were willing to bargain hard in favor of more extensive NGO participation in sensitive areas, such as dispute settlement.

The amicus curiae issue raises other concerns that cannot be easily resolved. Should there be rules of balance in brief submissions, so that both sides of a dispute get the benefit of outside expert support? Should developing country disputants receive legal or financial support in securing briefs favorable to their case? Should panelists be required to consider them, or even read them, in view of the heavy burden of background materials they often have to read and digest? The biggest potential benefit of NGO-generated briefs is the specialized expertise they bring to nontrade issues involved in trade disputes, especially regarding the environment. It will therefore be worth some effort by WTO members to explore ways to take advantage of this resource. Two developments suggest the possibility of a resolution to some of these problems. First, there is a broad range of NGOs across the political spectrum and an increasing depth of expertise that is likely to develop among competing NGOs, which together can facilitate a balanced representation of legal and technical expertise on both sides of DSU cases. In addition, WTO efforts and funding projects to provide legal resources and assistance to developing country members will, if successful, level the legal playing field. Finding a politically acceptable way to make their participation possible would benefit the WTO.

It is important to emphasize that granting observer status and even allowing the submission of amicus curiae briefs—if that happens at all—will not completely bridge the gap between the WTO and the advocacy NGOs most critical of it. As stated throughout this book, the best way to provide representation for focused transnational advocacy on nontrade issues is to develop corresponding transnational institutions. The WTO is providing increased access to information and is sponsoring forums for debate, so that the public discussion on trade policy can be better informed. It also currently includes environmental NGOs in trade-and-environment discussions through CTE meetings and may grant increased observer status in other WTO deliberations. These measures do not imply, however, a role for NGOs in WTO governance or rule making.

Nevertheless, the optimistic view is that increased flows of information between the WTO and NGOs will lead to a meeting of the minds between the trade community and WTO critics, insofar as interactions between them create better mutual understanding of their points of view. The assumption here is that information will flow both ways, not only, as Esty (1998) maintains, from the specialized NGOs to the WTO, but also in the opposite direction. In the wake of the Seattle protests, a dialogue between the WTO and its critics has opened up.

| Conclusion

The WTO is an intergovernmental organization, and its members are likely to want to keep it that way. For the collective WTO membership, the single common denominator is an interest in the gains from trade and the terms by which increased gains through trade liberalization and a rules-based system can be realized. A similar consensus on environmental and social goals and the means by which to achieve them has not come into existence. The state of world governance and cooperation, currently dominated by economic institutions, has therefore fallen short in accommodating other interests of global civil society. Until more institutional development occurs, both supporters of a purely trade-oriented WTO and supporters of the expanded influence on and participation of civil society groups in the WTO, or trade in general, are likely to remain unsatisfied.

Global citizenship is a concept in search of an institutional framework along social dimensions that parallel the global business dimensions of MNCs. NGOs are here to stay, just as MNCs are here to stay. Both are a natural consequence of the growing interdependence of the world's economies, the increased sensitivity to social and environmental concerns accompanying economic growth, and the expanded contact of people around the world through advancing technology and communications. They also have powerful roots in two prominent traits of modern civilization: the development and recognition of global public goods—social, humanitarian, environmental, and economic—and the development of international exchange and market opportunities. In this regard, it is important to remember that the global trading system not only facilitates exchange but is in itself a global public good (Birdsall and Lawrence 1999).

In structuring global systems of cooperation, the first and most important principle to follow is the efficient assignment of institutions to their respective tasks. In this respect, the dependence by civil society exclusively on direct representation and a decision-making voice in the WTO would be frustrating for both sides—and would ultimately cripple both trade and nontrade agendas. It would simply go directly against the economic interest of most WTO members to allow nontrade interests to tilt global trade rules away from their systemic role in trade liberalization. In addition, the lack of a credible process of global democratic representation would only lead to a proliferation of competing NGOs in efforts to maximize their influence. Lobbying structures at the domestic level would replicate themselves within the international organization, with no clear gain in democratic representation.[14]

In the meantime, the battleground will remain in domestic legislatures and national governments for both NGOs and MNCs. NGOs have entered the trade policy picture as a significant lobbying force and as such have aligned themselves in many cases with traditional protectionist forces on specific trade policy measures. With no international forum to provide them with direct representation, they work through the existing domestic political channels and focus on traditional international targets: trade policy and the WTO. MNCs, far from controlling the WTO, use their lobbying power to influence government policies, trade measures, and negotiating positions.

The role of NGOs in trade policy has varied according to the context of the debate. Advocacy NGOs have been most successful in pursuing their agendas when they have exploited communications technologies to mobilize popular dissent around major events or issues, such as high-profile antiglobalization demonstrations. As noted by Warkentin and Mingst (2000), NGOs have been effective in using the Internet in promoting large-scale participation in broadly defined populist issues that achieve resonance across a wide range of interests. Some NGOs will probably maximize their effectiveness as organizers of protests, rather than as information resources or crafters of compromise and policy in international institutions.

This dilemma brings us back to the political cartoon from the beginning of the chapter. The problem, it seems, is to fill in the blank panels of global governance. In addition to a "department of trade," the world needs departments of the environment, human rights, and social welfare. To be more precise, the world needs global organizations or expanded and strengthened conventions and treaties in these areas, founded on international agreements and backed up with resources and formal commitments to rules. To get there, it will be necessary to mobilize the political will of governments to move toward a broader system of international institutions. The necessary link is to establish domestic political channels to harness domestic interests for progressive steps toward transnational governance. This link will move the process forward—and away from the already overloaded WTO.

The increased role of other international organizations would provide new channels for the representation of civil society. An important aspect of this development from an institutional standpoint is that it would allow *national* representation to provide the means for transmitting the interests of civil society. National delegates to a world environmental or human rights organization, for example, would focus on the environment or human rights, not on trade. This would thereby create a more effective forum for the main issue at hand. In addition, NGOs would be in a position to play a more direct role in observing and even advising the organization in their areas of expertise. In the end, progress in solving global problems will continue to depend largely on the traditional system of sovereign countries representing their populations.

10

Conclusion
The Gains from
Trade and the
Global Commons

Our story began with a litany of fears and anxieties about globalization and the WTO, which led to several public, sometimes violent protests against the WTO and other global economic institutions in Seattle, Genoa, Davos, Washington, D.C., Quebec City, and Prague. After the terrorist attacks of September 11, 2001, the street protests abated but the anxieties remain. As the process of globalization continues and the work of the WTO moves forward with the Doha Round, the challenge for governments, NGOs, and businesses will be to find the political will to build the necessary institutions and cooperation to facilitate increased trade, economic growth, and progress on social and environmental issues.

A fanciful editorial cartoon attempts to capture the powerful nature of globalization and to show the limited impact of institutional structures on it. A mighty tiger marked "global economy" is rushing forward at breakneck speed, with a collection of miniature trade officials (dark suits again) labeled "WTO" clinging comically to its tail. They declare with mock authority, "We've decided not to do anything that might slow you down!" The WTO with its trade rules, it seems, has a tiger by the tail, a tenuous grasp on a force of nature beyond its control, but a force that can bring those willing to take the ride to higher standards of living and economic progress. Governments can, of course, jump off the rushing tiger and avoid globalization by closing off their markets, but they will be left behind. Fighting the WTO, apparently, would not stop the globalization tiger but would pull off many of those riding its tail. Can it be that the forces of globalization may also, through economic growth and its consequences, bring the world to greater levels of social and environmental welfare?

| Let the WTO Be the WTO

The main point of this book has been that the WTO and the GATT before it have accomplished good things for their members and for the world economy as a whole and that this work should continue. Trade liberalization has increased the availability of products and the level of productive efficiency and overall economic welfare to countries taking part in it. Trade has promoted technological advancement and economic growth, and in many ways it has brought countries closer together. What the WTO does best is keep markets open for international exchange because that is what all of its members want it to do, based on the consensus inherent in WTO membership. Not all countries have benefited equally from trade liberalization because they do not have equal access to global markets or the domestic capacity to take advantage of market opportunities. In order for trade to maximize its contribution to economic development, more must be done in these countries to build their political and economic stability, their basic physical and educational infrastructure, and their capacity for taking part in the global trading system.

Trade is one dimension, among many, of global society, and governments must strive to develop a system of global governance that recognizes a multidimensional world of economic, social, and environmental interests. Yet, it is important that the WTO continue its work unimpeded by divisive nontrade agendas. Introducing new environmental, labor, or human rights sections into the WTO cannot happen on the basis of the trade liberalization consensus that is the heart of the organization. The role for trade in such WTO amendments would be primarily negative—to punish WTO members with trade sanctions for noncompliance. Using the WTO in this manner would represent a betrayal of the organization's core principles.

Without a strong foundation of consensus on nondiscrimination and a rules-based system, the global trading system would weaken and probably collapse. Many countries would resort to a defensive posture of regional and other preferential trade agreements, seeking out exclusive trade allies and making market access contingent on unilateral or bilaterally negotiated criteria. Playing favorites is an easy state of mind for governments to slip into, and without binding WTO disciplines, trade relations would fragment. Trade volumes would shrink. International capital movements would also decline, along with national income and economic growth in most countries. We have seen this before in history: the protectionist trade wars of the 1930s and the collapse of world finance and trade, followed by worse events. We do not want to go there again.

The best way to address the fears associated with trade and globalization is to promote complementary domestic policies and international institutions, that will allow trade liberalization to proceed unencumbered by divisive adjustment and nontrade issues. For example, trade liberalization implies adjustment to import competition, which often means disruption and job displacement. Economic change in general is often disruptive, and economic research tends to indicate that technological change has played a larger role in disrupting labor markets and lowering the wages of low-skilled workers than trade. Yet, as with technology and other instigators of adjustment, trade is often an essential part of economic progress and growth. Countries with economic environments and policies that encourage their industries to integrate into the world economy tend to reap great rewards from it. Openness to global competition and access to efficient offshore suppliers, new technologies, and new markets is good for business and for the consumer. It is the cost of *not* adjusting that is high.

Nevertheless, change can be frightening, and the structural economic change that is taking place through the globalization of markets appears to pit workers in the advanced, environmentally conscious, politically stable developed countries against uneducated workers (including children) in poor countries with poor labor standards and little environmental protection to burden the production process. Yet the fundamental reason that the two markets are joined is this: wage rates are lower in poorer countries because of the relative abundance of labor and the stage of economic development there. This is an important part of the basis for mutually beneficial trade. Countries at this stage in their development will typically begin to produce simple manufactured goods that were once produced in great quantities by other countries that have now moved up the ladder.

At the same time, workers in advanced economies tend to have greater education and training, and they have the opportunity to combine their skills with more capital and technology than workers in poor countries. These differences, based on higher labor productivity, justify the wage premiums earned by workers in the richer countries. Some workers in developed countries with fewer skills, less training, and less education may be displaced from their jobs by import competition, and they will need to find new jobs. This process—structural adjustment advancing in all countries tied into the world economy—contributes significantly to efficiency and economic growth, and it is important that it move along unimpeded. Countries must adjust to structural economic changes and help their workers adjust, without impeding the necessary process.

The problem, therefore, is not the WTO. It is adjustment, and the solution lies in better domestic policies, with the appropriate mix of monetary and fiscal policies, adaptive educational programs, safety nets, labor market flexibility, and factor mobility that will promote the reallocation of resources from declining to growing activities and sectors of the economy. Not all workers suffer net losses from job displacement; young workers in the United States tend, for example, to gain in earnings after a job loss.[1] For those who do lose their jobs, trade is not usually the main reason in advanced industrialized countries. The need for adjustment assistance is best viewed in this regard as the result of numerous market forces, including technology, changes in population, changes in tastes, structural changes in economic activities, and other disruptive market developments, not just trade. Treating economic disruption as a generic phenomenon, with adjustment policies and possible relief for displaced workers based on broader criteria, would provide a better framework for dealing with the opposition to economic change and, especially, opposition to trade.

As for the competitive effect of low environmental and labor standards, these issues do not, in the vast majority of cases, create any unfair cost advantage in international trade. Environmental compliance costs in advanced economies continue to be a small portion of total production costs and are often linked with more productive technologies that offset the cost of pollution abatement. Child and sweatshop labor exist largely in nontraded sectors, and their usage in exported products has recently come under intense scrutiny, followed by significant internal and private monitoring to control or eliminate such practices in those sectors. Punitive trade sanctions would not be helpful because they would hurt the poorer workers themselves and undermine the economic basis for social progress. An alternative approach would be to encourage continued monitoring, diplomatic pressure, and positive inducements to improve labor conditions, while maintaining open trade policies. Although integration into the world trading system does not guarantee progressive policies in these areas, the associated increase in trade creates the opportunities for progress, and the linkage with the great majority of countries in the world creates strong incentives for progress.

Regarding the global problems of pollution, food safety, biodiversity, and related issues, environmentalists fear the WTO because they see trade policy rules, and even trade itself, as responsible for environmental degradation. Most economic research indicates, however, that trade activity does not harm the environment. To the extent that trade contributes to economic growth and technological advancement, it in fact helps to provide the foundation for improving environmental quality. Trade also contributes to the development process in poorer countries, which leads to higher levels of income and greater demand for a clean environment.

Trade policy rules incorporated in the WTO, on the other hand, are often alleged to hamper environmental enforcement measures by trumping unilateral, domestically imposed trade sanctions, which violate national sovereignty. Yet trade sanctions to enforce environmental standards are almost always uncalled for because there are better ways to attack the problem, beginning with multilateral agreements on pollution control or conservation. The fear of the WTO, once again, is often misplaced: it is the search for effective ways to achieve environmental goals that is most important. Those goals are best pursued in dedicated global environmental institutions and other international agreements, based on consensus and commitment among the countries taking part and with creative and progressive incentives for compliance.

Advocates of global labor and human rights standards harbor similar fears of the WTO and want trade rules to help reach their goals. They point to the UN Declaration on Human Rights and the ILO core labor standards, adopted by many countries, thereby justifying their incorporation into WTO trade rules. Yet the apparent consensus on human rights and standards does not necessarily imply an automatic consensus on implementation or on an enforcement mechanism. Trade sanctions impose real and potentially severe costs on both consumers and producers. In any case, such measures are extremely unlikely to achieve acceptance by the collective WTO membership. Instead, consensus on the means of reaching such goals is more likely through separate multilateral agreements that can incorporate positive inducements, moral suasion, public pressure, labeling agreements, diplomatic pressure, and other incentive mechanisms that do not carry the economic costs of trade restrictions. Trade sanctions, adopted by multilateral consensus, may sometimes play a role in moving toward these goals but may also conflict with WTO rules in the future. The best way to resolve these conflicts will be found within the framework of international law.

Policy Coherence

The world still has much to gain from trade liberalization. It also stands to gain from many other initiatives, including poverty alleviation, infrastructure and capacity building in poor countries, improved international aid and financial arrangements to support these goals, and, as already noted, better global environmental quality, human rights enforcement, and labor standards. The need for new international institutions to support the various goals of global society clearly implies a corresponding need for coordination among them, and this issue of policy coherence will be a daunting challenge. The current public debate over globalization has taught us that trade and all of these nontrade goals are interconnected. At the same time, it is often difficult to pursue one goal, past a certain point, without conflicting with other, equally compelling and beneficial goals.

In order to pursue these goals, new global institutions will need to be developed, and old ones will need to be strengthened. Specific proposals already exist for a world environmental organization (WEO) (Esty 1996) and a strengthened ILO (Elliott 2000). These are the two most important areas for global institutional development. A truly universal WEO may take many years to develop, but in the meantime, regional and smaller-scale multilateral agreements may be possible. Newell (2002) has suggested, for example, that a smaller subset of developed countries could conclude a global warming treaty without the need for a WEO. The protection of global human rights would benefit from a further strengthening and expansion of human rights conventions, with the possibility of establishing a global monitoring and investigation body. The ILO, on the other hand, provides the proper global forum for discussing labor standards and worker rights, but does not have consensus among its members on measures to encourage (or enforce) compliance. The proper approach is therefore for governments to find new ways to strengthen incentives for compliance.

Even among existing global economic institutions, a careful plan of coordination and cooperation would avoid many conflicts. This is a long-standing issue among existing organizations, particularly the Bretton Woods institutions: the International Monetary Fund, the World Bank, and the WTO.[2] In recent years especially, the IMF and World Bank have incorporated some trade policy conditionality into their program lending, which makes agreements on loans contingent on changes in tariffs, quotas, or other market access measures. The role of a country's trade policy environment in its economic development and performance is widely recognized. For example, there are direct connections among exchange rate stability, trade, debt repayment, and the resources available for development in poorer countries. For this reason, there are explicit coordination provisions in article III.5 of the WTO agreement regarding the Bretton Woods institutions. Even among these seemingly like-minded institutions, however, there are continuing problems of coordination.[3]

The problem of coherence extends to other levels of policymaking as well. Many countries tie their foreign aid to sourcing requirements that are economically inefficient. Trade ministries are often at loggerheads with finance and foreign affairs ministries. The dangers of damaging policy conflicts even within national governments are legion. Two recent proposals are worth exploring. The first is to use foreign aid to focus on specific goals, such as disease eradication and other measurable health standards in developing countries. The second is to offer incentives in foreign aid through untied grants or vouchers, which would be redeemable for a choice among development services, to countries that have established a track record of good performance with past aid.[4]

The point should be clear that a proliferation of international institutions will also require transparency, communications, and a structure for coordination among and between them on issues of common interest and competency. This will be especially important in cases where international agreements touch upon trade issues. Formal contact between the WTO and other organizations or signatories of international agreements in these areas can facilitate an early recognition of the possible problems of such measures and of the relative merits of alternative measures. The WTO has made significant progress in creating such a forum for trade and environment issues, the CTE, and the Doha agenda includes the issue of trade provisions in multilateral environmental agreements (MEAs). The WTO also has ties to the ILO, the UN Environmental Program (UNEP), and the UN Conference on Trade and Development (UNCTAD). Expanding contacts between the WTO and various NGOs even further would be a good idea, as suggested by Director General Supachai Panitchpakdi and Michael Young (2001).

For some critics of globalization, particularly those who see an expanding network of global institutions as a threat to national sovereignty, such coordination will smack of the ominous advent of "world government." This fear is misplaced. Regarding the WTO, the only real policy positions that can be taken on trade come from the collective decisions of the sovereign member countries themselves. The WTO Secretariat cannot really propose anything independently, because the WTO membership specifically wants it that way.[5]

There should be no illusions about the difficulties of forging new and stronger international institutions, despite the manifest need. Intellectual support is present; what is woefully lacking is political leadership.

Where Are the WTO's Friends?

Globalization appears to have placed governments, as well as organizations and interest groups that favor trade, on the defensive. While most of this study has attempted to analyze the opposition to the WTO, it is appropriate to ask, in conclusion, where are the WTO's friends? After so many years of apparently successful trade liberalization, why has it been so difficult for governments and those political constituencies that have clearly gained from trade liberalization to rally behind the concept of a rules-based, nondiscriminatory trading system, now that it is under fire from many quarters?

There is an old adage that all trade politics are domestic politics. In the end, the truth of this statement comes down to a recognition that national governments, guided by internal political considerations, hold the keys to power in any meaningful policy action regarding trade policy. Sovereign countries still run trade policy, even under the jointly agreed WTO rules, and domestic constituencies still have a major role to play in trade agendas. On trade, governments must lead, but they also depend politically on strong and visible pro-trade constituencies in order to push trade liberalization forward. This has been the pattern for several decades now.

The domestic adjustment costs of trade liberalization tend to be concentrated in certain import-competing industries, so political opposition to trade has traditionally come from predictable sources, in the form of lobbying activity to protect the interests of displaced workers and the owners of fixed capital. More recently, some NGOs have joined forces with industry opponents to trade in pursuing their agendas of social-chapter WTO reform as a turtle-teamster coalition. This alliance may play a role in the trade policy debate in national legislatures if efforts are not made to separate them.

Yet there are equally compelling reasons for those domestic parties who gain from trade to push their case also. The broad population of consumers has always been difficult to organize in favor of trade liberalization because of the wide dispersion of the consumer gains from trade. Therefore, the main domestic allies of trade liberalization have been export-oriented business. Such groups and businesses have historically played a major role in political coalitions to promote trade agreements. In recent years, the lack of strong and public business support for the WTO and multilateral trade liberalization has therefore been a major disappointment. In the past, export interests have been instrumental in pushing pro-trade agendas and energizing the trade negotiating agendas in the United States, Europe, and Japan in particular. In view of the recent attacks on the WTO, one might expect old friends to lend a word of support, and yet for the most part they have remained silent.

Part of the reason for the reticence of businesses in the WTO debate may reflect a sense of caution in public relations strategy. Much of the criticism of the WTO has focused on its alleged servitude to business, particularly multinationals. A loud and aggressive defense of the WTO by business interests may therefore risk inflaming antibusiness opposition to the WTO even further. Business is used to a calmer public audience when addressing trade issues, with antitrade voices concentrated in the significant, but predictable and recognizable, protectionist voices in the steel, textile, and other traditional manufacturing industries. The new opposition to the WTO has a strong populist element that often vilifies business as a coconspirator with the WTO in destroying the environment and national sovereignty as well as jobs. The new debate therefore requires a new set of debating points, and business groups have apparently been slow to work them out.

A subtle but important change has crept into recent trade negotiations that may go further in explaining the lack of interest by major business participants in defending the multilateral role of the WTO in opening markets. Since the conclusion of the Uruguay Round, there have been ongoing negotiations in specific sectors, such as information technology, telecommunications, and financial services. These talks followed separate tracks and have not involved the cross-market "horse trading" that typifies broader multilateral negotiations. They led to a set of sectoral agreements among narrower groups of (mostly wealthier) WTO members.[6] Aggarwal and Ravenhill (2001) argue that such narrowly focused agreements are detrimental because they allow strong pro-trade interests to achieve their own goals without having to put their political clout behind a broader multilateral, comprehensive trade negotiation. The big trade negotiations are ultimately much more beneficial to industries, consumers, and countries in general.

They also extend their benefits more broadly around the world, particularly to developing countries.

Narrow, sectoral trade negotiations are certainly attractive politically, particularly for the rich, advanced economies producing high-tech goods and services. They typically involve fewer countries, which often have similar trade interests and orientations, and promise to achieve a final agreement in relatively short order. Yet they can have a serious detrimental effect on the trading system by balkanizing the broader trade agenda into isolated issues with limited scope for reciprocal bargaining and resolution. The responsibility for this state of affairs rests squarely on governments, which may at times be sorely tempted by the promise of easy political gains and grateful business interests. Yet the broader interests of individual countries and the rest of the trading world are better served by the opportunity for multilateral trade negotiations to work. As noted earlier, it is not just a matter of maximizing the welfare of rich trading nations, but of giving poorer countries the chance to specialize, trade, and develop their way out of poverty. This, it would seem, is a matter of simple human decency, and it is why comprehensive, global trade negotiations are so important.

(Re)Building the Domestic Coalition for Trade Liberalization

The mobilization of antitrade political forces under a large, loosely organized but all-accommodating tent of protest reveals a number of possible reasons to oppose the WTO. Choose one from this partial list: environment, labor standards, child labor, human rights, national sovereignty, local job protection, autarkic self-sufficiency, hatred of multinational corporations, anticapitalism, sexism at WTO headquarters, unfair internal WTO governance, solidarity with Chiapas peasants in Mexico, Chinese political oppression, and resistance against U.S. cultural hegemony. The list goes on and on. A single line of reasoning fails to address all of the many varieties of accusations that have washed over the WTO like a public relations tidal wave. The WTO's traditional supporters seem to have been caught unprepared for such a barrage of postmodern, Internet-enabled, media-fueled protest.

This lack of forthright support must change. The WTO and the GATT before it worked for many years in relatively calm obscurity, a situation that was perhaps suited to the times. The gains from trade have always had a low public profile while the "victims" of trade liberalization have always won the headlines. The complicated but generally quiet diplomacy of trade negotiations sought to forge the required compromises that kept trade "problems" out of the headlines. So, no news was generally good news, and there was no perceived need for public relations programs to educate the public on the benefits of trade.

Now, globalization and trade policy are in the limelight, and there is a desperate need for a calm and reasoned, but public and direct, response to the anti-WTO protesters and more general anxieties over trade by both governments and those who are in the best position to explain the benefits of trade. Unfortunately, most post-Seattle government pronouncements on trade have tended so far to be feckless and uninspired.[7] Government statements declaring a commitment to promote "trade with a human face" come across as embarrassed rearguard actions, apologies for trade liberalization. President Clinton's declaration at the Seattle conference that labor standards should be enforced with WTO trade sanctions (discussed in chapter 1) was particularly damaging.

Some commentators believe that labor and environmental issues will hold trade liberalization hostage unless governments force the WTO to adopt social and green chapters (see Esty 2002; Destler and Balint 1999). The appeasement approach seems to regard the WTO as a big, accommodating agreement, with baskets for every issue. Throw in the environment, workers' rights, species protection, and any other hot-button issue, and there has to be some way that all the parties can work it out in the give and take of trade negotiations. These pages have tried to show, however, that this is a particularly dangerous gambit. The WTO is concerned with the benefits of the gains from trade, a proposition accepted by all its members, developed and developing, and it is essential for governments to begin thinking outside the WTO box if they want to see progress on nontrade issues of political importance. Put bluntly, no amount of persuasion, cajoling, bullying, or threats by the developed countries will move the developing countries as a whole to accept an erosion of this benefit. They may just as well leave the WTO, or remain in name only as parties to a moribund WTO agreement. There is no way to sugarcoat such a change in the WTO rules if they result in making market access contingent upon standards and terms dictated by developed countries. The problem lies not only in the existence of standards, but in how they would be formulated or modified, presumably under the heavy influence of developed country labor unions and protectionist interests, and how they would be monitored, presumably under developed country surveillance. The WTO itself has no resources to monitor compliance in these areas.

Furthermore, the notion that all such things are negotiable in a broad multilateral trade round does not hold water. What do the social clause proponents propose to offer as bargaining chips? At a minimum, one might imagine developing country demands for complete trade liberalization in textiles, apparel, and agriculture, radical reform or elimination of antidumping laws, and guaranteed exemptions or delays in TRIPs compliance, for starters. Yet these issues are nonstarters as trade agenda issues in many developed countries. Even so, the introduction of social chapters into the WTO would also require a large increase in the WTO bureaucracy and in the potential for dispute settlement, which implies increased financial burdens on member countries beyond what is already needed to manage the institution's operations effectively.

The U.S. and EU governments need to get beyond the view that such nontrade issues can only be handled politically within the WTO. At the same time, it is clear that global social issues are increasingly a part of domestic politics and must have a channel for policy and action. The goals of many environmental and social advocacy groups are compatible with a liberal, open trading system. Creating separate negotiating tracks to create new international agreements or organizations to deal with the nontrade issues would allow governments to promote environmental and labor issues while at the same time pursuing trade liberalization and maintaining the rules-based trade order. Representatives who might otherwise withhold support for the WTO would then have political cover to support both initiatives on separate tracks. In the meantime, the heavy posturing on linking new WTO social chapters to trade negotiations can only result in hopeless deadlock during future trade rounds.

In the end, there is still no substitute for leadership by governments in promoting trade liberalization, not only in international negotiations and organizations like the WTO but also at home. The mercantilist aspect of the WTO system, as noted in chapter 4, may make it difficult for some government officials to admit that trade agreements allow more imports into domestic markets or that WTO trade rules may prevent the government from restricting imports unilaterally. Yet the arguments in favor of trade are compelling. Trade means more choice and better-quality goods and services; trade means economic progress, access to new technologies, and higher incomes. Trade means more international investment and more stable relations with other countries, as they become more interdependent. The adjustment costs from trade can also be addressed forthrightly: governments should take steps to help those who are most vulnerable to economic change in general. Many environmental and other nontrade issues are also important, but they should be dealt with on separate tracks, where real progress on them can be made. Most government leaders know, in their heart of hearts, that trade is good. Now that the concept of the trading system is being challenged, they should stand up and say so.

| *The Doha Round and Beyond*

There were many anxious moments at the WTO ministerial meeting in Doha, Qatar, in November 2001, the first such meeting since the debacle in Seattle two years earlier. Yet, after much protracted debate, wrangling, and eleventh-hour haggling, the WTO members agreed to launch a new round of trade negotiations. The original business of Seattle was thereby finally completed. In addition, WTO members approved the accession of China and Chinese Taipei (Taiwan) and adopted a supplemental declaration to the TRIPs agreement that provided flexibility on access by poor countries to critical medicines.[8]

The Doha ministerial meeting touted the new trade negotiations as the "development round," and the Doha Declaration emphasizes this point often. The negotiating agenda contained a long list of issues, including agriculture, services, market access, TRIPs, investment, competition policy, WTO rules (dealing with unfair trade and preferential trade agreements), dispute settlement, and trade and the environment. There was disagreement as to whether some of these issues were actually on the negotiating agenda. India and some other developing countries, for example, opposed the inclusion of investment, competition policy, and other issues, although they finally allowed the inclusion of vague language in the declaration that deferred a decision until the interim assessment at the following ministerial meeting.[9]

In general, the developing countries were suspicious of an overly broad WTO negotiating agenda, which in the minds of many had worked to their detriment in the Uruguay Round's extension of the WTO into intellectual property protection. Issues such as these would involve commitments by developing countries, since they place relatively heavier compliance burdens on them than on developed countries, with no clear reciprocal benefits within the framework of the issues themselves. Burned once by TRIPs, they were twice shy. The agreed-upon terms of reference for the Doha Round conveniently paper over these differences with ambiguous statements of intent, as is typical in such negotiations. On the even more volatile issue of trade and the environment, the declaration carefully circumscribed the issue to address only such legalistic matters as the trade obligations of MEAs, with no indication of new environmentally based trade rules. The explosive issue of labor received only an acknowledgment of the ILO and core labor standards, and the upcoming agenda goes nowhere near that issue as a trade topic.

The declaration's focus on development issues includes commitments to special and differential treatment, capacity building, technical cooperation, and special efforts to integrate the least developed countries (LDCs) into the global trading system. While it is certainly politically important to emphasize the interests of developing countries in the Doha Round (and any future trade negotiations), their largest problems are a lack of financial and human resources and technical, physical, and governmental infrastructure, that is, shortcomings not directly related to trade. The bottom line is that, as in all trade negotiations, the outcome of the Doha Round will be judged economically successful to the extent that all countries, developed and developing, lower trade barriers and commit to nondiscriminatory market access rules. These are the results that will maximize the gains from trade for everybody.

The best outcome of the Doha meeting was that it brought multilateral trade negotiations back on track. In accomplishing this goal, it also showed evidence that some significant political forces against trade were being held in check in the major trading countries and that some fence mending had begun between developed and developing countries within the organization, although tensions simmered just below the surface, as described above. Issues of great importance to major players were included without specific commitments to controversial goals or outcomes. All of the WTO national delegations were therefore allowed to go home claiming victory.

The fragility of the groundwork for a new trade round is nothing new, and it is also nothing new to emphasize that the domestic political landscape for trade in the United States and Europe continues to be treacherous. In the new trade talks, however, the developing countries now have increased influence on the outcome of WTO negotiations. Like the Uruguay Round, the new Doha Round is set up as a single undertaking: the entire package of final agreements must in principle be acceptable to all WTO members, because there is no opting out of them on a selective basis. Based on the experience of the Uruguay Round, developing countries are likely to drive harder bargains.

Equally significant political divisions are emerging over trade and nontrade issues within and between the two largest trading powers, the United States and the European Union. For example, the U.S. Congress approved full WTO membership rights for China in a close vote in May 2000, after a long and acrimonious debate that highlighted China's dubious human rights record.[10] In an even closer vote, the U.S. Congress narrowly approved trade-negotiating authority (formerly known as "fast track") for the USTR, with most Democrats still insisting that provisions regarding labor and the environment be included in any trade agreements.[11] In the European Union, there is a bitter internal debate over the future of the Common Agricultural Policy, which also contains heavy protectionist measures. The European Union is reluctant to offer much in the way of reforms in agricultural policies, a position that puts it at loggerheads with the United States and other food-exporting countries.[12] In addition, the European Union has a strong interest in putting more green rules into WTO agreements, which will certainly provoke strong opposition from developing countries.

This sort of legislative trench warfare over trade policy shows that the threat to the WTO and the world trading system does not come primarily from the disruptive street protests themselves, but from the fact that many of these issues have struck a responsive chord among broader elements of the population in advanced industrial societies and, therefore, also among their politicians. Therein lies the problem and the main danger to the WTO: the confluence of traditional protectionism and efforts to incorporate nontrade issues may erode its focus on liberalizing market access rules to promote the gains from trade.

| Twelve Recommendations

It is time to take the matter of world governance of trade and nontrade issues seriously. In order to move in this direction and sustain a growth-generating trading system, governments have a lot of work to do. Here are twelve policy recommendations, based on the issues discussed in these pages:

1. The major economically advanced countries should take steps to negotiate new regional and multilateral agreements on the environment, moving toward the eventual creation of a global environmental organization. In addition, countries should strengthen the International Labor Organization as an institution with specific provisions to encourage and enforce compliance. They should also establish a global monitoring body for human rights, with multinational oversight and administration. Additional agreements on jurisdiction and the relationships between treaties and organizations regarding trade policy will also be necessary.

2. Governments must develop politically effective means of softening the hardship that accompanies economic change, while promoting measures to facilitate adjustment to change. These measures should not be confined to trade-related job losses, which are often difficult to identify, but should apply across the board to any job displacement. Programs should be carefully designed to provide incentives for completing the necessary economic adjustment. They should avoid subsidization of industries or any other measures that distort the allocation of resources in the economy and provide fuel for new trade disputes.

3. In conjunction with the previous item, governments should publicly promote the benefits of trade liberalization and seek to secure the broadest possible support among their industries and populations for it. They should avoid sectorally limited trade agreements and should work to the greatest extent possible toward the ultimate goal of multilateral trade liberalization.

4. The WTO should pursue an open dialogue with NGOs, through invitations to attend important WTO meetings, conferences, and exchanges of information.[13] The WTO Secretariat should establish a select advisory board of NGOs for regular contact and exchanges of views with the director general. At the same time, the terms of NGO participation in WTO activities, particularly in meetings, conferences, and dispute settlement matters, must be determined by negotiations among the WTO membership.

5. The WTO's dispute settlement process should, as much as possible, rely on a diplomatic arbitration model while retaining its current structure. Consensus, political dialogue, and negotiation should remain the guiding concepts of dispute resolution. The Dispute Settlement Understanding should provide strong motivations for both sides in a dispute to consider all possible alternatives to facilitate a mutually acceptable settlement. Sanctioned trade retaliation should remain a rare and last resort.

6. WTO member countries should take steps to accelerate the accession

of all remaining nonmember countries into the organization. For the poorest countries, the WTO should establish an advisory facility to help with the accession process and to train trade diplomats.

7. Governments from the wealthier WTO countries should provide additional funding for capacity building for poorer WTO member countries, including technical and legal training for trade officials, support for participation in dispute settlement proceedings, financial assistance in maintaining a minimal representative presence in the WTO, and aid for the technical infrastructure needed to comply with WTO obligations.

8. Government delegations should work together to develop a more inclusive internal governance system for the WTO. Governance should provide for the systematic representation of all interested WTO parties through some form of proxy, or "party" affiliation, for each specific issue.

9. Governments need to provide more funding for the operations of the WTO Secretariat in Geneva, particularly to finance the increased burden of dispute settlement case management and capacity building for developing country members.

10. The Doha Round and future trade negotiations should strike a balance between breadth and simplicity, with priority given to issues that affect the broadest number of trade categories and that have the broadest geographical impact. The focus should remain on liberalizing market access for goods and services along as broad a front as possible.

11. Economic development is a multidimensional process, and effective global development policies require coherence among all the different elements needed to make progress in this area. The rich countries must establish fundamental goals for development, such as health and disease eradication, and commit the necessary funds to achieve them. Trade, financing, debt relief, and aid policies should be coordinated through formal deliberations with and linkages among global economic institutions and national governments.

12. Trade-related intellectual property protection will remain the adopted problem child of the WTO for years to come, and it will be necessary for governments to find creative ways to adjust the terms of the agreement so that its costs and benefits for the collective WTO membership can be balanced in a mutually acceptable manner.

This is a package that combines global institutional reform, domestic policy reform, international cooperation, and the additional resource allocation to support it. Taken together, these recommendations suggest that the Doha "development" Round and future trade negotiations will benefit greatly if governments assign separate tracks to the labor and environmental issues, push for WTO reforms that improve internal governance, and implement policies at home that promote adjustment and receptiveness to trade liberalization.

Work on this book has been framed by two important events in the history of the WTO: the disastrous Seattle ministerial meeting in December 1999 and the more hopeful Doha ministerial meeting, which launched the new multilateral trade round in November 2001. In between, the sobering events of September 11, 2001, raised the consciousness of the global community on the importance—and fragile nature—of the world economy. Global stability in the future will depend on the alleviation of poverty, on improved welfare for the world's population, and on the ability to resolve international conflicts of all kinds through a comprehensive architecture of institutions. A well-functioning system of global trade has much to do with all of these requirements.

Harnessing the energy of the global economy "tiger" shown in the cartoon at the head of this chapter is therefore more than just an economic proposition. The gains from trade remain one of the most basic elements of human interaction across all peoples and all nations, and the potential benefits from it must not be squandered. The WTO provides a framework for capturing these benefits, which can serve as the foundation not only for economic growth and greater prosperity, but also for a more unified world economy. These benefits, in turn, may contribute to greater political stability, progress on human rights and labor standards, and efforts to secure a sustainable global environment.

Building the required global institutions to achieve these goals will not be easy. Since the years of the postwar boom, many governments have come to take the benefits of an integrated world trading system for granted and now risk reducing both economic growth and opportunities for poverty alleviation because of various protectionist and nontrade conflicts. Meeting the great challenge of creating global prosperity, peace, and stability will require governments to lay the foundation for international cooperation and conflict resolution in both trade and nontrade dimensions. The WTO is a part of that foundation, which is already in place, and it needs the continued support and commitment of its members to the integrity of its core goals. Governments must now build the other blocks of the foundation alongside the WTO, so that each can do its job in supporting the future of the global commons.

Notes

Introduction

1. After the accession of China in 2001, the WTO represented well over 90 percent of the world's population. In early 2003, there were twenty-five countries negotiating accession, including Algeria, Andorra, Azerbaijan, Bahamas, Belarus, Bhutan, Bosnia Herzegovina, Cambodia, Cape Verde, Ethiopia, Kazakhstan, Lao People's Democratic Republic, Lebanese Republic, Nepal, Russian Federation, Samoa, Saudi Arabia, Serbia and Montenegro, Seychelles, Sudan, Tajikistan, Tonga, Ukraine, Uzbekistan, Vietnam, and Yemen. The current WTO membership, combined with this list, leaves only a handful of countries with no immediate prospects of joining, including Iran, Iraq, Democratic People's Republic of Korea (North Korea), Libya, Somalia, and Syria. WTO News Item, "WTO Membership Rises to 146," April 4, 2003.

2. A list of World Trade Center tenants is located at http://www.washington post.com/wp-srv/nation/articles/wtc_lz.html.

3. The subsequent al-Qaeda attack on the resort town on Bali in October 2002 showed a similar strategy of economic terrorism: a well-placed bomb to intimidate incoming visitors and thereby destroy the tourism industry in the area.

4. Reich (1998) and other authors in his edited volume provide an overview.

5. See Davis (2001), for a post–September 11 assessment of trade as a strategy to diminish terrorism.

6. The U.S. State Department characterizes the following countries as supporting state-sponsored terrorism: Cuba, Iran, Iraq, Libya, North Korea, Sudan, and Syria. George Gedda, "Iran Ranked No. 1 Terrorist Country by State Department," Associated Press Newswires, May 1, 2001. Cuba is in fact a WTO member, having joined in 1995 as a legacy member of the GATT, but the United States has invoked the

WTO national security clause to deny Cuba treatment as a normal WTO member by the United States. Sudan was negotiating for WTO accession in 2003 (see n. 1).

7. Ibid. Algeria, Ethiopia, Lebanon, Uzbekistan, and Yemen were negotiating for WTO accession in 2003.

Chapter 1

1. A list of participating NGOs is located at the WTO Web site, www.wto.org, as document ngoinseattle_e.htm, "Non-Governmental Organizations (NGOs): List of NGOs Attending Seattle."

2. Interview with Seattle *Post-Intelligencer*, November 30, 1999. Published December 1, 1999, p. A1.

3. www.globalexchange.org/economy/rulemakers/toptenreasons.html.

4. Buchanan (1998).

5. www.geocities.com/CapitolHill/Lobby/8771/wwwto2.html.

6. http://www.cuts-india.org/Twin-sal.htm.

7. In addition to the anti-WTO Websites indicated in the text, a sample of publications critical of the WTO includes Danaher and Burbach (2000); Working Group on the WTO/MAI (1999); Shrybman (2001).

8. Ostry (2001) cites the case of the World Bank's Narmada dam project, which was canceled in 1993, largely as a result of NGO lobbying. See also O'Brien et al. (2000).

Chapter 2

1. Feenstra (1998) describes an important extension of the gains-from-trade model to include specialization not only between industries, but also within the value chain of individual industries in a country, a concept he calls *vertical specialization*. Increasing international capital mobility allows firms to break down their production processes into component stages and assign each stage to the most efficient production location in the global resource market. The practical significance of this idea receives support from the observation of increasing outsourcing of intermediate inputs in manufacturing in most industrialized countries.

2. Other important assumptions are that perfect competition prevails, technology is fixed within a country, input costs are fixed, labor and capital cannot move outside the country, and no trade barriers or transportation costs impede trade. The discussion emphasizes the mobility factor and full employment assumptions because they provide the most direct political links to lobbying for trade restrictions.

3. This proposition is known as the Stolper-Samuelson theorem. It is based on the Heckscher-Ohlin model of trade, which modified the Ricardian model to explain how a country's endowment of the factors of production (labor, capital) ultimately determines the pattern of trade. Stolper-Samuelson is extremely important to our understanding of trade policy because of the way it identifies the economic interests of different groups in various trade policy regimes.

4. See Feenstra (1998) and n. 1.

5. The firm could set up a subsidiary in the foreign country for local production and sales to jump inside the tariff wall, but this strategy shifts the risk over to the

realm of tax policy and regulation of foreign direct investment in the host country, which may be discriminatory or unpredictable. These issues eventually entered trade negotiations in the Uruguay Round, which resulted in the TRIMs (trade-related investment measures) agreement.

6. WTO rules do not require all tariffs to be bound, although this is the ultimate goal. In the Uruguay Round of trade negotiations, 99 percent of the imports of developed countries and 60 percent of the imports of developing countries became bound. These negotiations resulted in an increase of bound tariffs from 70 percent to 88 percent of all industrial products. See Schott and Buurman (1994), pp. 62–63.

7. See Brander and Spencer (1984), p. 204. After explaining the possible economic benefits of tariffs and other government intervention, the authors conclude: "Finally, it should be emphasized that our arguments should not be taken as support for using tariffs." Similar disclaimers can be found in Helpman and Krugman (1989), pp. 185–86, and in several chapters by various authors in Krugman (1986).

8. The economic case for using antidumping and countervailing duties is very narrowly defined, and the laws in practice are subject to political abuse. See Finger (1993) and Boltuck and Litan (1991).

9. See Kaul, Grunberg, and Stern (1999), particularly the contribution by Birdsall and Lawrence, "Deep Integration and Trade Agreements." Yarbrough and Yarbrough (1992) develop the underlying theory of transaction costs in international trade relations and the role of trade agreements to reduce these costs.

10. Irwin (2000) and others note that many countries have unilaterally opened their markets to imports, apparently without WTO incentives. However, Schott (2003) observes that these countries often demand WTO "credit" for these measures in subsequent trade negotiations, and that even so, unilateral trade liberalization rarely reduces entrenched domestic protectionism as much as do multilateral negotiations.

Chapter 3

1. See U.S. International Trade Commission (1999). The estimate is based on data for 1996. Most of the gains would occur as a result of removing protective barriers against textile and clothing imports.

2. It is true that other workers in declining industries gain from protection, to the extent that they enjoy higher wages and benefits financed by the proceeds of a protected market, and they may even be able to finish their working careers before the industry is forced to adjust. However, the "legacy costs" (unfunded pensions and benefits) of retired workers in the U.S. steel industry show that commitments to workers by protected firms can complicate the adjustment process and increase its financial cost. See Ikensen (2002).

3. The escape clause has always been politically "expensive" to use because it requires governments to apply it in a most-favored-nation (MFN) manner, that is, the trade restriction cannot usually target individual countries, even those that can be identified as the source of the import surges. In addition, any increase in protection above the bound tariff rates from trade negotiations requires compensatory tariff reductions or their equivalent for all affected member exporters.

4. See http://www.doleta.gov/tradeact/2002act_index.asp for a summary. The new provisions expand eligibility to more worker groups, increase existing benefits,

provide tax credits for health insurance coverage assistance, and increase timeliness for benefits receipt, training, and rapid response assistance.

5. The proposal by Kletzer and Litan (2001), for example, is largely incremental with respect to the payments system, building on the existing unemployment insurance program and requiring an estimated additional outlay of $4 billion.

6. See Scheve and Slaughter (2001) and Kull (2000).

Chapter 4

1. For an early history of the GATT, see Curzon (1965), pp. 70–103, and Dam (1970), pp. 10–22.

2. See www.wto.org/english/thewto_e/secre_e/budget03_e.htm. Budget contributions come from member countries based on their share of international trade. For a general discussion of the WTO's activities and budget, see Blackhurst (1998).

3. In some cases, panels must judge cases in which no WTO rule is alleged to have been violated, but where some damage has been caused to the trading interest of a WTO member by a specific practice or policy. Most cases discussed in this study fall in the rules-violation category.

4. See Hoekman and Mavroidis (2001). Costa Rica and Venezuela won cases against the United States on cotton textiles and gasoline regulations, respectively.

5. Hoekman and Mavroidis (2001), pp. 133–34, discuss the political economy of a government's decision to go ahead with a case, in light of its impact on the national economy, possible retaliation, or other repercussions.

6. The disputes on foreign sales corporations (FSCs), beef hormones, and bananas date back to 1973, 1987, and 1993, respectively. See Stehmann (2000); Kerr and Hobbs (2002); Valles and McGivern (2000). On the original manifestation of the FSC challenged in the GATT, the Domestic International Sales Corporation (DISC), see Dryden (1995).

7. The EU moved in 2001 to close the banana dispute with the required changes in legislation; see *Journal of Commerce*, December 21, 2001. In addition, the beef hormones case moved closer to resolution in 2001; see "French Seek to End Hormone Row," *Agra Europe*, August 17, 2001, p. EP/2. The latest version of the FSC case was in part a U.S. response to the unresolved beef hormones case and may similarly lead to U.S. acquiescence to the WTO decision, pending final resolution of the beef hormones issue. See Sally Schuff, "FSC Ruling Sets Stage for EU," *Feedstuffs*, August 27, 2001, p. 1.

8. U.S. implementing legislation to ratify the results of the Uruguay Round included a provision that a legislative commission would review any WTO panel rulings against the United States, reserving the right of the U.S. Congress to withdraw from the WTO if it were dissatisfied with the decisions.

9. See the discussion in chapter 6 on the shrimp/turtles case. Focused aid to provide the needed resources for environmental protection, for example, may be able to prevent acrimonious trade disputes.

10. The ACWL Web site address is www.acwl.ch/MainFrameset.htm. Hoekman and Mavroidis (2001), pp. 139–45, discuss the ACWL and related strategies for assisting developing countries in dispute settlement cases. For WTO funding of technical assistance, see WTO press release PRESS/277, March 8, 2002, "Pledging Conference to Provide Sound Financial Basis for Doha Agenda." Principal financial support

for the ACWL as of early 2003 came from the nine developed country members: Canada, Denmark, Finland, Ireland, Italy, Netherlands, Norway, Sweden, and the United Kingdom.

Chapter 5

1. See the discussion of sovereignty in Barfield (2001), pp. 7–9. Barfield also elaborates on several theories of international law and politics and their implications for trade relations.

2. Krasner (1999), pp. 9–25, cited in Barfield (2001).

3. See Hainsworth (1995) for an overview of sovereignty issues regarding various aspects of the Uruguay Round agreements.

4. See WTO, article X. Schott and Buurman (1994), pp. 138–39, and Jackson (1998), p. 177, provide brief explanations of this arrangement.

5. Nonmarket economies provide an even more extreme example of economic sovereignty, in which the state asserts absolute control over most, if not all, economic activity, including the determination of prices, incomes, and outputs according to a centralized plan.

6. On industrial location, see Levinson (1996). On the California effect, see Vogel (1995).

7. Charnovitz (1992), p. 11; Bhagwati and Srinivasan (1996).

8. "Understanding on Rules and Procedures Governing the Settlement of Disputes," annex 2, article 3.2 of the WTO agreement, in World Trade Organization (2000).

9. Ibid.

10. Elmslie and Milberg (1996). See also Wolffgand and Feuerkake (2002).

Chapter 6

1. Public Citizen's Global Trade Watch, which owns the rights to this image, declined to grant permission for its use in this volume. The GATTzilla image can be viewed at www.citizen.org/publications/release.cfm?ID=5154.

2. Siebert (1996) lists six WTO guidelines that are in dispute in the debate: (1) use of trade policy only when it is the most appropriate means of addressing an environmental issue; (2) principle of nondiscrimination; (3) invoking an exception to WTO rules (as defined in GATT article XX) only when it is absolutely necessary; (4) limiting trade measures to address environmental issues only within a country's territorial sovereignty; (5) nonapplicability of domestic environmental standards to foreign production processes; and (6) use of consumer demand criteria rather than production processes' similarity in defining a "like" product for purposes of trade policy.

3. This issue resurfaced in a 1997 WTO dispute panel request by Malaysia, Thailand, and Pakistan regarding a U.S. import ban against shrimp caught with nets that harm turtles (Frances Williams, "WTO to Probe U.S. Shrimp Row," *Financial Times*, February 26, 1997, p. 6). For various perspectives on the tuna panel cases, see Hudec (1996), Horwitz (1993), Petersmann (1993), and Charnovitz (1993).

4. After intense lobbying by Mexico, attempts by the U.S. Commerce Depart-

ment in 2003 to expand the scope of acceptable fishing methods certified as "dolphin-safe" were overturned in U.S. federal court. In the meantime, the major U.S. tuna canneries continued to abide by the more restrictive "dolphin-safe" standards, effectively excluding most imported tuna caught with purse seine and driftnets. See Miller and Croston (1999) and John Authers, "Tuna Dispute Runs Deeper Than the Death of Dolphins," *Financial Times*, June 23, 2003, p. 20.

5. GATT article XX(g) allows the use of trade restrictions, which may include provisions based on the method of production (i.e., types of nets used), to promote the conservation of exhaustible natural resources. See Shaw and Schwartz (2002), pp. 146–49, for a discussion.

6. Labeling can also be a tricky issue. Opponents to the beef imports may press for a prominently displayed skull and crossbones. Supporters of the imported beef may insist on an innocuous content statement in fine print. Yet even this controversy gets closer to a viable solution to the dispute than the seemingly endless trade litigation that has occurred so far.

7. The trend in recent trade negotiations has in fact been to eliminate exceptions to open trade rules rather than to add new ones, as shown by the Uruguay Round's success in bringing agriculture and textiles, not to mention services, intellectual property, and trade-related investment, under multilateral trade rules.

8. Wilson (1996) offers an economic analysis and critique of the race-to-the-bottom argument. Cass and Boltuck (1996) discuss the legal issues associated with the application of the argument to antidumping and countervailing duty laws.

9. In the debate, this issue often appears to boil down to a fundamental disagreement over the nature of absorptive capacity and the legitimacy of economic criteria in environmental policy. Buckley (1993), for example, derides the notion of absorptive capacity, as well as economic efficiency and welfare criteria for environmental policy.

10. See the discussion on bargaining within regional trade agreements under the subheading "Steppingstones to a Comprehensive International Agreement." Despite the high profile of the NAFTA environmental chapter, its actual effectiveness in harmonizing environmental standards in North America is debatable. The European Union, with its deeper integration of legal structures, is better positioned to achieve harmonization along the lines of a sovereign state.

11. Hilton and Levinson (2000). See reviews of the literature by Dean (1992), Levinson (1996), Ferrantino (1997), and World Trade Organization (1999), pp. 35–46.

12. Haq et al. (2001) examine environmental costs to European firms, and the authors conclude that "properly designed regulation need not increase costs" (p. 137). A U.S. Environmental Protection Agency study (1997) concluded that early estimates of the compliance costs of the U.S. Clean Air Act were greatly exaggerated. Hilton and Levinson (2000) studied the compliance cost among U.S. firms and found no systematic evidence of a "pollution haven" effect nor of a race to the bottom.

13. The profile of environmental quality may not be uniformly increasing, however. Grossman and Krueger (1991) and Shafik and Bandhyopadhay (1992) present evidence that sulfur dioxide concentrations and deforestation, respectively, tend to increase as countries reach middle-income status and to decrease thereafter. Some types of pollution tend to decline consistently with increases in per capita GDP, while others increase as countries become richer. In general, however, the wealth

effect tends to increase both the resources available for improving environmental quality and the demand for it. See Ferrantino (1997), pp. 46–48.

14. Hillman and Ursprung (1992) and Hoekman and Leidy (1992), for example, suggest that economic incentives allow protectionist interests to "capture" environmental issues for their own purposes.

15. Antidumping and countervailing duty law reform proposals that incorporate new environmental criteria in calculating manufacturing costs may provide such an example of green protectionism. Examples include the U.S. Congress's proposed Pollution Deterrence Act of 1991 (see Subramanian 1992, p. 137) and the Gorton amendment to the Clean Air Act of 1990 (Charnovitz 1992, p. 343).

16. Environmental groups that feel hostility toward the free-trading system itself usually exhibit that hostility openly. See Nader et al. (1993).

17. Unfortunately, the history of heavy trade protection for this industry raises further suspicions; canned tuna continues to receive tariff protection far above the manufacturing average. See Hufbauer and Elliott (1994), pp. 50–51.

18. The European Union's principled approach on this issue did not prevent it, however, from applying its own environmental rules to imports of furs caught by leg traps. See Esty (1995).

19. See Esty (1994) and Runge (2001), pp. 399–426, for more detailed treatment.

20. Hufbauer, Schott, and Elliott (1990), pp. 92–104, conclude that economic sanctions tend to be effective in forcing an alteration in a target country's behavior or policy if the goals are modest, the target country is weak, and trading links are strong.

Chapter 7

1. The Universal Declaration was adopted as UN General Assembly Resolution 217A(III) on December 10, 1948. Related declarations include the International Covenant on Civil and Political Rights (United Nations Treaty Series 1976, 999: 171) and International Covenant on Economic, Social, and Cultural Rights (UNTS 1976, 993:14531). Texts of these documents are available at www.hrweb.org/legal/undocs.html.

2. See Stirling (1996), p. 39

3. See Ward (1996), pp. 620–21.

4. We are assuming a consensus-based system; a single dominant country could theoretically impose a *pax Romana* standard of human rights, or any other standard.

5. See Stirling (1996), pp. 5–6.

6. International Convention on the Suppression and Punishment of the Crime of Apartheid, November 30, 1973, 13 ILM 50; Convention on the Prevention and Punishment of the Crime of Genocide, December 9, 1948, 78 UNTS 277; Convention against Torture and Other Cruel, Inhuman, or Degrading Treatment or Punishment, pmbl. GA Res. 39/46, UN GAOR, reprinted in 23 ILM 1027 (1984).

7. See Hufbauer, Schott, and Elliott (2003), pp. 1–17.

8. UN-led sanctions alone resulted in an annual cost to South Africa of $116 million from 1963 to 1978 and $523 million from 1979 to 1985. Intensified sanctions by the United Nations and the United States led to an estimated annual cost of over $1 billion from 1985 to 1994, when the apartheid regime ended. The cost of sanc-

tions to South Africa over the entire period ranged from 1.2 to 1.9 percent of GNP. Hufbauer, Schott, and Elliott (2003), Case 62–2, UN v. South Africa.

9. See Stirling (1996), pp. 25–32.

10. See "U.S. Prisons Accused of Violating Torture Ban," *St. Petersburg Times*, May 16, 2000, p. 2A.

11. UN Document A/55/342, "Globalization and Its Impact on the Full Enjoyment of All Human Rights: Preliminary Report of the Secretary-General, Fifty-fifth Session of the General Assembly," p. 4. Cited in Lim (2001), p. 278.

12. See Stirling (1996). The prison labor provision is contained in GATT article XX(e), part of the General Exceptions section.

13. See Sub-Commission on the Promotion and Protection of Human Rights, "The Adverse Consequences of Economic Sanctions on the Enjoyment of Human Rights," UN Document E/CN.4/Sub.2/2000/33, June 21, 2000.

14. The United Nations, which administered the Iraq sanctions, struggled to find a way to impose sanctions without harming the general population of the country. See "Cosmetic Surgery," *Economist*, May 16, 2002, p. 44, for a discussion of reforms that would have permitted Iraq to import more consumer goods while continuing restrictions on imports of military and strategic goods. Saddam Hussein's government in Iraq fell in April 2003 following an invasion led by U.S. and British forces.

15. Hufbauer, Schott, and Elliott (2003). The author is grateful to these authors for providing advance information from the third edition.

16. Ibid. The authors compiled a list of nine "dos and don'ts" to follow: (1) don't bite off more than you can chew; (2) do pick on the weak and helpless; (3) do pick on allies and trading partners, but remember that good friends are hard to come by and even harder to lose; (4) do impose the maximum cost on your target; (5) do apply sanctions decisively and with resolution; (6) don't pay too high a price for sanctions; (7) don't suppose that, where sanctions will fail, covert maneuvers or military action will necessarily succeed; (8) don't exaggerate the importance of international cooperation with your policies and don't underestimate the role of international assistance to your target; and (9) do plan carefully: economic sanctions may worsen a bad situation.

17. The Jackson-Vanek amendment, passed by the U.S. Congress and signed into law in 1974, was designed to make trade between the United States and the Soviet Union contingent on Soviet reforms to allow Jewish emigration. Its more general application in recent years has been to allow the United States to invoke the WTO nonapplication clause against new WTO members, such as the Kyrgyz Republic, Moldova, and Armenia, based on those countries' emigration policies. Nonrecognition can be revoked if the country's policies are changed.

18. See Irwin (1996), chap. 10.

19. The ILO report, "A Future without Child Labor," is available at http://www.ilo.org/public/english/standards/decl/publ/reports/report3.htm.

20. Graham (2000).

21. Edgren (1979).

22. See the ILO Web site, www.ilo.org.

23. www.ilo.org/public/english/about/mandate.htm.

24. See www.ilo.org/public/english/standards/norm/enforced/index.htm, with special reference to the Convention regarding Freedom of Association and Protection of the Right to Organize.

25. The text appears at www.ilo.org/public/english/standards/decl/declaration/ text/tindex.htm.

26. See Watson, Flynn, and Conwell (1999), pp. 67–76, who conclude that the consensus view outside the United States, Norway, and perhaps a few other countries is that labor issues should be kept out of the WTO. See also Charnovitz (1997), pp. 131, 156.

27. If ILO conventions did include provisions for specific trade sanctions, then they would have to be reconciled, through principles of international law, with signatories' WTO obligations. Yet this is how the conflict *should* be addressed: as a matter of ordering competing international obligations, as discussed in chapter 6.

28. For a discussion of international codes regarding multinational corporations, see Mousouris (1988) and Kolodner (1994).

29. See Prakash and Williams (2000). For a more skeptical view, see Bernasek and Porter (1997).

Chapter 8

1. Many of these ideas originated with the classical economists Smith, Mill, and Ricardo, among others. See, for example, Meier and Baldwin (1957).

2. The terms of trade are usually measured as the ratio of the index of a country's export prices to the index of its import prices. Many developing countries typically rely on commodity exports for their foreign exchange earnings and therefore for their ability to finance imported goods. Therefore, the perception that commodity prices would continue a downward trend created the fear that developing countries would continue to face balance-of-payments difficulties at least until (and if) they "graduated" to the status of manufacturing exporters.

3. See Schott and Buurman (1994) for a description of the tentative nature of trade liberalization in agriculture. There is great difficulty in measuring progress in this sector, since any reduction of one type of protection can be replaced by other forms of protection.

4. Among WTO members that use these laws, the majority of AD and CVD cases tend to involve iron, steel, other base metals, chemicals, and plastics. See WTO press release PRESS/287, April 22, 2002.

5. See Lindsey and Ikenson (2001). For general critiques of unfair trade law, see Finger (1993) and Boltuck and Litan (1991).

6. Figures quoted by Maskus (2000) are in 1995 dollars. The list of countries studied is not comprehensive, but they do show a net loss (transfer of consumer welfare) of $1.66 billion for EU countries outside Germany, $555 million for Japan, and $1.3 billion for Canada. Among developing countries, losses are $1.2 billion for Brazil, $665 million for India, $562 million for Mexico, $143 million for South Africa, and $97 million for Colombia.

7. See the WTO Web site for the full text of the Doha Declaration and the Declaration on the TRIPs Agreement and Public Health, www.wto.org. Panagariya (2002) discusses the implications of the Doha Declaration for developing countries regarding TRIPs and other issues.

8. Khor (2000) regards the lack of representation as the root cause of the WTO's main shortcomings.

9. Schott and Watal (2000) note that larger green-room consultations also included developed countries such as Australia, New Zealand, Norway, and Switzerland; one or two countries with transitional economies; developing countries such as Chile, Colombia, Egypt, Hong Kong, Mexico, Pakistan, South Africa, and South Korea (in addition to India and Brazil); and the ASEAN countries of Brunei, Indonesia, Malaysia, Philippines, Singapore, and Thailand. Most smaller, poorer countries do not participate due to lack of resources. Even so, one-half to two-thirds of the participants in a typical WTO green-room meeting come from developing countries.

10. The IMF and World Bank executive boards combine a set of eight permanent members with sixteen seats shared by groupings of the remaining members. See Blackhurst (2001), p. 303.

11. Krueger (1999); Wolf (2001). The WTO dispute settlement system does not guarantee that, for example, a legal victory by St. Kitts over the United States will completely level the playing field and set everything right. Large countries have always flouted the rules and used all their powers of bargaining and intimidation to pursue their interests, even in violation of international obligations and laws. Yet without a system of third-party review and binding settlement, like the WTO dispute process, the domination of large over small countries is a foregone conclusion.

Chapter 9

1. See the *Economist*, January 29, 2000, pp. 25–27. This figure includes only international NGOs and does not distinguish between those with primarily an issue advocacy mission and those involved mainly with activities such as food and foreign aid distribution or other similar services. There are also purely domestic NGOs, which number in the millions.

2. http://www.un.org/MoreInfo/ngolink/brochure.htm. See the Web site for the Union of International Associations, http://www.uia.org/uiadocs/orgtypea.htm, for a discussion of the difficulty in defining *nongovernmental organization* precisely.

3. Public Citizen's Trade Watch (www.citizen.org/trade/) was active in the anti-MAI campaign.

4. Lizza (2000) discusses these issues with regard to the advocacy organization Public Citizen's Global Trade Watch.

5. http://www.unglobalcompact.org/. See also UN press release SG/SM/7203, November 2, 1999.

6. See "Campaigns: Alliance for a Corporate-Free UN," http://www.corpwatch. org/campaigns/PCC.jsp?topicid=101, sponsored by Corpwatch, an issue advocacy group.

7. Firms tend to file unfair trade law petitions based on market structure factors, degree of unionization, capital intensity, import penetration, market share, employment trends, the international structure of the firm's supply chain, and the risk of retaliatory actions by rivals, especially those that also have access to these laws. See Feinberg and Hirsch (1989) for an empirical study of the determinants of filing cases. Many MNCs will be reluctant to file unfair trade law cases because such a strategy weakens their case for open markets and may expose them to retaliatory actions in kind by foreign rivals.

8. Section 301 was originally introduced in the Trade and Tariff Act of 1974, with amendments in 1984 and 1988. See Bhagwati and Patrick (1990), Bayard and Elliott (1994), and Ostry (1997).

9. In the United States, trade policy has been largely relegated to the executive branch since the Reciprocal Trade Agreements Act of 1934, which was designed to prevent legislatively generated tariff "logrolling," which reached its peak in the Smoot-Hawley Act of 1930. Schattschneider (1935) presents the classic account of this process.

10. It is important to remember that the principle of reciprocity dominates WTO-sponsored trade negotiations, which means in essence that governments come to the table to swap concessions on market access. In this regard, only sovereign governmental entities with jurisdiction over trade policy can take part in multilateral trade negotiations.

11. See Ullrich (2000), pp. 77–79. At critical stages of trade negotiations, a small number of participants may find it necessary to strike a deal on an individual issue in order to allow the larger multilateral negotiations to proceed. While the content of the deal as it pertains to all of the participants typically becomes public eventually, the deal itself may be negotiated in secret, away from press coverage, lobbyists, and other potentially interested parties who may disrupt the negotiations. Similarly, at earlier stages of a dispute settlement, the conflicting parties are encouraged to negotiate an out-of-court settlement, or sometimes they may use a mediator. In these cases, the principle of confidentiality serves to allow the parties to reach a settlement more easily. See Cot (1972), pp. 159–68.

12. Robertson (2000) suggests a system of NGO accreditation in the WTO that would require NGOs to divulge their membership numbers, financing, purpose, and the positions they claim to represent, with submitted information subject to formal auditing. This standard would also presumably apply to business NGOs and other interest groups that participate in WTO activities.

13. This is not to say that NGOs from less-developed countries (LDCs) are uniformly opposed to NGO participation in the WTO. Political economy considerations suggest that some trade unions in LDCs or with strong LDC representation, for example, may stand to benefit from higher labor standards, to the extent that their implementation would shift labor demand toward their members.

14. A competing assessment from some legal commentators presents the possibility of an institutional evolution of the WTO system into a broader agreement on non-trade issues. This line of reasoning rests on the presumed ability of the WTO Dispute Settlement Understanding to establish new international law and on an adaptive theory of organizations that includes necessary adjustments to the changing needs of the members they serve. The main problem with this view is that it assumes that WTO rulemaking can go beyond the gains-from-trade consensus, which is the foundation of the WTO's legitimacy. See Trachtman (1999).

Chapter 10

1. Hipple (1999), pp. 15–32, notes that workers aged 25–34 who had lost a job in 1995–1996 increased earnings by an average of 5.5 percent by early 1998.

2. Among the many studies on policy coordination among these institutions, see Vines (1998); Michalopoulos (2001), chap. 11; and Bergsten (1994).

3. See Michalopoulos (2001), pp. 233–42. Some IMF and World Bank conditionality provisions have worked at cross-purposes with the WTO obligations of the recipient country. In addition, it has often been difficult to incorporate autonomous

trade liberalization measures mandated by conditionality provisions into the broader framework of WTO multilateral reciprocal trade negotiations, especially regarding tariff bindings.

4. See Wolf (2002); Sachs (2001); and Sachs (1999), which is also available at the Harvard Center for International Development Web site, http://www.cid.harvard.edu/cidinthenews/articles/sf9108.html.

5. Michalopoulos (2001), pp. 240–42 and n. 9, relates his experience with "representing" the WTO, which does not have a clearance procedure for official policy positions on specific issues, since that would imply unanimity on them among the entire membership, which is a virtual impossibility.

6. The Information Technology Agreement was concluded in 1996, followed by the Global Agreement on Basic Telecommunications and the Financial Services Agreement in 1997. All were concluded within the WTO framework, but without participation by the entire WTO membership.

7. The major exception was U.S. trade representative Robert Zoellick's spirited defense of the trading system (Zoellick 2001), which is discussed in the introduction.

8. See Schott (2002); and "The Doha Round: Seeds Sown for Future Growth," *Economist*, November 17, 2001, p. 65. The official ministerial declaration, WTO Document WT/MIN(01)/DEC/1, adopted November 14, 2001, is available at the WTO Web site, www.wto.org.

9. Panagariya (2002) examines the controversy over these so-called Singapore issues, which were originally debated at the 1996 Singapore ministerial meeting. See www.wto.org for the full text of the Doha Declaration and other related documents.

10. The vote on granting China "permanent normal trade relations" (thereby permitting full WTO benefits to China by the United States once Chinese accession to the WTO occurred) was 237–197 in the U.S. House of Representatives; two-thirds of the Democrats and one-quarter of the Republicans voted against the bill. See "A Much-Needed Victory," *Economist*, May 25, 2000, p. 27.

11. See Max Baucus, "The Trade Act of 2002," speech presented at the Institute for International Economics, February 26, 2002, www.iie.com/papers/baucus0202.htm. Senator Baucus (D-Montana) is chair of the Senate Finance Committee. See also Bhagwati (2001). The political price for the narrow legislative victory apparently also included some separate protectionist measures applied subsequently to steel and softwood lumber imports, as well as increased subsidies to agriculture. Other traditional protectionist issues persist in the U.S. Congress, including strong opposition to antidumping reform and textile trade liberalization, both of which became major issues during the Doha Round negotiations.

12. The conclusion of the Uruguay Round was held hostage for years to a resolution of differences between the United States and the European Union over agriculture, which also hindered progress in the Doha Round.

13. The WTO announced that 647 NGOs were eligible to attend the fourth Ministerial Conference in Doha, Qatar, in November 2001. WTO press release, August 10, 2001. By the beginning of the conference, 365 NGOs had registered to attend (see www.wto.org/english/forums_e/ngo_e/doha_attend_e.doc). The distant location and fears of travel in the months following the terrorist attacks of September 11, 2001, appeared to keep NGO attendance down. See Murray Hiebert, "Globalization: Violence Is Out of Fashion," *Far Eastern Economic Review*, November 15, 2001, p. 26.

Bibliography

Books and Articles

Aggarwal, Vinod, and John Ravenhill (2001). "How Open Sectoral Agreements Undermine the WTO." *Asia-Pacific Issues*, no. 48 (February).

Awtle, John M., and Gregg Heidebrink (1995). "Environment and Development: Theory and International Evidence." *Economic Development and Cultural Change* 43, no. 3: 603–25.

Bach, Jonathan (1999). "U.S.–EU Trade Issues." *Foreign Policy in Focus* 4, no. 37 (www.foreignpolicy-infocus.org).

Balassa, Bela (1980). "The Process of Industrial Development and Alternative Development Strategies." *Essays in International Finance* 141 (December): 4–11.

Balasubramanyam, V. N., and M. A. Salisu (1991). "Export Promotion, Import Substitution and Direct Foreign Investment in Less Developed Countries." In *International Trade and Global Development: Essays in Honor of Jagdish Bhagwati*, edited by A. Koekkock and L. B. M. Mennes. London and New York: Routledge.

Barfield, Claude (2001). *Free Trade, Sovereignty, Democracy: The Future of the World Trade Organization*. Washington, D.C.: AEI Press.

Bayard, Thomas O., and Kimberly Ann Elliott (1994). *Reciprocity and Retaliation in U.S. Trade Policy*. Washington, D.C.: Institute for International Economics.

Bergsten, C. Fred (1998). *Fifty Years of the GATT/WTO: Lessons from the Past for Strategies for the Future*. Washington, D.C.: Institute for International Economics.

——— (1994). "Managing the World Economy of the Future." In *Managing the World Economy: Fifty Years after Bretton Woods*, edited by P. B. Kenen. Washington, D.C.: Institute for International Economics.

Bernasek, Alexandra, and Richard C. Porter (1997). "Private Pressure for Social Change in South Africa: The Impact of the Sullivan Principles." *Review of Social Economy* 55, no. 2 (Summer): 172–93.

Bettcher, Douglas W., Derek Yach, and G. Emmanuel Guindon (2000). "Global Trade and Health: Key Linkages and Future Challenges." *Bulletin of the World Health Organization* 78, no. 4: 521–35.

Bhagwati, Jagdish (2002). "The Poor's Best Hope." *Economist*, June 20, pp. 24–26.

——— (2001). "Break the Link between Trade and Labour." *Financial Times*, August 29, p. 14.

——— (1998). "Fifty Years: Looking Back, Looking Forward." Paper presented at the Symposium on the World Trading System, Geneva, Switzerland, April 30.

——— (1988). *Protectionism.* Cambridge, Mass.: MIT Press.

Bhagwati, Jagdish, and Arthur Lehman (1999). "On Thinking Clearly about the Linkage between Trade and the Environment." Paper presented at the Conference on Environment and Trade at the Kiel Institute for World Economics, Kiel, Germany, July.

Bhagwati, Jagdish, and T. N. Srinivasan (1996). "Trade and the Environment: Does Environmental Diversity Detract from the Case for Free Trade?" In *Fair Trade and Harmonization: Prerequisites for Free Trade?* Vol. 1, edited by J. N. Bhagwati and R. E. Hudec. Cambridge, Mass.: MIT Press.

Bhagwati, Jagdish, and Hugh T. Patrick, eds. (1990). *Aggressive Unilateralism: America's 301 Trade Policy and the World Trading System.* Ann Arbor: University of Michigan Press.

Birdsall, Nancy, and Robert Z. Lawrence (1999). "Deep Integration and Trade Agreements: Good for Developing Countries?" In *Global Public Goods: International Cooperation in the 21st Century,* edited by Inge Kaul, Isabelle Grunberg, and Marc Stern. New York: Oxford University Press.

Blackhurst, Richard (2001). "Reforming WTO Decision-Making: Lessons from Singapore and Seattle." In *The World Trade Organization Millennium Round: Freer Trade in the Twenty-First Century,* edited by K. G. Deutsch and B. Speyer. London and New York: Routledge.

——— (1998). "The Capacity of the WTO to Fulfill Its Mandate." In *The WTO as an International Organization,* edited by Anne O. Krueger. Chicago: University of Chicago Press.

Blackhurst, Richard, and Arvind Subramanian (1992). "Promoting Multilateral Cooperation on the Environment." In *The Greening of World Trade Issues,* edited by K. Anderson and R. Blackhurst. Ann Arbor: University of Michigan Press.

Boltuck, Richard, and Robert E. Litan, eds. (1991). *Down in the Dumps: Administration of the Unfair Trade Laws.* Washington, D.C.: Brookings Institution.

Brander, James, and Barbara Spencer (1984). "Tariff Protection and Imperfect Competition." In *Monopolistic Competition and International Trade,* edited by Henry K. Kierzkowski. Oxford: Clarendon Press.

Buchanan, Patrick (1998). "Address to the Chicago Council on Foreign Relations." November 18. See www.freerepublic.com/forum/a365e6ad15eb8.htm.

Buckley, Ralf (1993). "International Trade, Investment and Environmental Regulation: An Environmental Management Perspective." *Journal of World Trade* 27: 101–48.

Burtless, Gary, et al. (1998). *Globaphobia: Confronting Fears about Open Trade*. Washington, D.C.: Brookings Institution.

Carothers, Thomas, William Barndt, and Mustapha Kamel al-Sayyid (1999). "Civil Society." *Foreign Policy* 117 (Winter): 18–22.

Cass and Boltuck (1996). "Antidumping and Countervailing-Duty Law: The Mirage of Equitable International Competition." In *Fair Trade and Harmonization: Prerequisites for Free Trade?* Edited by Jagdish Bhagwati and Robert E. Hudec. Cambridge, Mass.: MIT Press.

Charnovitz, Steve (2000). "World Trade and the Environment: A Review of the New WTO Report." *Global Environment and Trade Study*, www.gets.org.

———— (1999). "Addressing Environment and Labor Issues in the World Trade Organization." In *Trade in the New Economy*, pamphlet, Progressive Policy Institute, November.

———— (1997). "Trade, Employment and Labour Standards: The OECD Study and Recent Developments in the Trade and Labor Standards Debate." *Temple International and Comparative Law Journal* 11: 131–156.

———— (1993). "Environmentalism Confronts GATT Rules: Recent Developments and New Opportunities." *Journal of World Trade* 27, no. 2: 37–54.

———— (1992). "GATT and the Environment: Examining the Issues." *International Environment Affairs* 4, no. 3: 11.

Chishti, S. (2000). "Democratic Decision Making in the World Trade Organization: An Assessment." *International Studies* 37, no. 2: 85–96.

Cline, William R. (1997). *Trade and Income Distribution*. Washington, D.C.: Institute for International Economics.

Collins, Susan M. (1998). *Imports, Exports, and the American Worker*. Washington, D.C.: Brookings Institution Press.

Cot, Jean-Pierre (1972). *International Conciliation*. London: Europa.

Cottier, Thomas (2000). The WTO and Environmental Law: Some Issues and Ideas. Trade and Development Centre (World Bank/WTO) On-line Essay No. 1 (www.itd.org/issues/essay1.htm).

Covelli, Nick (1999). "Public International Law and Third-Party Participation in WTO Panel Proceedings." *Journal of World Trade* 33, no. 2: 125–39.

Crick, Bernard (1968). "Sovereignty." In *International Encyclopedia of the Social Sciences*. Vol. 15, edited by David L. Sills. New York: Macmillan.

Curzon, Gerard (1965). *Multilateral Commercial Diplomacy: The General Agreement on Tariffs and Trade and Its Input on National Commercial Policies and Techniques*. New York: Praeger.

Dam, Kenneth (1970). *The GATT: Law and International Economic Organization*. Chicago, Ill.: University of Chicago Press.

Danaher, Kevin, and Roger Burbach, eds. (2000). *Globalize This! The Battle against the World Trade Organization and Corporate Rule*. Monroe, Maine: Common Courage Press.

Davis, Bob (2001). "Trade Craft Is Employed on War's Economic Front." *Wall Street Journal*, October 29, p. A1.

Dean, Judith (1992). "Trade and the Environment: A Survey of the Literature." In *International Trade and the Environment*, edited by Patrick Low. Washington, D.C.: World Bank.

Deardoff, Alan V., and Robert M. Stern (2000). "What the Public Should Know about Globalization and the World Trade Organization." Paper presented at the Conference on Globalization: Trade, Financial, and Political Economy Aspects, Athens, Greece, May.

Denny, Charlotte (2001). "Cheap Labour, Ruined Lives." *The Guardian*, February 16, p. 21.

Destler, I. M., and Peter J. Balint (1999). *The New Politics of American Trade: Trade, Labor and the Environment.* Washington, D.C.: Institute for International Economics.

Dryden, Steve (1995). *Trade Warriors: USTR and the American Crusade for Free Trade.* New York: Oxford University Press.

Edgren, Gösta (1979). "Fair Labour Standards and Trade Liberalisation." *International Labour Review* 118: 523.

Elliott, Kimberly Ann (2000). "Getting beyond No! Promoting Worker Rights *and* Trade." In *The WTO after Seattle*, edited by J. Schott. Washington, D.C.: Institute for International Economics.

Elmslie, Bruce, and William Milberg (1996). "Free Trade and Social Dumping: The Lessons from the Regulation of U.S. Interstate Commerce." *Challenge* 39, no. 3: 46–53.

Environmental Protection Agency (1997). *The Benefits and Costs of the Clean Air Act, 1970–1990.* Washington, D.C.: EPA.

Esty, Daniel (2002). "The World Trade Organization's Legitimacy Crisis." *World Trade Review* 1. 1: 7–22.

——— (1998). "Linkages and Governance: NGOs at the World Trade Organization." *University of Pennsylvania Journal of International Economic Law* 19, no. 3: 709.

——— (1996). "Greening World Trade." In *The World Trading System: Challenges Ahead*, edited by Jeffrey Schott. Washington, D.C.: Institute for International Economics.

——— (1995). "The Case for a Global Environmental Organization." In *Managing the World Economy: Fifty Years after Bretton Woods*, edited by P. B. Kenen. Washington, D.C.: Institute for International Economics.

——— (1994). *Greening the GATT: Trade, Environment, and the Future.* Washington, D.C.: Institute for International Economics.

Evans, John W. (1971). *The Kennedy Round in American Trade Policy: The Twilight of the GATT?* Cambridge, Mass.: Harvard University Press.

Feenstra, Robert C. (1998). "Integration of Trade and Disintegration of Production in the Global Economy." *Journal of Economic Perspectives* 12, no. 4: 31–50.

Feinberg, Robert M., and Barry T. Hirsch (1989). "Industry Rent Seeking and the Filing of 'Unfair Trade' Complaints." *International Journal of Industrial Organization* 7. 3: 325–40.

Ferguson, Louise (2000). "Barrier Breaking." *Asian Business* 36, no. 1: 15.

Ferrantino, Michael J. (1997). "International Trade, Environmental Quality, and Public Policy." *World Economy* 20, no. 1: 43–72.

Finger, J. M., and L. Alan Winters (1998). "What Can the WTO Do for Developing Countries?" In *The WTO as an International Organization*, edited by Anne O. Krueger. Chicago: University of Chicago Press.

Finger, J. M., ed. (1993). *Antidumping: How It Works and Who Gets Hurt.* Ann Arbor: University of Michigan Press.

Frankel, Jeffrey A., and David Romer (1999). "Does Trade Cause Growth?" *American Economic Review* 89, no. 3: 379–99.

Fratianni, Michele, and John Pattison (2001). "International Organizations in a World of Regional Trade Agreements: Lessons from Club Theory." *World Economy* 24. 3: 333–58.

General Agreement on Tariffs and Trade (1992). "Trade and the Environment." *International Trade* 1: 19–39.

Gillham, Patrick F., and Marx, Gary T. (2000). "Complexity and Irony in Policing and Protesting: The World Trade Organization in Seattle." *Social Justice* 27, no. 2: 212–36.

Godley, Wynne (1999). *Interim Report: Notes on the U.S. Trade and Balance of Payments Deficits.* Jerome Levy Economics Institute of Bard College, Annandale-on-Hudson, New York.

Gonderinger, Lisa (2000). "Despite Charges and Counter-Charges, Prague Shines through after Riots." *Prague Post,* October 4, p. 5.

Gordon, Bernard K. (2003). "A High-Risk Trade Policy." *Foreign Affairs* 82, no. 4: 105.

Graham, Edward M. (2000). *Fighting the Wrong Enemy: Antiglobal Activists and Multinational Enterprises.* Washington, D.C.: Institute for International Economics.

Griswold, Daniel T. (2000a). "WTO Critics Trade Away Truth for a Sound Bite." Cato Institute Commentary, January 2, www.catoinstitute.org/dailys/01-03-00b.html.

———— (2000b). *WTO Report Card: America's Economic Stake in Open Trade.* Center for Trade Policy Studies.

———— (1999). *Trade, Jobs, and Manufacturing: Why (Almost All) U.S. Workers Should Welcome Imports.* Center for Trade Policy Studies.

Groombridge, Mark A. (2000). "China's Long March to a Market Economy: The Case for Permanent Normal Trade Relations with the People's Republic of China." *Trade Policy Analysis,* no. 10, Cato Institute's Center for Trade Policy Studies. Washington, D.C.: Cato Institute.

Grossman, Gene, and Alan Krueger (1991). "Economic Growth and the Environment." *Quarterly Journal of Economics* 110, no. 2: 353–77.

Hainsworth, Susan (1995). "Sovereignty, Economic Integration, and the World Trade Organization." *Osgoode Hall Law Journal* 33. 3: 584–622.

Haq, Gary, et al. (2001). "Determining the Costs to Industry of Environmental Regulation." *European Environment* 11: 125–39.

Helpman, Elhanan (1999). "The Structure of Foreign Trade." *Journal of Economic Perspectives* 13, no. 2: 121–44.

Helpman, Elhanan, and Paul Krugman (1989). *Trade Policy and Market Structure.* Cambridge, Mass.: MIT Press.

Hillman, Arye, and Heinrich Ursprung (1992). "The Political Economy of Interactions between Environmental and Trade Policies." In *The Greening of World Trade Issues,* edited by K. Anderson and R. Blackhurst. Ann Arbor: University of Michigan Press.

Hilton, Francis G., and Arik Levinson (2000). "Measuring Environmental Compliance Costs and Economic Consequences: A Perspective from the U.S." Draft for World Bank conference, Quantifying the Trade Effect of Standards and Regulatory Barriers: Is It Possible? Washington, D.C., April 24.

Hipple, Steve (1999). "Worker Displacement in the Mid-1990s." *Monthly Labor Review* (July): 15–32.

Hodgson, Geoffrey M. (1998). "The Approach of Institutional Economics." *Journal of Economic Literature* 36: 166–92.

Hoekman, B. M., and Michel Kostecki (1995). *The Political Economy of the World Trading System*. Oxford: Oxford University Press.

Hoekman, B. M., and Michael P. Leidy (1992). "Environmental Policy Formation in a Trading Economy: A Public Choice Perspective." In *The Greening of World Trade Issues*, edited by K. Anderson and R. Blackhurst. Ann Arbor: University of Michigan Press.

Hoekman, B. M., and P. C. Mavroidis (2001). "WTO Dispute Settlement, Transparency and Surveillance." In *Developing Countries and the WTO: A Pro-Active Agenda*, edited by B. Hoekman and W. Martin. Oxford: Blackwell.

Horwitz, Thomas (1993). "International Environmental Protection after the GATT Tuna Decision: A Proposal for a United States Reply." *Case Western Reserve Journal of International Law* 25: 55.

Howse, Robert (2002). "From Politics to Technocracy—and Back Again: The Fate of the Multilateral Trading Regime." *American Journal of International Law* 96, no. 1: 94–117.

——— (2000). "Democracy, Science and Free Trade: Risk Regulation on Trial at the World Trade Organization." *Michigan Law Review* 98: 2329.

Hudec, Robert E. (1996). "GATT Legal Constraints on the Use of Trade Measures against Foreign Environmental Practices." In *Legal Analysis*, vol. 2 of *Fair Trade and Harmonization*, edited by J. Bhagwati and R. E. Hudec. Cambridge, Mass.: MIT Press.

Hudnall, Shannon (1996). "Towards a Greener International Trade System: Multilateral Environmental Agreements and the World Trade Organization." *Columbia Journal of Law and Social Problems* 29, no. 2: 175–94.

Hufbauer, Gary Clyde, and Kimberly Ann Elliott (1994). *Measuring the Costs of Protection in the United States*. Washington, D.C.: Institute for International Economics.

Hufbauer, Gary Clyde, and Daniel H. Rosen (2001). "Steel: Big Problems, Better Solutions." Washington, D.C.: Institute for International Economics.

——— (2000). "American Access to China's Market: The Congressional Vote on PNTR." Washington, D.C.: Institute for International Economics.

Hufbauer, Gary Clyde, Jeffrey J. Schott, and Kimberly Ann Elliott (2003). *Economic Sanctions Reconsidered: History and Current Policy*. 3d ed. Washington, D.C.: Institute for International Economics.

——— (1990). *Economic Sanctions Reconsidered: History and Current Policy*, 2d ed. Washington, D.C.: Institute for International Economics, case 62–2, "UN vs. South Africa," pp. 346–59.

Ikensen, Dan (2002). "Steel Trap: How Subsidies and Protectionism Weaken the U.S. Steel Industry." *Cato Institute Center for Trade Policy Studies* 14: 6–7.

Irwin, Douglas (2000). "Do We Need the WTO?" *Cato Journal* 19, no. 3: 351–57.

——— (1996). *Against the Tide: An Intellectual History of Free Trade*. Princeton, N.J.: Princeton University Press.

Jackson, John H. (2000). "Dispute Settlement and the WTO." In *Seattle, the WTO, and the Future of the Multilateral Trading System*, edited by Roger B. Porter and

Pierre Sauvé. Cambridge, Mass.: John F. Kennedy School of Government, Harvard University.

————— (1999). "Fragmentation or Unification among International Institutions: The World Trade Organization." *New York University Journal of International Law and Politics* 31, no. 4: 823–31.

————— (1998). "Designing and Implementing Effective Dispute Settlement Procedures." In *The WTO as an International Organization*, edited by Anne Krueger. Chicago: University of Chicago Press.

————— (1989). *The World Trading System: Law and Policy of International Economic Relations*. Cambridge, Mass.: MIT Press.

Johnson, Harry G. (1967). *Economic Policies toward Less-Developed Countries*. New York: Praeger, for the Brookings Institute.

Johnson, Ian (1999). "China Retreats on Concessions Made for WTO." *Asian Wall Street Journal*, May 7, p. 4.

Julius, DeAnne (1994). *International Direct Investment: Strengthening the Policy Regime*. Washington, D.C.: Institute for International Economics.

Kaul, Inge, Isabelle Grunberg, and Marc A. Stern, eds. (1999). *Global Public Goods: International Cooperation in the 21st Century*. New York: Oxford University Press.

Kerr, William, and Jill Hobbs (2002). "The North American–European Union Dispute over Beef Produced Using Growth Hormones: A Major Test for the New International Trading Regime." *World Economy* 25, no. 2: 283–96.

Kessie, Edwini Kwame (1999). "Developing Countries and the World Trade Organization: What Has Changed?" *World Competition* 22, no. 2: 83–110.

Khor, Martin (2000). "Seattle Debacle: Revolt of the Developing Nations." In *Globalize This! The Battle against the World Trade Organization and Corporate Rule*, edited by Kevin Danaher and Roger Burbach. Monroe, Maine: Common Courage Press.

————— (1999). "A Comment on Attempted Linkages between Trade and Non-Trade Issues in the WTO." In *The Next Trade Negotiating Round: Examining the Agenda for Seattle*, edited by J. Bhagwati. New York: Columbia University Press.

Kletzer, Lori G., and Robert E. Litan (2001). *A Prescription to Relieve Worker Anxiety*. Washington, D.C.: Institute for International Economics.

Kolodner, Eric (1994). "Transnational Corporations: Impediments or Catalysts of Social Development?" Occasional Paper No. 5, United Nations Research Institute for Social Development. Geneva: UNRISD.

Kovski, Alan (1997). "EPA Bows to Venezuela on Gasoline Import Rules." *Oil Daily*.

Krasner, Stephen (1999). *Sovereignty: Organized Hypocrisy*. Princeton, N.J.: Princeton University Press.

Krueger, Anne (1999). "The Developing Countries and the Next Round of Trade Negotiations." *World Economy* 22, no. 7: 909–32.

————— (1980). "Trade Policy as an Input to Development." *American Economic Review* 70 (May): 288–92.

Krugman, Paul (2000). "Reckonings: The Magic Mountain." *New York Times*, January 23, p. 15.

Krugman, Paul, ed. (1986). *Strategic Trade Policy and the New International Economics*. Cambridge, Mass.: MIT Press.

Kull, Steven (2000). "Americans on Globalization: A Study of U.S. Public Attitudes." Paper presented at the Program on International Policy Attitudes, University of Maryland, March 28.

Lash, William H., III, and Daniel T. Griswold (2000). "WTO Report Card II: An Exercise or Surrender of U.S. Sovereignty?" Trade Briefing No. 9, Cato Institute's Center for Trade Policy Studies. Washington, D.C.: Cato Institute.

Lawrence, Felicity (2002). "The Sweatshop Generation." *The Guardian*, June 12, p. 17.

Levinson, Arik (1996). "Environmental Regulations and Industry Location: International and Domestic Evidence." In *Fair Trade and Harmonization: Prerequisites for Free Trade?* Vol. 1, edited by J. N. Bhagwati and R. E. Hudec. Cambridge, Mass.: MIT Press.

Lewis, Howard, and J. David Richardson (2001). *Why Global Commitment Really Matters!* Washington, D.C.: Institute for International Economics.

Lim, Hoe (2001). "Trade and Human Rights: What's at Issue?" *Journal of World Trade* 35, no. 2: 245.

Lindsey, Brink (1999). "The U.S. Antidumping Law: Rhetoric versus Reality." Trade Policy Analysis No. 7, Cato Institute's Center for Trade Policy Studies. Washington, D.C.: Cato Institute.

Lindsey, Brink, and Dan Ikenson (2001). "Coming Home to Roost: Proliferating Antidumping Laws and the Growing Threat to U.S. Exports." *Cato Institute Center for Trade Policy Studies* 14 (July): 30.

Lindsey, Brink, et al. (1999). "Seattle and Beyond: A WTO Agenda for the New Millennium." Trade Policy Analysis No. 8: Cato Institute's Center for Trade Policy Studies. Washington, D.C.: Cato Institute.

Lizza, Ryan (2000). "Silent Partner." *New Republic* 22 (January 10): 22–25.

Loy, Frank (2001). "Public Participation in the World Trade Organization." In *The Role of the World Trade Organization in Global Governance*, edited by Gary P. Sampson. Tokyo: United Nations University Press.

Lukas, Aaron (2000). *WTO Report Card III: Globalization and Developing Countries.* Washington, D.C.: Cato Institute, Center for Trade Policy Studies.

McCalman, Phillip (1999). "Reaping What You Sow: An Empirical Analysis of International Patent Harmonization." Working Paper, Economics Department, University of Wisconsin-Madison, June.

Macchiaverna, Francesca (1998). "The Reformulated Gasoline Case: International Trade's Impact on U.S. Environmental Policy." *South Carolina Environmental Law Journal* 7: 129.

Marceau, Gabrielle (2001). "Conflicts of Norms and Conflicts of Jurisdictions: The Relationship between the WTO Agreement and MEAs and Other Treaties." *Journal of World Trade* 35, no. 6: 1081–131.

Maskus, Keith E. (2000). "Intellectual Property Issues for the New Round." In *The WTO after Seattle*, edited by J. Schott. Washington, D.C.: Institute for International Economics.

—— (1998). "The International Regulation of Intellectual Property." *Weltwirtschaftliches Archiv* 134: 186–208.

Mazur, Fay (2000). "Labor's New Internationalism." *Foreign Affairs* 79, no. 1: 79–93.

Mehta, Pradeep S. (1999). "The Freezing Effect: Will It Escalate?" Paper presented at the Conference on the Agenda for Seattle, Columbia University, New York City, July 22–23.

Meier, Gerald M. (1995). *Leading Issues in Economic Development*. New York: Oxford University Press.

Meier, Gerald M., and R. E. Baldwin (1957). *Economic Development: Theory, History, Policy*. New York: Wiley.

Michalopoulos, Constantine (2001). *Developing Countries in the WTO*. New York and Hampshire: Palgrave.

Miller, Carol J., and Jennifer L. Croston (1999). "WTO Scrutiny v. Environmental Objectives: Assessment of the International Dolphin Conservation Program Act." *American Business Law Journal* 37, no. 1: 73–125.

Moore, Mike (1999). "It Is Vital to Maintain and Consolidate What Has Already Been Achieved." Press release at the Third WTO Ministerial Conference, Seattle, Washington, December 7.

Moritsugu, Erika (2002). "The Winding Course of the Massachusetts Burma Law: Subfederal Sanctions in a Historical Context." *George Washington International Law Review* 34, no. 2: 435–82.

Moulson, Geir (2000). "Free-Trade Backlash Fears Cloud World Elite Gathering." Associated Press Newswires, January 31, 2000.

Mousouris, Sotirios (1988). "Codes of Conduct Facing Transnational Corporations." In *Handbook of International Business*. 2d ed., edited by I. Walter and T. Murray. New York: Wiley.

Mun, Chak (1999). "Linkage of Environmental and Labor Standards." Paper presented at the Conference on the Agenda for Seattle, Columbia University, New York City, July 22–23.

Nader, Ralph, et al. (1993). *The Case against Free Trade*. San Francisco, Calif.: North Atlantic Books.

Newell, Peter (2002). "A World Environmental Organization: The Wrong Solution to the Wrong Problem." *World Economy* 25, no. 5: 659–71.

Noland, Marcus (1999). "Learning to Love the WTO." *Foreign Affairs* 78, no. 5: 78–92.

Norstrom, Hakan, and Scott Vaughan (1999). *Trade and Environment*, Special Studies 4, WTO Publications. Geneva: World Trade Organization.

O'Brien, R., et al. (2000). *Contesting Global Governance: Multilateral Economic Institutions and Global Social Movements*. Cambridge and New York: Cambridge University Press.

Ostry, Sylvia (2001). "The WTO after Seattle: Something's Happening Here, What It Is Ain't Exactly Clear." Paper presented at the American Economic Association meeting, New Orleans, January 5–7.

——— (2000). "Making Sense of It All: A Post-Mortem on the Meaning of Seattle." In *Seattle, the WTO and the Future of the Multilateral Trading System*, edited by Roger B. Proter and Pierre Sauvé. Cambridge, Mass.: John F. Kennedy School of Government, Harvard University.

——— (1997). *The Post–Cold War Trading System: Who's on First?* Chicago, Ill.: University of Chicago Press.

Oxley, Alan (1999). "Poor Environmental Policy: The Fundamental Problem in the 'Trade and Environment' Debate." Paper presented at the Conference on the Agenda for Seattle, Columbia University, New York City, July 22–23.

Panagariya, Arvind (2002). "Developing Countries at Doha: A Political Economy Analysis." *World Economy* 25, no. 9: 1205–234.

——— "TRIPs and the WTO: An Uneasy Marriage." Paper presented at the Conference on the Agenda for Seattle, Columbia University, New York City, July 22–23.

Panitchpakdi, Supachai (2002). "Balancing Competing Interests: The Future Role of the WTO." In *The Role of the World Trade Organization in Global Governance*, edited by Gary P. Sampson. New York: United Nations Publications.

Panitchpakdi, Supachai, and Michael Young (2001). "The Evolving Multilateral Trade System in the New Millennium." *George Washington International Law Review* 33, nos. 3–4: 419–49.

Peacock, Alan (1999). "The Communitarian Attack on Economics." *Kyklos* 52: 497–510.

Petersmann, Ernst-Ulrich (2000). "The WTO Constitution and Human Rights." *Journal of International Economic Law* 3, no. 1: 19–25.

——— (1993). "International Trade Law and International Environmental Law: Prevention and Settlement of International Environmental Disputes in GATT." *Journal of World Trade* 27, no. 1: 43–81.

Porter, Michael E., and Claas van der Linde (1995)."Toward a New Conception of the Environment-Competitiveness Relationship." *Journal of Economic Perspectives* 9, no. 4 (Fall): 97.

Prakash, Sethi, and Oliver Williams (2000). "Creating and Implementing Global Codes of Conduct: An Assessment of the Sullivan Principles as a Role Model for Developing International Codes of Conduct: Lessons Learned and Un-learned." *Business and Society Review* 105, no. 2 (Summer): 169–200.

Preeg, Ernest H. (1995). *Traders in a Brave New World: The Uruguay Round and the Future of the International Trading System.* Chicago, Ill.: University of Chicago Press.

Presley, Mari (1998). "Sovereignty and Delegation Issues regarding U.S. Commit-ment to the World Trade Organization's Dispute Settlement Process." *Journal of Transnational Law and Policy* 8, no. 1: 173–96.

Putnam, Robert D. (1988). "Diplomacy and Domestic Politics: The Logic of Two-Level Games." *International Organization* 42, no. 3: 427–60.

Reich, Walter, ed. (1998). *Origins of Terrorism: Psychologies, Ideologies, Theologies, States of Mind.* Washington, D.C.: Woodrow Wilson Center Press.

Riedel, James (1991). "Strategy Wars: The State of Debate on Trade and Industrial-ization in Developing Countries." In *International Trade and Global Development: Essays in Honor of Jagdish Bhagwati*, edited by A. Koekkock and L. B. M. Mennes. London and New York: Routledge.

Robertson, David (2000). "Civil Society and the WTO." *World Economy* 23, no. 9: 1119–134.

Rose, Andrew (2002). "Do We Really Know That the WTO Increases Trade?" Center for Economic Policy Research Discussion Paper No. 3538. London: CEPR.

Runge, C. Ford (2001). "A Global Environmental Organization (GEO) and the World Trading System." *Journal of World Trade* 35, no. 4: 399–426.

Rutgeerts, Ann (1999). "Trade and Environment: Reconciling the Montreal Proto-col and the GATT." *Journal of World Trade* 33, no. 4: 61–86.

Sachs, Jeffrey (2001). "After Genoa." *Financial Times*, July 24, p. 15.

——— (1999). "Helping the World's Poorest." *Economist*, August 14–20, pp. 11–12.

Sampson, Gary P. (2001). "Overview." In *The Role of the World Trade Organization* in *Global Governance*, edited by Gary Sampson. Tokyo, New York, and Paris: United Nations University Press.

——— (2000). "The World Trade Organization after Seattle." *World Economy* 23, no. 9: 1097–118.

Sbragia, Alberta M. (2000). "Environmental Policy: Economic Constraints and External Pressures." In *Policy-Making in the European Union*, 4th ed., edited by Helen Wallace and William Wallace. New York: Oxford University Press.

Schattschneider, E. E. (1935). *Politics, Pressures and the Tariff*. New York: Prentice-Hall.

Scheve, Kenneth F., and Matthew J. Slaughter (2001). *Globalization and the Perceptions of American Workers*. Washington, D.C.: Institute for International Economics.

Schott, Jeffrey J. (2003). Correspondence with the author.

——— (2002). "Reflections on the Doha Ministerial." *Economic Perspectives* 7, no. 1 (January). www.iie.com/publications/papers/schott0102.htm.

——— (2000). "Toward WTO 2000: A Seattle Odyssey." *Federal Reserve Bank of St. Louis Review* 82, no. 4 (July–August): 11–30.

Schott, Jeffrey J., ed. (2000). *The WTO after Seattle*. Washington, D.C.: Institute for International Economics.

Schott, Jeffrey J., and Johanna W. Buurman (1994). *The Uruguay Round: An Assessment*. Washington, D.C.: Institute for International Economics.

Schott, Jeffrey J., and Jayashree Watal (2000). "Decision Making in the WTO." In *The WTO after Seattle*, edited by Jeffrey J. Schott. Washington, D.C.: Institute for International Economics.

Sforza, Michelle (1998). "MAI Provisions and Proposals: An Analysis of the April 1998 Text." Public Citizen Global Trade Watch. www.citizen.org/trade/issues/mai/articles.cfm?ID=7415.

Shaffer, Gregory C. (2001). "The World Trade Organization under Challenge: Democracy and the Law and Politics of the WTO's Treatment of Trade and Environment Issues." *Harvard Environmental Law Review* 25, no. 1: 1–93.

Shafik, N., and S. Bandhyopadhay (1992). "Economic Growth and Environmental Quality: Time-Series and Cross-Country Evidence." World Bank Policy Research Working Paper WPS 904. Washington D.C.: World Bank.

Shaw, Sabrina, and Risa Schwartz (2002). "Trade and Environment in the WTO: State of Play." *Journal of World Trade* 36, no. 1: 146–49.

Shrybman, S. (2001). *The World Trade Organization: A Citizen's Guide*. 2d ed. Toronto: Canadian Centre for Policy Alternatives and Lorimer.

Siebert, Horst (1996). "Trade Policy and Environmental Protection." In *The World Economy: Global Trade Policy 1996*, edited by Sven Arndt and Chris Milner. Oxford: Blackwell.

Slater, Johanna (2000). "Managers and Managing: Mattel Backs Campaign to Check Overseas Plants." *Wall Street Journal Europe*, July 6, p. 34.

Smith, Frances B. (2000). "World Trade, Consumers . . . and Seattle." *Consumers' Research Magazine* 83, no. 1: 34–35.

Srinivasan, T. N. (1999). "Developing Countries in the World Trading System: From GATT, 1947, to the Third Ministerial Meeting of WTO, 1999." *World Economy* 22, no. 8: 1047–64.

Stehmann, Oliver (2000). "Foreign Sales Corporations under the WTO." *Journal of World Trade* 34, no. 3: 127–56.

Stirling, Patricia (1996). "The Use of Trade Sanctions as an Enforcement Mechanism for Basic Human Rights: A Proposal for Addition to the World Trade Organization." *American University Journal of International Law and Policy* 11, no. 1: 1–46.

Strauss, Andrew L. (1996). "From Gattzilla to the Green Giant: Winning the Environmental Battle for the Soul of the World Trade Organization." *University of Pennsylvania Journal of International Economic Law* 19, no. 3: 769–821.

Subramanian, Arvind (1992). "Trade Measures for the Environment: A Nearly Empty Box?" *World Economy* 15, no. 1: 135–52.

Taylor, Annie, and Caroline Thomas (1999). *Global Trade and Global Social Issues*. London and New York: Routledge.

Tierney, John (2000). "The World of Child Labor." *The World and I* 15, no. 8 (August): 54.

Trachtman, Joel P. (1999). "The Domain of WTO Dispute Resolution." *Harvard International Law Journal* 40, no. 2: 333–77.

———— (1997). "The Theory of the Firm and the Theory of the International Economic Organization: Toward Comparative Institutional Analysis." *Northwestern Journal of International Law and Business* 17, no. 2–3: 470–555.

Ullrich, Heidi (2000). "Stimulating Trade Liberalization after Seattle." Conference Paper, New Directions in Global Governance, University of the Ryukus, Okinawa, Japan, July 19–20.

United Nations Conference on Environment and Development (1992). "Rio Declaration on the Environment and Development." In *International Legal Materials*. New York: United Nations.

U.S. International Trade Commission (1999). "The Economic Effects of Significant U.S. Import Restraints: Second Update." Investigation No. 332–325. Washington D.C.: U.S. International Trade Commission.

Valles, Cherise, and Brendan McGivern (2000). "The Right to Retaliate under the WTO Agreement." *Journal of World Trade* 34, no. 2: 63–84.

Vermulst, Edwin, and Folkert Graafsma (2001). "WTO Dispute Settlement with Respect to Trade Contingency Measures: Selected Issues." *Journal of World Trade* 35, no. 2: 209–28.

Vesely, Milan (2000). "The WTO Shambles: Dateline USA." *African Business* 251 (February): 22–24.

Viner, Jacob (1950). *The Customs Union Issue*. New York: Carnegie Endowment for International Peace.

Vines, David (1998). "The WTO in Relation to the Fund and the Bank: Competencies, Agendas, and Linkages." In *The WTO as an International Organization*, edited by Anne Krueger. Chicago, Ill.: University of Chicago Press.

Vogel, David (1995). *Trading Up: Consumer and Environmental Regulation in a Global Economy*. Cambridge, Mass.: Harvard University Press.

Wallich, Lori (2000). "Is Free Trade Actually Free?" Letter to Editor. *Wall Street Journal*, April 28, p. A19.

Ward, Halina (1996). "Common but Differentiated Debates: Environment, Labour and the World Trade Organization." *British Institute of International and Comparative Law Quarterly* 45, no. 3: 592–632.

Warkentin and Mingst (2000). "International Institutions, the State, and Global Civil Society in the Age of the World Wide Web." *Global Governance* 6, no. 2: 237.

Watal, Jayashree (2000). *Intellectual Property Rights in the World Trade Organization: The Way Forward for Developing Countries*. New Delhi: Oxford University Press; London: Kluwer Law International.

Watson, Peter S., Joseph E. Flynn, and Chad C. Conwell (1999). "Multilateral Approaches to Trade Liberalization." In *Completing the World Trading System*. London: Kluwer Law International.

Weinstein, Michael, and Steve Charnovitz (2001). "The Greening of the WTO." *Foreign Affairs* 80, no. 6 (November–December): 147–56.

Whalley, John (1999). "Special and Differential Treatment in the Millennium Round." *World Economy* 22, no. 8: 1065–94.

Wilson, John Douglas (1996). "Capital Mobility and Environmental Standards: Is There a Theoretical Basis for a Race to the Bottom?" In *Fair Trade and Harmonization: Prerequisites for Free Trade?* Vol. 1, edited by J. N. Bhagwati and R. E. Hudec. Cambridge, Mass.: MIT Press.

Wilson, John S. (2002). "Standards, Regulation and Trade: WTO Rules and Developing Country Concerns," In *Development, Trade and the WTO: A Handbook*, edited by Bernard Hoekman, Aaditya Mattoo, and Philip English. Washington D.C.: World Bank.

Winestock, Geoff (1999). "EU, U.S. Squabble over Agenda for WTO: Europe Wants Broad Discussions at Millennium Round." *Wall Street Journal Europe*, October 25, p. 4.

Wolf, Martin (2002). "Making Aid a Better Investment." *Financial Times*, March 13, p. 15.

——— (2001). "Broken Promises to the Poor." *Financial Times*, November 21, p. 14.

——— (1987). "Differential and More Favorable Treatment of Developing Countries and the International Trading System." *World Bank Economic Review* 1, no. 4: 647–68.

Wolffgand, Hans-Michael, and Wolfram Feuerkake (2002)."Core Labour Standards in World Trade Law: The Necessity for Incorporation of Core Labour Standards in the World Trade Organization." *Journal of World Trade* 36, no. 5: 883–901.

Working Group on the WTO/MAI (1999). *A Citizen's Guide to the World Trade Organization*. New York: Apex Press.

World Trade Organization (2000). *The Legal Texts: The Results of Uruguay Round of Multilateral Trade Negotiations*. Cambridge, UK: Cambridge University Press.

——— (1994). "The Structure and Organization of Work during the Transition from the GATT to the WTO." Press release GW/02, June 24.

Yang, Guifang, and Keith Maskus (2001). "Intellectual Property Rights and Licensing: An Econometric Investigation." *Weltwirtschaftliches Archiv* 137, no. 1: 58–79.

Yarbrough, Beth, and Robert M. Yarbrough (1992). *Cooperation and Governance in International Trade*. Princeton, N.J.: Princeton University Press.

Zoellick, Robert B. "Unleashing the Trade Winds." *The Economist*, December 7, 2002, pp. 27–29.

——— (2001). "Countering Terror with Trade." *Washington Post*, September 20, p. A35

Zoellick, Robert B. (2002). "Unleashing the Trade Winds." *The Economist*, December 7, 2002, pp. 27–29.

Web sites

www.acwl.ch/MainFrameset.htm (Advising Center on WTO Law), downloaded July 8, 2003.

"Campaigns: Alliance for a Corporate-Free UN." Downloaded from http://www.corpwatch.org/campaigns/PCC.jsp?topicid=101, July 8, 2003.

www.hrweb.org/legal/undocs.html (Human Rights Web), downloaded July 8, 2003.

"Non-Governmental Organizations (NGOs): List of NGOs Attending Seattle." Downloaded from www.wto.org/english/forums_e/ngo_e/ngoinseattle_e.htm, downloaded July 8, 2003.

http://www.unglobalcompact.org/portal/ (The Global Compact: Human Rights, Labor, Environment), downloaded July 9, 2003.

"World Trade Center Tenants." Downloaded from http://www.washingtonpost.com/wp-srv/nation/articles/tower1.html, downloaded July 9, 2003.

Index

globalization
  fear of, 4–5, 7, 18–19, 22–25
  human rights standards and, 133–34
  labor standards and, 139–40
global resource market, 36, 204n1
Gore, Al, 20
Gorton amendment, 209n15
governance, global. *See* global governance
governance, internal, 211–12nn8,9
  developing countries and, 12, 26–27,
    30, 148, 160–62, 166
  protest groups and, 28, 30, 31
government intervention, 24–25, 53,
    113–14
  human rights standards and, 127
  restraints on, 40–42, 46
GPA (government procurement agree-
    ment), 73
Graafsma, Folkert, 85
Great Depression, 68–69
Greenpeace, 29, 170
green-room negotiations, 26, 30, 83, 160–
    64, 211–12nn8,9
GSP (generalized system of preferences),
    73, 75
Gulf War (1991), 132

harmonization, 96, 98, 114–15, 155, 157,
    208nn9,10
Havana Charter, 140
Heckscher-Ohlin model of trade, 204n3
Hoekman, B. M., 88
Hufbauer, Gary Clyde, 129, 133, 210n15
human rights standards, 20, 28–30, 50,
    189–90
Hussein, Saddam, 132, 210n14

ILO (International Labor Organization),
    26, 98, 128, 135, 137–38, 141–45,
    190–92, 211n27
IMF (International Monetary Fund), 4,
    68
  internal governance and, 82, 162,
    212n10
  policy coherence and, 18, 78, 191, 213–
    14nn2,3
import competition, 20, 22, 23, 27–29,
    35–36, 42, 75, 136
import substitution industrialization (ISI),
    153–54
import surges, 44, 60, 205n3
industrial location, 96, 104
Information Technology Agreement,
    214n6

intellectual property (IP) protection, 18,
    21, 26, 27, 107, 120, 157–60
interdependence, economic, 93–97
internal governance. *See* governance, in-
    ternal
International Bank for Reconstruction and
    Development. *See* World Bank
international codes of conduct, 144–45,
    211n28
international customary law, 128
international institutions. *See* global institu-
    tions
International Trade Organization (ITO),
    68, 82
investment, 40–42, 151, 204–5n5
isolationism, 29, 98
ITO (International Trade Organization),
    68, 82
IWW (Industrial Workers of the World),
    25

Jackson, John H., 87, 101
Jackson-Vanek amendment, 134, 210n17
job displacement, 23, 27, 49, 52–54, 61–
    62, 136, 189, 213n1
Johnson, Harry, 150

Kennedy, John F., 69
Kennedy Round, 69–70
Kletzer, Lori G., 61, 206n5
Krasner, Stephen, 94
Krugman, Paul, 22

labeling, 109, 112, 117, 208n6
labor code of conduct, 144–45
labor standards, 20, 28–30, 50, 126, 135–
    45, 189–90, 211n26
labor unions, 21, 23, 53–54, 62, 116, 136
Law of Unintended Consequences, 99
LDCs. *See* developing countries
Lehman, Arthur, 110
Lewis, Howard, 62
Litan, Robert E., 61, 206n5
lobbying
  agriculture and, 17
  environmental standards and, 122
  global governance and, 168–74, 176,
    184
  intellectual property (IP) protection and,
    18
  by multinational corporations, 40
  of national governments, 79
  by NGOs, 31–32, 204n8
  protectionism and, 53–54

Long, Olivier, 82
lumpenproletariat, 21

macroeconomic policies, 23, 61–63
MAI (Multilateral Agreement on Investment), 171–73, 212n3
market access
    developing countries and, 149, 151–52, 154, 156
    environmental standards and, 107, 112
    gains-from-trade theory and, 39–42, 204–5n5
    reciprocity in trade agreements and, 75
market failure, 113–14, 153
market signaling, 51
Marrakesh agreement, 78, 180
Marx, Karl, 21
Marxist models, 152
Maskus, Keith E., 157
Mavroidis, P. C., 88
McCalman, Phillip, 157
MEAs (multilateral environment agreements), 73, 120–21, 192
medical emergencies, 160
mercantilist philosophy, 38
MFA (Multifiber Agreement), 17, 27, 156, 165
MFN (most-favored nation) clause, 41, 69, 73–74, 76–77, 85, 107, 134, 205n3
Michalopoulos, Constantine, 164
minimum wage, 99, 126, 140–41
Ministerial Conference (WTO), 80
MNCs. *See* multinational corporations
Montreal Protocol, 123
Moore, Mike, 82–84, 162, 163
morally based unilateral trade sanctions, 98–99, 145–46
moral suasion, 142–44, 173
Multifiber Agreement (MFA), 17, 27, 156, 165
Multilateral Agreement on Investment (MAI), 171–72
multilateral environmental agreements (MEAs), 73, 120–21, 192
multilateral trade agreements, 78–79
multilateral trade negotiations, 69–71, table 4.1, 78–80, 116–18, 140–41, 193–94, 197–98, 214n6
multinational corporations (MNCs)
    developing countries and, 27
    global governance and, 167–85, 212n7
    human rights standards and, 129
    labor standards and, 138–39, 144–45, 211n28

market access and, 40, 57–58
opposition to, 6, 11–12, 21–22, 25, 28, 110, 116, 122

Nader, Ralph, 25, 171
NAFTA (North American Free Trade Agreement), 75–77, 97, 103, 109, 115, 120, 123, 208n10
Narmada dam project, 204n8
national environmental practice codes, 115
national governments, 79, 175–78, 184, 192, 213n9
national security exemptions, 44
national treatment of imported goods, 41
negotiated trade restraints, 18, 24, 107, 110
neo-Luddite groups, 30, 49
Newell, Peter, 191
New York Times, 8
NGOs (nongovernmental organizations)
    dispute settlement and, 27, 86–87
    global governance and, 167–85, 192, 212n1, 213nn12,13
    influence of, 19, 31
    internal governance and, 30
    labor standards and, 142
nondiscrimination, 41, 107, 109, 117
nontariff barriers (NTBs), 69–71, 73, 156, 211n4
nontrade goals, 29, 89, 159, 177–78, 188, 195–96, 198, 213n14. *See also* environmental standards; human rights standards; labor standards

OECD (Organization for Economic Cooperation and Development), 144, 172–73
optimum tariff, 43
Organization for Economic Cooperation and Development (OECD), 114, 172–73
Ostry, Sylvia, 31, 204n8
outsourcing, 36, 54–55, 171, 204n1
Oxfam, 170

Panitchpakdi, Supachai, 82–84, 162, 192
patents, 18, 120, 157–58, 160, 211n6
peril point tariff rate floors, 69
Perot, Ross, 29, 97
pharmaceutical industry, 18, 159
political leverage, 134
political strategies, 37–42, 45–46
political will, 87–88, 135, 144
pollution standards, 29, 114–17, 120, 208n12

pornography, 139
Porter, Michael E., 115
Prebisch, Raul, 153–54
precautionary principle, 111–12
price system, 51, 74
prison-labor exception, 131, 142–45, 210n12
profit motive, 5–6, 28
prostitution, 139
protectionism, 17, 23, 28–29, 34
  adjustment problem and, 48–65
  agriculture and, 27
  anti-WTO activists and, 89
  developing countries and, 156, 157–60, 211nn3,4
  environmental standards and, 116–17, 209nn14-17
  labor standards and, 136, 140, 142–43
  national sovereignty and, 97
  trade restrictions and, 43–45, 205n7
protest groups. *See* anti-WTO protests
PTAs (preferential trade agreements), 76–77
Public Citizen's Global Trade Watch, 171, 207n1, 212n4
Public Citizen's Trade Watch, 25, 29, 170, 212n3
public opinion, 12, 29, 121, 170
public policy issues, 60–63
public relations, 26, 180–83, 192–96, 214nn5,7

al-Qaeda, 7, 9, 203n3
quotas, 17, 22, 43–44, 56, 58–59, 136

race-to-the-bottom effect, 103, 106, 114–15, 208nn8,12
Ravenhill, John, 193
reciprocity in trade agreements, 39, 41, 75, 78, 154–55, 161, 179, 213n10
reform contraints, 31, 88–91, 155–56
reformulated gasoline case, 108, 110
representation, 79, 178–80
restricted trade. *See* trade restrictions
retaliatory measures
  developing countries and, 159
  dispute settlement and, 78, 81, 85–86
  environmental standards and, 107, 111–12
  human rights standards and, 130
  labor standards and, 144
  national sovereignty and, 99–100
  WTO and, 45
retraining, 30, 53

Ricardo, David, 35–37, 38, 204nn1-3
Richardson, J. David, 62
Rio summit (1992), 123
Rio summit (1992). Declaration on the Environment and Development, 106
risk, 9, 40–42, 46, 204–5n5
Rose, Andrew, 46
Ruggiero, Renato, 82–83

Sachs, Jeffrey, 159
safeguard laws, 18, 85, 156
safety net policies, 49, 62, 153
Salinas, Carlos, 83
sanctions, trade, 50
  environmental standards and, 24, 107, 118–20, 122–24, 189–90, 209n20
  human rights standards and, 129–35, 209–10nn8,14,16
  labor standards and, 140, 143–46, 211n27
  morally based, 98–99
  nontrade goals and, 11, 89–91
Save the Children Fund, 137
Schott, Jeffrey J., 129, 133, 162, 210n15
Schwartz, Risa, 108
scientific evidence, 111–12, 118, 121
scientific tariff, 115
"Seattle Man," 21–22
Seattle ministerial meeting, 80, 201
  developing countries and, 27–28
  director general (DG) and, 83–84
  dispute settlement and, 88
  global governance and, 160–62, 171–72
  labor standards and, 195
  opposition to, 5, 15–16, 19–22
sea turtles, 24, 108, 109–10, 206n9
Secretariat. *See* WTO Secretariat
September 11 terrorist attacks, 7–11
Shaffer, Gregory C., 176
Shaw, Sabrina, 108
shrimp/turtle case, 24, 108, 109–10, 206n9
Siebert, Horst, 207n2
Sierra Club, 29
Singapore ministerial meeting, 16, 80
"single undertaking" agreement, 17
slavery, prohibition of, 128–29
Smith, Adam, 38
Smoot-Hawley Act (1930), 213n9
social dumping, 93, 140
social standards, 11–12, 24–25, 89–90, 96
South African apartheid, 129, 145, 209–10n8
sovereignty, economic, 95–96

sovereignty, national, 23–24, 28–30, 92–124, 207nn1,3
  developing countries and, 27
  dispute settlement and, 18, 84–87, 99–101
  environmental standards and, 119
  human rights standards and, 129–30, 132
special and differential (S&D) treatment, 73, 152–55, 161, 165
specialization, 22, 35–37, 136, 149, 151, 172, 204n1
SPS (sanitary and phytosanitary), 73, 107, 155
Srinivasan, T. N., 98, 144
standards of living, 97, 139, 140, 146, 148
state-sponsored terrorism, 10, 203–4n6
steel industry, 23, 57, 60, 62, 136, 205n2
Stirling, Patricia, 128
stockholders, 58–59
Stolper-Samuelson theorem, 204n3
Subramanian, Arvind, 118
Sullivan Principles, 129, 145, 173
sunk costs, 40–41
Sutherland, Peter, 83
sweatshop labor, 20, 137–40, 145, 189

tariff binding, 41, 43, 154, 205n6
tariff reductions, 17, 22, 38, 41–42, 46, 56, 69–71
tariffs, 29, 34, 43–45, 58–59, 60, 136, 149–50, 205n7
tariff spikes, 17
technical NGOs, 171
technical standards, 107
technological change, 23, 52, 54–56, 115
terms of trade, 153, 211n2
terrorism, 7–10, 203nn3,5
textile industry, 17, 26, 44, 58–59, 155, 156
theory of comparative advantage, 35–37, 204nn1-3
Third World Network (TWN), 30
Third World Trade Network, 170
Tokyo Round, 71, 161
torture, 130, 132
tourism industry, 203n3
TPRM (trade policy review mechanism), 73–74
trade adjustment assistance (TAA), 61–63
Trade and Tariff Act (1972), 212n8
trade barriers, 153, 156
trade liberalization, 12
  developing countries and, 148–49, 153–54, 156, 165

domestic coalition for, 192–96, 214nn5,7
  environmental standards and, 116–17, 121, 123–24
  GATT and, 17–18, 69–71
  human rights standards and, 131, 145
  labor standards and, 139, 145
  opposition to, 24–25, 31–32, 36
  political strategies for, 37–42, 45–46
  PTAs and, 76–77
trademark violations, 120, 157
trade restrictions, 29–30, 34, 42–45, 60. See also quotas; tariffs
  developing countries and, 156
  environmental standards and, 109, 116, 120, 122, 208n5
  human rights standards and, 131–34
  labor standards and, 138, 140
  market failure and, 114
trade secrets, 157
trade theory, 33–47, 76
trade wars, 85, 87
transaction costs, theory of, 151, 205n9
Treaty of Westphalia, 94
TRIMs (trade-related investment measures), 74, 172, 174, 204–5n5
TRIPs (trade-related intellectual property) measures
  developing countries and, 18, 120, 155, 157–60, 164, 197, 211n6
  global governance and, 172, 174
  in Uruguay Round, 18, 74, 120
tuna/dolphin case, 107, 108–9, 112, 207–8nn3,4, 209n17
turtle-teamster coalition, 193

UNCTAD (UN Conference on Trade and Development), 153, 192
unemployment compensation, 61, 206n5
unilateral sanctions, 134
unilateral trade restrictions
  economic nationalists and, 29–30
  environmental standards and, 117, 119
  human rights standards and, 133
  intellectual property (IP) and, 159
  national sovereignty and, 23, 101–2
United Auto Workers, 28
United Nations, 98, 181, 209–10nn8,14
United Nations. Charter on Human Rights, 103
United Nations. Conference on Trade and Development (UNCTAD), 153, 192
United Nations. Department of Public Information, 169–70